DISCARD

Welcome to
HELL

Letters & Writings
from Death Row

Second Edition

Compiled and edited,
with a new introduction,
by Jan Arriens

foreword by Sister Helen Prejean
preface by Clive Stafford Smith

Northeastern University Press
Boston

Advisor in Criminal Justice to Northeastern University Press
Gil Geis

Copyright 1991, 1997, 2005 by Jan Arriens
An earlier version of this book was originally published in 1991 in Great Britain by
Ian Faulkner Publishing Ltd. as *Welcome to Hell: Letters and Other Writings by
Prisoners on Death Row in the United States.*

Library of Congress Cataloging-in-Publication Data
Welcome to hell : letters & writings from death row / compiled and edited, with a new
introduction, by Jan Arriens ; foreword by Sister Helen Prejean ; preface by Clive
Stafford Smith.— 2nd ed.
p. cm.
ISBN 1-55553-636-0 (pbk.)
1. Death row inmates—United States—Correspondence. 2. Death row—United
States. 3. Capital punishment—United States. 4. Prisoners' writings, American.
I. Arriens, Jan.
HV8699.U5W45   2005
365'.6'092273—dc22   2004018289

Royalties from the sale of this book are being donated to the Louisiana Crisis
Assistance Center in New Orleans to support its work on behalf of Death Row
prisoners and indigent prisoners in capital trials.

Designed by Diane Levy

Composed in Times Roman by Coghill Composition, Richmond, Virginia. Printed and
bound by Thomson-Shore, Inc., Dexter, Michigan. The paper is Nature's Natural,
an acid-free stock.

MANUFACTURED IN THE UNITED STATES OF AMERICA
08 07 06 05 04   5 4 3 2 1

To Sam, Leo, and Mali

Contents

Foreword

Who wants a guided tour into Hell—even in a book? Who wants to go there? Only Dante risked such a subject, but even he didn't write about pure Hell. In his *Divine Comedy* he also takes us into Purgatory, the purifying place, and into Paradise, the place of pure bliss.

Why would anyone in their right mind want to descend into the hellish experience of Death Row inmates awaiting execution?

Because we read books to stretch us, to expand our human experience, to test our philosophical categories, to grow in humanness. And we read books because we're curious as hell. We want to know. We want to probe and test popular assumptions to see for ourselves if they hold up. Assumptions such as: Death Row inmates are nothing more than a bunch of losers, a bunch of animals, unfit to live on the face of the earth, disposable human waste. They have raped, stabbed, shot, tortured, and killed—and given half a chance they'll do it all again. They are not human like us.

They don't have the same sorts of hopes and fears as we, do they? And they sure as hell don't need friends or the sort of friendship that their English and Irish pen-pals in LifeLines give.

Really?

I've been in the company of such *unfit-to-live-among-us-scum* for fourteen years now and accompanied several of them to their executions in the electric chair. I know how much these letters mean to men who have little in the way of friendship on Death Row. Contact with someone in the outside world goes a long way in that place where letters are rare and visits rarer.

Take this guided tour around Hell—guided by those who should know: the prisoners themselves. This is a book that speaks from the heart to the heart. Hopes, fears, anguish, desolation, anger—they're all here. Many people have said that this is one of the most powerful and moving books they have ever read. I agree. There isn't a page that doesn't make us laugh, cry, or shout.

This book is *their* story—the story of those cast aside by society.

Not human like we are? Come and see for yourself.

Sister Helen Prejean, CSJ
Author of *Dead Man Walking*

Preface

I was sitting in an oppressively hot room in Mississippi just after midnight on May 20, 1987. Edward Johnson was sitting in front of me, strapped into the gas chamber. I was required to be in the observation room because I was Edward's lawyer. Around me were a dozen people who had volunteered to be there, as witnesses to his execution. The two or three guards present were shaken, obviously moved by the impending death of a young black man they had known and liked. A reporter from the Fox Broadcasting Corporation was chattering excitedly at his first execution, noting all the minute details of the death machine, and discussing how a poor black boy had had his first ever shrimp for dinner that night.

Those who knew Edward—even supposedly hardened prison guards—were horrified at this spectacle. Those who never knew Edward behaved with the inhumanity that—in their ignorance—they attributed to him. Those who have produced this book have helped dispel a little of the ignorance and inhumanity that pretends to justify the death penalty.

When I first came to the South to work against the death penalty, I was twenty, just back from a holiday tour around the world. I spent several months living next to Death Row, visiting those who soon became my many friends inside. To begin with I was rather nervous. The death penalty was certainly wrong in theory, but I shared all of our misperceptions, both as to the Birdmen of Alcatraz who would be caged up inside, and because I could not think that anyone in prison would want to talk to me about the freedom I—a do-gooder who got to go home every evening—so obviously enjoyed.

Soon, I received more from the friendships than I could ever give. That much was made particularly clear when I recently celebrated a birthday. It had been a tough month, with the United States Supreme Court handing down some decisions that made the world a much darker place for those on Death Row—darker also for me in my work, but so much darker for those waiting on Death Row, lying under the sword of Damocles. On the day itself, I received an "Order" signed by twenty of my clients on Death Row in Mississippi, headed by "Chief Justice" Sam Johnson, one of the most eloquent contributors to this book:

IN THE COURT OF THE HEARTS OF THOSE WHO CARE
STATE OF HOPEFULNESS

We who care for
Clive A. Stafford Smith   } No. 7-9-91

Order of Enjoyment and Happiness

This August body, after first giving full consideration to all the facts surrounding the date of July 9th, 1991, hereby Orders that the above named Clive A. Stafford Smith, on that Day and Date, be the Happiest that he has ever been; that he know that all of us are in full accord in wishing him the Happiest of Birthdays.

It is so Ordered!

Done, this the 5th Day of July, 1991.

Samuel B. Johnson
Chief Justice of the Court

I doubt that there has ever been a birthday present that has meant more to me. Such kindness does not often appear in our often-cruel world, and I see it far more frequently among the men and women on Death Row than in the halls of justice.

In this book, you will meet some of the people on Death Row. You will hear of several people who may very well be innocent—it is frightening to think that at least three hundred innocent people have been convicted of capital offenses in the United States in this century. Most of the people who write in this book, however, probably committed murders as violent as anything you have ever imagined. They talk about it, and I want you to know that you would hear them apologize much more profusely for their often-momentary loss of control if I had not censored some of their words to protect them from the legal consequences of their remorse.

In any event, this is not a book about crime. When you have read to the end, you may wonder whether it would be fair for the world to judge you if all people knew was what they read in a tabloid newspaper, under a three-inch headline. Indeed, in the end, this is a book about people. It is not a book about stereotypes. One writer is hopeful, one fearful, one resigned. One writer is poetic, one passionate, one simple. One writes of purity, one of murder. One writer struggles to better himself; one, to better his neighbor. Whatever the motives, the results may be perverse: the downtrodden may struggle to help educate his friend, without realizing that society is more likely to execute a retarded person who learns to read and write.

The purpose of this book is not to canonize everyone on Death Row, though some goodness will shine through the storm clouds. Reality is etched in shades of gray, and we never expect perfection or utter evil of an acquaintance in everyday life. However, whether that acquaintance becomes a firm friend or an unmitigated enemy, very rarely do we ultimately wish his or her execution.

Though the condemned people are all individuals, in some respects life on Death Row is black and white. My friends are the discarded waste of society, awaiting society's incinerator. When I went to see one middle-aged retarded black man, Johnny, I was the first person he had seen from outside the prison in five years. I used to despair that the few of us working here could hope to visit the three thousand Johnnies more than once a year ourselves, while at the same time provide them with legal representation.

Then along came LifeLines—over sixteen hundred strong and growing—kind people lending a helping, human hand to those despised men and women who are most in need. First, a pen-pal in the United Kingdom or Ireland would write and send a few stamps to a person with nothing. Next, some friends would come all the way to the United States to visit. What was once an acorn was already a sapling, and only neglect could prevent it from becoming the broadest, tallest tree in the forest of decency.

By the end of this book, you probably will have cried—as I often have for Edward, Billy, Wes, Roosevelt, Henry, Leo—as you hear the bell toll for one of your new friends. There is no escaping the tragedy of what we are still planning to do to Sam, Joe, Susie, Bryan, Sabrina, Bobby . . .

Yet the Phoenix rises from the ashes. Just as the state of Mississippi executed Edward Johnson—in my opinion, an error even according to their own rules—Paul Hamann was making a BBC documentary that would carry Edward's tragedy across the world. Edward's final wish was that we all would work to help the friends he was leaving on Death Row.

However sad his death was, Edward helped to make many things possible: Paul's documentary *Fourteen Days in May* grew out of Edward's death; LifeLines grew out of the film; and this book grew out of LifeLines. I hope that friendship will grow out of this book for you.

Clive Stafford Smith
Director, Louisiana Crisis Assistance Center

Acknowledgments

My thanks go out to all those who have helped produce this book, especially those who provided the material—both prisoners and pen-pals. They have not been individually named because some sixty prisoners have contributed to the book and in some cases the possibility of identification is best avoided.

Particular thanks for their help with the text are due to Hilary Sheard, former LifeLines coordinator for Texas; Rachel Day, former LifeLines treasurer and now a Death Row attorney in Florida; Mandy Bath of Amnesty International; and Suzanne O'Callaghan, who has done so much to help with the distribution of the first (British) edition. Past and present LifeLines coordinators have also provided invaluable assistance in putting the book together. Above all, I am indebted to Tori Burbridge, the LifeLines secretary, for her help in compiling material and for her constructive suggestions and unfailing encouragement and support.

I owe a debt of great gratitude to Nadir Dinshaw for his support in many ways. I am deeply grateful to Clive Stafford Smith for the inspiration he has provided for our letter-writing movement and for his contributions to the book, and to Sister Helen Prejean for her foreword and her kindness and help to many LifeLiners who have visited the United States.

I want to thank Paul Hamann of the BBC for his generous permission to reproduce the photographs taken in Parchman Penitentiary,

Mississippi, in 1987. David Herman has kindly allowed the drawing sketched in his cell at Ellis Unit 1, Huntsville, Texas, to be used.

I am grateful to Avon Books for permission to reprint the article by Clive Stafford Smith in Chapter 11, and to *The Other Side* for permission to reprint the article by Sam Johnson also appearing in that chapter.

Introduction

This book sets out to give a voice to the three thousand men and women on Death Row in the United States through the letters they have written to people on the outside. For periods of up to 20 years they have spent 23 hours a day in cells measuring 6 feet by 9 feet, waking each day to the knowledge that the state is actively trying to take their lives. Some crack, but others rise above their circumstances. In doing so, they can be confronted with their true selves and touch depths in a way that most of us never do. Those of us writing to them—some three thousand people in the United Kingdom and Ireland—often gain at least as much from the prisoners as we are ever able to give them. To correspond with someone under permanent threat of death, to gain an insight into their backgrounds and to share their innermost feelings is at once extraordinarily inspiring and humbling.

This book attempts to show the human face of Death Row—to show that the death penalty is not about statistics but about individual human beings. Above all I hope that when people read what the prisoners have written they will feel as strongly as I do that whatever these men may have done, they have not forfeited their right to live.

Assuredly, many have committed crimes that fill us with loathing and anger, and I can well understand the deep, unbridled fury and desire for retribution that victims' families and friends so often feel. Many relatives and friends of victims would, I am sure, feel appalled that anyone would be so naïve as to write to these condemned men and women and offer them nonjudgmental support and friendship. All I can say is that through the letter writing, we have seen a totally different side of the men and women on Death Row.

The prisoners provide deeply affecting glimpses into their wretched childhoods and an all-too-familiar pattern of sexual and physical abuse, poverty, neglect, lack of love, cut-short education, and unemployment followed by petty crime, alcohol and drug abuse, and more serious offenses—until something goes hideously wrong. Their already-fragile self-esteem is then further shattered by the hostility of a system that offers no hope or support but remorselessly seeks—often for periods of seven, ten, or more years—to take their lives.

This book consists mostly of excerpts from the prisoners' own letters. They speak with their own voices, which are far more eloquent and telling than mine could ever be. In particular, I have tried to let the "inner child" of each person speak—the child turned into an alcoholic at six or a male prostitute at eight, physically and sexually abused and deprived of the love and support most of us take for granted. For many, Death Row is the first time they have been able to listen to the anguish of their own "inner child."

I thank them all for agreeing to the publication of these extracts. The identity of some of the prisoners has been hidden or disguised because they show a side of themselves that they have not revealed to anyone before—let alone to prison authorities. For legal reasons, too, anonymity often has had to be preserved.

In some cases, these considerations have meant that admissions of guilt have had to be excluded, thereby giving the impression that rather more prisoners protest their innocence than is actually the case. Where appropriate, the letters have been left unedited to preserve authenticity.

This book is also the story of LifeLines. It may strike American readers as odd and perhaps offensive that so many people in Britain and Ireland are writing to men and women who have caused such terrible misery and suffering (in fact, few of those on Death Row are women—just 49 out of 3,000). There are various reasons. First, not everyone on Death Row is a serial killer or pathologically disturbed. Many are ordinary people for whom life has gone hideously wrong, and who would give anything to undo their past. Some are innocent and later are released. Second, the death penalty was abolished in Britain thirty years ago, and many people in Britain are horrified that it still exists in a civilized society. Third, separation by the Atlantic also adds an element of reassurance that some American people might find lacking. Fourth, people are appalled at the cat-and-mouse appeals system in the United States and the extraordinary length of time that prisoners spend on Death Row. Fifth, people change on Death Row, and it is to this change that the members of LifeLines respond.

Perhaps most important of all, the correspondence has flourished because of what the prisoners bring to it. Anger, demands for money, and pornographic outpourings do bring some efforts at correspondence to an abrupt and unhappy end. In most cases, however, the correspondence has proved unexpectedly equal and two-way. Had the prisoners not given as much as they have, LifeLines and the many extraordinary relationships that have been built up never would have happened.

Introduction to the Second Edition

In the fifteen years since LifeLines was founded, the number of prisoners on Death Row in the United States has risen by more than half to 3,500. Some prisoners have been on Death Row for a quarter of a century. They endure underground maximum-security prisons without natural lighting, reduced association with other prisoners, tighter visiting restrictions, and the absence of the limited work programs once in existence. Few prisons allow hobby and craft materials, and access to health facilities is a great source of concern among prisoners.

The right to appeal has been curbed, especially in Texas, which executes more people than any other state. The U.S. Supreme Court has ruled that a state can execute an innocent person as long as due process has been observed.

At the same time, past and present members of the Supreme Court have expressed their misgivings about the death penalty. In Illinois, outgoing Governor George Ryan—a Republican—declared a moratorium out of concern about the ability to administer the death penalty fairly, announcing a blanket commutation upon leaving office in January 2003. Internationally, the United States is becoming increasingly isolated, especially as one of the very few countries that still execute minors.

Another important trend is the use of life without parole. A growing number of Death Row prisoners with overturned sentences face this punishment, which extends no hope for change, reform, or reward. The extreme challenge that this poses to prisoners as they go through the appeal process has been an unmistakable theme in recent correspondence. They find themselves asking whether this is truly an alternative.

The new chapters in this edition focus on the ways prisoners have learned to cope with periods of imprisonment (often in excess of life sentences in other countries) under the threat of eventual execution, and the knowledge that the only realistic alternative is life without parole.

Given the increasingly dehumanizing living conditions and the prospect of permanent incarceration (if their appeals succeed), prisoners need support through correspondence all the more. Over the years, LifeLines has put some six thousand people in touch with prisoners on Death Row. Not all these people are still writing, but LifeLines has found a pen-friend for every prisoner on Death Row who wants one.

Two themes often dominate their letters: the terrifying, traumatic, soul-destroying efforts by the state to take their lives (often over many years), and the first true flowering of many of them as human beings. Death Row, for some prisoners, provides the first period of true stability in their lives. Most arrive on the Row as young adults after childhoods filled with deprivation and inconceivable abuse. Some educate themselves, read extensively, and discover previously hidden abilities. But on the Row they must depend on their own resources. So, in the depths of their privation they reach out to fellow prisoners and, when possible, people in the outside world, through correspondence. If the system does not overwhelm them, they can discover that they are, in fact, intelligent and talented human beings.

Welcome to Hell

1

Beginnings

What an extraordinary role chance plays in our lives. One evening in November 1987 I had nothing in particular to do and idly switched on the television. It was a program about a young black man executed in Mississippi—a program that earlier I had decided not to watch because I thought it would be altogether too depressing.

Within minutes I was riveted. Fourteen Days in May *remains the most compelling television documentary I have ever seen.*

For reasons that remain obscure, the BBC had been permitted to take its cameras into the maximum security unit of Parchman Penitentiary in Mississippi in May 1987 and film the last fourteen days in the life of Edward Earl Johnson. As the documentary proceeded, the viewer felt a terrible sense of impotence at what was happening, which was so manifestly wrong—whatever one's views on the death penalty. Edward Earl Johnson radiated a very special quality: a quiet charm and honesty, a simplicity, a guilelessness. Guards, the chaplain, the attorneys—all expressed their liking for Edward Earl and clearly did not want the execution to proceed.

The voice of humanity, however, came from the least-expected quarter: the other prisoners. Three other prisoners were interviewed in the film. The words of one in particular affected me profoundly. At ten minutes past 10 P.M., less than two hours before the scheduled execution, one of the prisoners said quietly but with great feeling: "Everyone here is dying tonight—a part of them. I can never be the same after this. We're supposed to be vicious and cruel, but this goes beyond anything that anyone could ever do."

Those words were to change my life. My overwhelming reaction was one of astonishment that a prisoner was able to say exactly what I was feeling but was unable to express. I remember breaking down at that point, engulfed with grief as the legal machine rolled on inexorably to execute a human being who was so obviously liked and respected and who had so much to offer.

I knew then that I would have to write to the man who had spoken those words.

After finding out their names from the BBC, I wrote to all three prisoners. At that stage I did not know which was which, and I sent each of them the same letter. Their names were Leo Edwards, John Irving, and Sam Johnson. In my letter I said:

I am writing this letter to you after having seen the television film *Fourteen Days in May* about Edward Johnson, in which you were interviewed.

What I want to say is that I was deeply moved by the film, not just by Mr. Johnson's extraordinary dignity and composure, but also by the humanity, insight and sensitivity you each displayed. When one of you said that part of you was dying with Mr. Johnson, that was exactly what we as viewers felt: part of us, too, was dying. And in the same way, part of Edward Johnson lives on, through you and through those of us reached on television by his personality.

The terrible execution of Edward Johnson and the reaction of others to it, notably yourselves, is an outstanding example of how something deeply worthwhile and important can come out of darkness. It is almost as though we human beings only really discover the depths of our humanity and spirituality when life is most against us.

A few days before the film was shown here, the bomb went off in Enniskillen in Northern Ireland, killing many people at a war remembrance ceremony. One of the lasting impressions of that terrible incident has been the dignity of the father of a 22-year-old nurse who was killed, who said he bore no one any bitterness, and that he could only accept that it was somehow part of a greater plan. Because of his words, which moved the nation, his daughter certainly did not die in vain, but may well have helped bring about reconciliation between Catholics and Protestants in Northern Ireland.

In the same way, Edward Johnson's death, and your plight, have moved many people deeply and been a source of great inspiration and, somehow, hope. If there are times when you wonder how on earth your life could have taken such a turn, please know that there are many people who wept at your wonderful words and whose lives have been touched by yours. I shall never forget the extraordinary qualities you displayed.

Yours sincerely,
(Mr.) Jan Arriens

All three replied. The first letter I received was from Leo Edwards. I had never received a letter that moved me more. It read as follows:

Hello Mr. Arriens   12.12.87

I sincerely pray that this letter finds you and all your loved ones in God's complete grace and care.

I received your most uplifting letter a day ago (I wasn't sure if you wanted to here back from any of us or not?) and was very happy to hear about the effect the film "14 Days in May" had on you and hopefully others, and that it was beneficial in some way.

When I decided to be interviewed for the film my prayers and hope's were that it (the film) would open everyone's eyes to this useless and deceiving taking of life.

There was a time when I thought that there should be a Death Penalty for *certain* crimes, such as rape and murder and child abuse and murder, but (I am not sure who said this, but, I do think he was right) "If any man should die, then no man should live."

But the Death Penalty in this country and many others is politically and economically motivated, there is also the fact that the vast majority of the population just doesn't care, until it's *their* loved ones in this (having a death sentence) situation.

But there are many of us here who don't have family or anyone to help us with our struggles with the courts or in our mere survival, such as hygienic materials, warm clothing, a proper law research library and food that I wouldn't give to my dog! The problems we face here are many but as you're probably saying to yourself, "The biggest problem we face is staying alive."

Please forgive me Mr. Arriens for expressing my frustrations and problems to you in this letter because that was *not* my intention.

I wrote you this letter to let you know that your letter and feeling's were of great importance and highly appreciated by myself and the others here.

I also wanted to let you know that if there is anything you need to know, or would like, to continue to write (or someone you know who would like to write) me or anyone else here. Your/their letters will be warmly excepted, and all questions will be answered.

So once again "Thank You!" for your letter and concern.

If you would like to write back I will be more than happy to hear from you.

May God be between you and harm and all the empty places you walk.

Sincerely
Leo Edwards
M.S.U. Co.P.
Parchman, Ms. 38738

How was it possible for someone in his position to display so much concern about me, as though he were investing me with strength, instead of leaning on me? Above all, how could someone in the bleakest and darkest of situations worry about the "empty places" in which I walked?

A few days later a second letter arrived. It was from Sam Johnson. I quote it in full because of the impact it made on me and all who read it.

Dear Jan,   7 December 1987

In oneness of heart, mind, and spirit I greet you while praying that this will find you, your family and everyone fine and in the very best of health and all else that's good and of God.

Thank you for your letter that I received today and, even more than this, thank you for caring enough to write.

I cannot say that I am doing fine but I am coping with my situation as best as I possibly can and, with the help of God, I feel certain that I will be able to endure this and overcome it eventually.

I hope that you have no objections to my addressing you by your first name and please, if you respond to my letter, call me "Sam." Last names sound so "formal" and "impersonal." I would enjoy corresponding with you and will enjoy even more developing a friendship with you.

Jan, I am from New York and am here without family or friends. I am innocent of the crime I've been convicted of and struggle daily to prove my innocence. This New Year's Eve will mark six (6) years that I have been here. I came here with three other individuals. Two of them are cousins and are from the town that this tragedy occurred. The other individual I met while I was in New Orleans. I met the guy that killed the Officer on the same day that we came here. Jan, I won't try to portray myself to you as an Angel or as a person with a lily white character. I am not a person of violence and have never in my life seriously hurt anyone.

We were stopped by a Highway Patrolman for no other reason than that there were four Blacks in a car together. I was driving but was not speeding or violating any other rules of the highway. After stopping us the Officer searched me and asked that I stand at this car while he searched my car. The front seat passenger (Charlie) was searched by the Officer and then told to stand at the Officer's car where I was already standing. Charlie did this. The Officer then searched the front seat of my car. He found nothing illegal in my car at that time. Finishing with his search of the front seat, he then told the other two individuals (Otis and Anthony) to exit the car and stand where Charlie and I were standing at his (the Officer's) car. Otis was sitting on the rear passenger's side of the car and got out and came back to where Charlie and I were standing. Anthony, who was sitting in the rear behind the driver, got out of my car. Instead of coming to where the three of us were standing, Anthony walked between the cars to where the Officer was bent over in the back seat and stabbed him in the back. I had never seen the knife that he had and it was several months afterwards that I found out that he (Anthony) had known the Officer and that he knew that the Officer had killed a Black man 10 months before we were stopped. Anthony told Otis, his cousin, that he killed the Officer because he was scared that after the Officer found the checks he was going to kill us.

Anyway, after I saw Anthony stab the Officer I tried to stop him. I ran to my car where Anthony and the Officer were, at this time, struggling and tried to take the knife from Anthony. He cut me with the knife in two places in my right hand. (I'll trace a picture of the cuts on the back of this page.) I screamed at him that he had cut me. He then dropped the knife and continued to struggle with the Officer. Charlie and Otis had ran back to my car while this was happening. Anthony and the Officer struggled by me and I ran to my car with intentions of leaving Anthony. I got to my car but couldn't get it started because my hand was so bloody and kept slipping off the key. Charlie reached over me and started the car. By the time that this happened we heard a gunshot and then Anthony got back into my car and told me to "drive." Jan, I was so panic filled at this time I couldn't do anything but what he told me. I drove. None of us at this time knew whether he still had the knife or the gun and all of us were panic filled.

I drove to a deserted area that Anthony told me to and then jumped out of my car and tried to run away from Anthony and all that had happened. We all tried to run away from him. He told us not to run and we stopped. Anthony was wearing a white sweater that was filled with blood and he told Charlie and myself to help him take it off. We did this and Charlie threw the sweater in some bushes near the railroad tracks that were close by. "Fear" isn't the correct word for what I was that day but it's the only word that I know that can come close to describing the feelings that were within me then. After helping him take off the sweater, Charlie and I ran aimlessly away from him. He stole another car, picked Otis up in it and then drove to where Charlie and myself were and picked us up in it. We knew nothing else to do but get in and we got in the car. Anthony drove for about a half a block and then pulled over and told me to drive the car because he was "too nervous" to drive. I didn't want to but I drove the car and followed his directions on where to go. Roadblocks had already been set up and we were caught a short while later. It was God's Grace that we weren't killed at the roadblock because the Officers there shot the car we were in into total destruction. Anthony knew several Officers who were at the roadblock and told them that Charlie and I killed the Officer. We were almost beaten to death. As I've said, Anthony and Otis were from the town that this happened in and all of their family lived in this town. I didn't find this out until after my trial but Anthony's family were pretty influential in this town and used their influence to buy him out of this trouble. He was allowed to be the State's witness against us and testified that I stabbed the Officer and then ordered Charlie to shoot him.

Here are some facts that weren't allowed to be brought out at my trial. Anthony testified that I was wearing the sweater and that in stabbing the Officer, my hand slipped down onto the knife and that's how I got the cuts in my hand. He also said that, after stabbing the Officer, I changed hands with the knife and tried to get the Officer's gun away from the Officer with my bloody hand. Jan, the knife was a butcher's knife and had one cutting edge to it. *If* I had used the knife and cut myself while using it there is NO WAY that I could have two cuts in my hand in the positions that these cuts are in my hand. *If* I had worn the sweater, as he said I did, there is NO WAY that my blood wouldn't have been on it SOMEWHERE. *If* I had struggled with the Officer and tried to take his gun away from him with my bloody hand, as he said I did, there is NO WAY that my blood wouldn't have been on the Officer or on his clothes or that his blood wouldn't have been on me or my clothes.

Jan, *none* of my blood was on the Officer or on his clothes nor was any of his blood on me or on my clothes. My fingerprints weren't found on the knife or on the gun (no fingerprints were found on either of these items). Jan, three people (white) who had no involvement in this tragedy and knew none of us identified Anthony as the man they saw struggling with and perhaps stabbing the Officer. They testified to this at my trial but yet and still I was found guilty solely upon Anthony's testimony and sentenced to die.

Jan, God knows that I didn't kill the Officer or anyone else but I sit here on death row and this State is doing all in its power to execute-murder me. My case is before the United States Supreme Court at this time and we are waiting for them to make a decision on whether to overturn my death sentence. My attorneys seem optimistic about things but there is no way to know at this time what exactly the court is going to do in my case. I hope and pray that they will see fit to overturn my case but I just don't know. Looking back at the tragedy that was Edward Earl Johnson I know that it's possible for me to be killed by these people. I pray that I won't be killed although I know that I may be.

I tell you about me and what has happened to me because if I am killed I'll at least know that someone other than my family and someone outside of this country knows of the tragedy that was Sam Johnson. I can't begin to tell you how hard all of this has been upon me, Jan. I haven't seen any of my family since I've been here and I never knew that loneliness could hurt so very much. I don't mean to cry upon your shoulder but speaking about this place one can find very little that's happy to speak about. I've written an essay about the tragedy that was Edward and it's going to be published in "The Other Side" I think in January. I'm not sure that it's published in your country or not but I'm supposed to get an "author's copy" of the essay and, when I do, I'll send it to you if you want me to. Let me know, OK?

I think and feel that the tragedy that is America must be brought to the attention of the world and I thank God for allowing the essay about Edward and the film about him to be seen. None of us here has seen the film but, from what you say about it, I don't think that Edward died completely in vain. Paul Hamann (the producer) and his staff all are very wonderful people and I'll cherish their memories for as long as I live. Jan, I don't know what else to say in this at this time. If you or anyone that you know would like to correspond with me I'll be more than happy to write. I'm open and honest about myself and I would like to develop a friendship with you. Thank you for writing and may God bless you and yours always and ALL WAYS.

Sam

For three days after receiving Sam's letter, I went about in something of a daze as I tried to absorb the notion of a possibly innocent man spending six years on Death Row. Here was something utterly beyond my normal frame of reference. While doing my best not to abandon my critical faculties, I found something persuasive and genuine about Sam's letter. I wrote in reply that what he was having to endure was beyond my comprehension and that I felt a desperate, impotent rage at the tragedy that had befallen him. I wrote:

Sam, let me share the pain with you—without going off into mystical flights of fancy, I do have very deep-seated beliefs, as evidently do you, that there is something greater beyond ourselves, and that we are not the separate islands we imagine ourselves to be, but much more closely interconnected than we realize.

Sam, it is only a tiny comfort, but in this world in which there is so much injustice and unfairness, things change as others get to hear of it and are stirred into action (like the abolition of slavery), and because of the publicity given to Edward, and your part in that, you are part of the small, visible spearhead of the vast body of injustice that produces change. There are others whose voice isn't heard at all, and you must represent them. Have courage—it is people like yourself who help our world move forward, however slowly.

I shall be thinking of you specially on New Year's Eve.

At 12:01 A.M. on New Year's Eve, 1987, Sam wrote:

Very many thanks for your kind and inspirational letter that I received today and hearing from you lifted my spirits immensely.

Jan, I honestly feel that if light were shed on the things that happened to me in this tragedy I would gain my freedom. Today marks the sixth year that I have been here. Jan, this place is HELL and I kid you not in the least little bit. Let me not let thoughts of hell make this a "sad" letter.

The "desperate, impotent rage" that you speak of mirrors almost exactly my feelings. I never dreamed that something like this could happen not only to me but to anybody. I am not sure that I can even begin to explain to you how I feel being caught up within this vicious system. But, even so and, like you, I feel, think and *believe* that God is going to free me from within the belly of this beast. I look forward with eagerness to the time when I will be able to accept your invitation to visit you in your country. In my mind's eye I, too, have a picture of myself coming through Heathrow and you meeting me (smile). Let's touch hearts in prayer and believe that the pictures that are in our mind's eye will soon become reality.

This government preaches and teaches that we are all equal. Equality shouldn't mean that the next person is equal to you but that you are equal to the next person. If I was equal to *them* I wouldn't be in this situation. My rights would have been safeguarded from the moment that this tragedy occurred. No, Jan, I don't think or feel that life has dealt me a fair hand but I won't sit here and not try to change my situation because I feel sorry that life hasn't dealt me a fair hand. I can't give up, Jan.

The correspondence with Sam almost instantly developed an extraordinary closeness. Through his writings the power of Sam's personality radiated with great immediacy to others, and this has been a critical factor in the evolution of the LifeLines pen-friends group in the United Kingdom. In May 1988, impressed by the letters from Death Row, the Hartington Grove Quaker Meeting in Cambridge, England, organized that most English of events, a cream tea in a village garden. We raised £270 ($400). News of this improbable event reached the ears of the local newspaper, which sent a journalist, Merrilyn Thomas, to interview me.

The story she published led to inquiries from twenty-five people in the Cambridge area volunteering to write. It also uncovered the fact that Clive Stafford Smith, the (then) Atlanta-based British lawyer who represented Edward Earl Johnson and who featured prominently in Fourteen Days in May, *came from a village just twenty miles from where I lived. We met in summer 1988—when he also persuaded Merrilyn that there was a book to be written about Edward Earl and Death Row generally.*

Fourteen Days in May *was rescreened in September 1988, together with* The Journey, *a documentary that sought to establish the identity of the real killer for whose crime Edward Earl was executed. Also in September the British Quaker weekly* The Friend *published an article of extracts from Sam's letters. This boosted the number of people writing to about sixty.*

In November and December of 1988 I took advantage of the low airfares and flew out to the United States to meet Sam. He was all that I had expected. Sam came in smiling so broadly that the guard said, "Hey, what's up with you, man," and forgot to manacle him. This happy chance meant that we were able to shake hands through the small metal hatch. We spent five hours together. It was as though we had known each other all our lives.

In all I met nine inmates in Mississippi and three in Georgia, spending about an hour with each. Most of the men came from tragic backgrounds, having suffered as children from violence, broken homes, and often sexual abuse, and lapsing as they grew up into a world of drugs, alcohol, and petty larceny. For some of them, like Leo Edwards, I discovered to my astonishment that Death Row represented the first period of real stability in their lives. Although a number of them had committed terrible deeds, many of them were on Death Row because of a single instance of lost control. Because of the way that poverty (and hence poor legal representation), mental retardation, lack of education, and race are associated with the death penalty in the southern states, very few of those on Death Row fall into the category of cold and vicious psychopaths, and this was certainly true of those I met.

In February 1989, Merrilyn Thomas went out to Mississippi to gather information for her book. Just seven months later, Life on Death Row *was published.*

In May of that year, I called the first national meeting of letter writers. Just over forty people came, from all over Britain. The speaker was *Paul Hamann, the producer and director of* Fourteen Days in May, *who told us how the film had come to be made. No American TV crew had ever been allowed to film on Death Row, and it took eighteen months of negotiating before the call came from Parchman, Mississippi. It was an experience that was to change not only Paul's life but the lives of the film crew and all of us who now have pen-friends on Death Row.*

Paul spoke of the games of chess he played with Edward Earl—a good player—and of the genuine affection he and the film crew developed for him. As he came to know the man, Paul's initial skepticism about his protestations of innocence was dispelled, and he became convinced that he was witnessing a terrible miscarriage of justice.

Edward, "the calmest man in the prison," encouraged the anguished producer to carry on filming to the end, not for himself but for everyone on Death Row. Paul and his crew, though increasingly distressed, continued filming until thirty minutes before the execution.

When this moment came, the crew filmed Paul as he embraced Edward and said good-bye, fumbling for words. At the crew's insistence, this scene, in which the BBC dropped its mask and the director suddenly appeared on screen, was not cut.

A report in a national newspaper on this conference brought over two hundred new letter writers. A major event in the organization's growth was the publication of the British edition of Welcome to Hell *in late 1991. Several months later, in early 1992, the BBC screened a forty-minute documentary on the correspondence between Ray Clark on Death Row in Florida and Mary Grayson in England (see Chapter 9, "The Pee-Pee Dance"). As a result of this program, LifeLines received sixty-five hundred letters from viewers wanting to write—a figure that staggered even the BBC. With the influx of new members it became possible to say in 1992 that every prisoner on Death Row who wanted to had been supplied with a British or Irish pen-pal. By 1996, the LifeLines organization had put an estimated five thousand people in touch with prisoners on Death Row in the United States. Many, however, do not sustain the correspondence or drop out of the organization. At present, probably about three thousand people are writing, and LifeLines' membership is sixteen hundred.*

LifeLines puts out a quarterly newsletter, with articles by letter writers and prisoners as well as information on the organization and activities such as conferences. It has also organized creative-writing competitions for the inmates, which gave rise to a collection of prisoners' prose and poetry entitled Out of the Night, *edited by Marie Mulvey Roberts. LifeLines has regional groups and a team of counselors to help if the correspondence runs into problems or if a prisoner faces execution.*

LifeLines holds two conferences a year. Speakers have included Clive Stafford Smith, Marie Deans, Susan Cary, and Sister Helen Prejean (who spoke of the events she was later to describe in Dead Man Walking*); Death Row attorneys from California, Florida, and Alabama; the Reverend Jo Ingle (author of* Last Rights*); Pat Bane, the chairperson of the U.S. organization Murder Victims Families for Reconciliation, who spoke from personal experience of having lost a loved one; and Betty Foster, the mother of the juvenile offender Chris Burger, who was executed in Georgia in November 1993.*

From the outset, LifeLines has not been a campaigning or political organization: it exists to provide support for people who, whatever they may have done, spend years trying to avoid the death chamber, often with minimal outside support. A charitable organization, the An-drew Lee Jones Fund, which grew out of LifeLines, supports British people studying law in the United States with a view to representing Death Row prisoners.

Quite deliberately, LifeLines has not at any point sought to mount an organized drive to recruit new letter writers. Instead, we have grown organically, as a result of TV films, radio interviews, articles, and talks. By and large, people have come forward because they have been touched by the human qualities of the men on Death Row—qualities most of us had not expected to encounter.

2

Killing Our Mistakes

There are at present a little over 3,000 men and 49 women on Death Row in the United States. A number have been there since the death penalty was reintroduced in 1976. Thirty-eight of the states have brought back the death penalty, although as of February 1996 four had not yet imposed death sentences and twelve had not carried out any executions. Until recently a map of the United States with the executing states shaded in was virtually a map of the Confederacy in the Civil War. The five main executing states were Texas, Florida, Virginia, Louisiana, and Georgia. Eight of the top-ten executing states are former Confederate states; the other two are Missouri and (most recently) Illinois.

In 1972, the United States Supreme Court ruled that the death penalty constituted "cruel and unusual punishment." This ruling followed a five-year period from 1967 in which the use of the death penalty had been suspended. In 1976, however, the Supreme Court allowed individual states to bring back the death penalty. Since then, as of February 1996, there have been 322 executions and 43 suicides, there have been 72 commutations, and 1,480 convictions or sentences have been reversed. Something like three hundred prisoners are added to Death Row each year.

What those figures mean is that out of a total of a little over forty-seven hundred people who have entered the portals of Death Row since 1976, just under 7 percent have been executed and a little over 30 percent have come off Death Row. Allowing for the fact that many of those now on Death Row will also have their convictions or sentences overturned, it is clear that a very substantial proportion of those who spend years of uncertainty awaiting possible execution in fact end up getting off Death Row.

The death penalty is arbitrary and capricious: just one out of every one hundred convicted murderers is sentenced to death. These are by no means always the worst offenders.

Just over 50 percent of those on Death Row are members of minority groups, compared with a national average of 12 percent. A number of rigorous academic studies have uncovered strong evidence of racism in the administration of the death penalty. Since the reintroduction of the death penalty in 1976, it took until 1991—the 188th execution—for the first white man to be executed for murdering a black victim.

The United States Supreme Court affirmed in 1989 that states could execute people who committed their offense at the age of sixteen—an age at which all but a handful of countries would treat them as juveniles. The United States is one of only six or seven countries—including Iraq and Iran—known to have executed juvenile offenders in recent years.

The death penalty also bears on the poor. Defense lawyers maintain that no one able to buy proper counsel gets the death penalty. It is the black, the poor, the undereducated, and the retarded who are particularly at risk.

The arbitrary and discriminatory nature of the legal system has been powerfully summed up by one of its victims, Ronald Spivey, on Death Row in Georgia since 1976:

America's death rows are made up of entirely different people than you have been told are there.

They are, for the most part, socially deprived because of actual handicaps that are not recognized as legal handicaps.

Some are emotionally handicapped because they were never in a healthy environment where they could learn to give proper responses to the normal frustrations of everyday life. A majority were abused physically or mentally and as a result, suffer from an extreme lack of self-esteem. Abused children usually believe they are at fault and the cause of the abuse, by being somehow bad. They feel they are not a good child or it wouldn't be happening to them. So they grow up with an overload of guilt and they don't know what they were guilty of that justified a parent or parents' abuse of them. They have, as a consequence, absolutely no sense of self-worth.

Some are retarded, cheated by their genes of a whole mind. Some of them are childlike, to a pitiful degree. Some of them are totally insane and have been for many years. In some cases, the defense *and the prosecutor's psychiatrist* all said the person was insane before, during and after the crime. Yet, the prosecutor asked for and got the death sentence. Why do this, knowing of the insanity? Because there is ten times the media coverage of a death penalty trial than there is of a normal trial. It keeps the prosecutor's name before the voters. Many death sentences are the result of going to trial just prior to elections. Normally, in some cases, a death sentence wouldn't be sought, but because of the impending election and multiplied media coverage, the prosecutor can't resist the lure of the additional limelight. So, someone gets a death sentence for a crime much less shocking to the conscience than others the prosecutor has let off with a life sentence.

Always, in such cases, the defendant is poor and his family is without political influence in the community. Perfect socio-economically deprived fodder for the prosecutor's discriminatory judicial grist mill.

These insane ones are not kept in the state mental hospital because you can't, by law, execute an insane person. So, they are kept on death row as if they were mentally healthy, so they can be executed when their time comes. Some are racially deprived and live their entire lives there knowing certain doors were forever closed to them. This is not an era of racial progress, but of racial decline. Doors that were once open, or at least opened a crack, are being systematically slammed shut. This is advocated in the highest levels of our present regime. This power structure feels too much was given too fast, so let's take some back.

All people on death row have one thing in common: they are poor and can't afford the high-powered attorneys that can, at the very least, give you a very good chance at a life sentence.

Most are economically deprived and raised in poverty or near poverty. So many doors are closed to them, too. They grew up in poor neighborhoods, where the majority had limited horizons. The collective sense of hopelessness that exists among the poor contributes to reduced expectations.

All these areas of deprivation, singly or combined, mean a lack of local community and political influence. So they get the death sentences the other 95% convicted of the same crime do not.

By definition, these people on America's death row constitute a specific class. Even though they differ ethnically and religiously, they have one or more of these areas of deprivation in common, or they wouldn't have a death sentence.

America is killing the economically deprived, those of the lower socioeconomic strata, killing the insane, killing the retarded, killing illiterates, killing the emotionally crippled, killing the childishly immature and mentally undeveloped, killing the socially disenfranchised and the politically powerless of our society, killing those so criminally abused as children that they never had a chance to develop normally to a well-balanced human being. Their minds were stunted, twisted and mentally and emotionally destroyed as children.

We are killing the weaker of the species. We kill our mistakes. The financially strong and socially fortunate survive and the weak perish . . . just like the jungle animal kingdom.

Ron Spivey also describes what it feels like to be up against the assembled legal forces of the state:

When a deprived person of this lower socioeconomic class has to defend him or herself against the state's imposition of the death sentence as a pauper or near pauper, this person is stripped of the socially recognized necessities when in conflict with the awesome overwhelming power of the state judiciary. This defendant has neither powerful relatives nor political influence to any degree, nor the money necessary to pay for a defense strong enough to avoid the death sentence.

He or she is naked, devoid of the armor of social and financial power and position necessary to survive an encounter with the inexorable machinery of the state. The state's power is most awesomely displayed when wielded against a social pauper who stands alone in this conflict, who must piteously appeal to the state, the very one trying to kill him or her, for the paltry funds the state reluctantly gives in amounts so picayune as to permit only an inadequate semblance of even a poor defense.

For all these reasons, I ask you to accept the definition of those on death row, as a cognizable class of socioeconomically deprived. I ask you to recognize the use of the death sentence as an act of social genocide.

The following (necessarily anonymous) statement by an inmate provides a graphic illustration of what Ron Spivey describes.

I have been under psychiatric care since age eleven. I have been in the State Mental Hospital four times. I have spent half of my life in prisons. In 1965 I was diagnosed as a person with severe emotional problems who, under prolonged stress, goes into psychotic rages.

There should be no legal way for me to buy, borrow, trade for, or be given a handgun or any other gun. In the winter of 197-, my wife left me and took her three daughters by her first husband and our one-year-old daughter. My world was in ruins. The pain and depression were beyond belief. I started drinking to numb the pain, and this led to losing a fine franchise business. I took tranquilizers, trying desperately to fight off the soul-numbing depression. Three days after the most lonely and miserable Christmas of my life, I was taking tranquilizers and drinking all day. I had a confrontation with three men. One became physically aggressive. I just snapped and went completely out of my mind. Because I had a handgun when I went berserk that horrible night in December 197-, a true American hero lost his life. Officer X, a 14-year police veteran, was moonlighting at a shopping center to earn extra money for his wife and children. During that night of madness I shot five total strangers, and two died. I caused great suffering and emotional trauma to others that night as well. I have been on Death Row for 15 years. My guilt and the horror of that night have haunted me constantly. This prison; nothing on Earth; no one, can punish me like my conscience has done. Without a gun, I couldn't possibly have done those terrible things. Somehow we must wake up and see to it that laws are passed to rid us of the millions upon millions of guns in our society and see to it that no more are carelessly sold in the U.S.A.

John Lamb, a white prisoner who has been on Death Row in Texas since 1983, writes:

My trial lawyers did more to convict me than the District Attorney did but I didn't know then what I know now as far as the law goes. It's hard to blame my lawyers—I realize they have to live in their communities and live with the DA for years. I do blame the process; the public puts so much pressure on the DAs to get a conviction on a capital case that the rules governing a fair trial go right out the window. A DA could end up losing his job, his future, if a press-covered case ends up in acquittal or not guilty. Knowing how much a career means, how can I say I blame them? To prove my point examine: before my trial the DA offered me a 40-year sentence. My lawyers tell me, "If we can get that phony confession thrown out, they can't convict you of anything," so I refused the 40 years. So my lawyer comes back and says, "Believe it or not the DA said, make him an offer." Once again I said "No!" So my trial lawyers had me sign an affidavit releasing them of blame, stemming from me not accepting the plea bargain. Boy was that a mistake. By relieving my trial lawyers of fault I gave them the green light to sell me out.

I've had three execution dates. On my second one I was without a lawyer; my counsel quit without telling me anything. I used the media to inform everyone I was without counsel. They went to the ACLU [American Civil Liberties Union] and NAACP [National Association for the Advancement of Colored People] offices and in concert they said, "We are running out of money and pulling up stakes." The Houston newspapers printed it, they decided to use me as an example. My trial lawyer returned from vacation two days before my date. He found out I was going to be executed unless I found a lawyer. He filed a writ charging ineffective counsel at the trial on himself.

This place is like no other place. The conditions are the worst I've ever seen or heard of, we need all the support we can get.

Walter Correll, a young white prisoner, wrote to his pen-friend Paul Allison, a journalist in Liverpool, England, about his childhood. On his sixth birthday his father—a heavy drinker—

took me by my feet and started beating my head on the floor until it was bleeding. I didn't know it then but this was to be just one of many beatings I would receive just because things weren't going the way dad wanted them to.

Well, for a long time mom put up with the beatings until she got smart to the way dad would start drinking. If he wasn't drinking he would come home from work on time but if he was drinking he was always late. So to keep herself and me from getting beat up she would take us kids and walk around the streets until dad would go to sleep. It didn't matter if it was raining or snowing we had to walk the streets to keep from getting beat up. When you are a little kid you don't think about what's going on you just make a game of it and that's what we did.

Walter also wrote about the circumstances of his trial and sentencing:

The day of the hearing came and there were a lot of people there to help me so the judge wouldn't sentence me to death. People from the foster homes were there, teachers from the schools I was in, family and friends. I found out things about myself that I never knew before. They were saying that I had brain damage and other things wrong with me. Then my dad got on the stand and told the judge about how hard my childhood was. I was watching the judge to see what his reaction would be, but it stayed the same. After everyone had finished talking the judge told me to stand up. I wasn't sure my legs would be able to hold me up so I grabbed the table and pulled myself up. I was crying and really didn't hear all the judge said but when he said "I sentence you to death" I heard that and I just broke down.

I don't really know if I walked from the court room or if the guards carried me, but when I walked into the cell block the guys asked me what the judge had given me. When I said, "He sentenced me to death," they thought I was joking. Then the guard told them they had to lock up so I could get my stuff out of the cell. Now these were guys I had been with for nine months and now they had to be locked away from me. Hearing the guard say this made me feel as if I had some kind of an illness these people could catch. It also made me feel like I wasn't good enough to be around other people. When I walked in to get my stuff the guys wanted to shake my hand, but the guard told me not to get near them. I asked him what they were going to do to me if I did shake their hands and he looked at me real funny. I know I saw a tear in his eyes when I said this.

After I had packed my stuff and told the guys good-bye the guard took me back downstairs and put me in this small cell all by myself. They were going to take me to the state prison that day. It was already four o'clock and I didn't see why I couldn't just stay at the jail until the morning. While in the little cell I called my parents and told them they were moving me that day and then I called the lawyer and thanked him for nothing. He had the nerve to ask me why I was so mad at him. He told me that he had done the best job he could and all I could do was think to myself, I petty [sic] the next guy he defends.

After I got off the phone Vicky came to the door and asked me how I was doing. She was one of the guards working at the jail and she also testified at the hearing saying that I shouldn't be given a death sentence. When she asked me this I started crying and couldn't stop. She told me she was sorry she couldn't help me any more than she did, but I told her that she did her best and that I was very grateful. She even got the other guard to open the cell door so she could give me a hug. While we were hugging she started crying and had to leave. I can't say for sure, but I think a lot of the guards knew I wasn't guilty, but there was nothing they could do.

A prisoner in a midwest state wrote to his pen-pal as follows:

My Mom was a very beautiful lady who married at age 14, and had four pups by the time she was 20. She divorced my Dad when I was 8, and I blamed her, exclusively, for banishing my God-like father. She and I deteriorated in our relationship steadily for the next five years to the point where we *thought* we hated each other and I went to be a ward of the court. I hated her again for not attending my trial, and I didn't find out for years that the trauma of my impending trial had caused her to be hospitalized. We reunited five years ago when she visited me here on my birthday, and she visited each birthday after that. She died last year. She was 47 years. Our last visit was over three hours long. We laughed the whole time, we held hands and we reaffirmed our mother-son bond that had been tarnished but not destroyed. After her death, my sister found a private room that my Mom had set up as *my* room. She had poems I'd written her, baby pictures, letters I'd written her, Mother's Day cards. And there were two lengthy letters to me—started but never finished. They remain my most highly valued possession.

With respect to his parents, the way in which his pen-friend shares his letters with her husband dredges up a painful memory.

I wanted to comment on what you said about Peter only reading my letters if invited. I was touched by it. I love to see that kind of respect. It shouldn't be strange and surprising to me, but it is, I'm sorry to admit. My parents had basic contempt. Fistfights and profanity directed at each other, and us kids, was so common that it began to be viewed as a nuisance rather than another tragedy. 1978 found me watching the World Series, my Mom is on the floor, my step dad (340 lbs.) is sitting on her, beating her in the face, and I screamed for them to shut up, I'm trying to watch TV. That was one of the worst beatings I ever saw my Mom take, and I was cold to it. I had only come home for the weekend (from the children's home) because my granny (my mother's step mom) had died. I cry, sometimes, thinking about how indifferent I had become.

From Mecklenberg, Virginia, Joe O'Dell has written to Audrey Elcombe, of Bury St. Edmunds, England:

The Court assigned me a "Drunk" for an attorney . . . the man knew absolutely "No" Law, and he told me to plead not guilty by reason of temporary insanity! I told him he must be crazy and that I was not pleading anything but "Innocent" due to the fact that I was innocent. To make a long story short . . . I "fired" him and took the case upon myself, and for the 21 months that they held me in solitary confinement, I wrote by hand 179 legal motions and presented myself in Court 55 times, and fought 13 scientists and a multitude of other witnesses that they threw at me . . . I had *nothing* to fight with, and they would not allow me to bring in witnesses that would prove my innocence. My witnesses were threatened, and they brought in a man I had never seen before in my life, and he told the Jury that I confessed the crime to him in jail! Of course this man made the story up from what he read in the newspapers to get him and his wife out of jail on five serious charges that carried a life sentence in prison! The man told the court that I confessed, but the only problem was, what he told was totally inconsistent with *any* of the scenarios of the crime, and it would have been impossible to have happened. I don't think anybody believed him, but he provided the "element" of the crime that was needed to convict me. He connected me to the crime with his lies, and without the lies, there was *no* connection to me and the crime at all.

I fought the case for five grueling weeks. I done a fair job of defending myself against the astronomical odds, but here I was *alone*, with *nobody* up against the whole State of Virginia, all that their inexhaustible resources could supply, and a courtroom full of the victim's family influencing the jury. I had two ex-judges on my jury.

Audrey, you have no idea of the horror that goes on in the United States. Our country has become so decadent and full of political corruption. People in America *do not care* if a person is *innocent* or *guilty* as long as there is *someone* to pay for a crime!

Many of my friends that have been sentenced to die and then found innocent are going around the United States and getting on national television telling their stories. One, Joseph Green Brown, spent 14 years on Death Row in Florida, and was measured and fitted for his "Burial" suit, and signed the funeral arrangement papers . . . and then was found innocent and released! Can you imagine the "Transition" shock of in one moment getting ready to die, and the next being released into the hot sunshine of Florida? Another friend of mine, Guy Gordon Marsh, spent 14 years in prison for a murder he did not commit, and finally proved his innocence and was released. By the Grace-of-God did he escape dying in the Electric Chair. Another friend of mine, Jerry Banks, spent five years on Georgia's Death Row, was proven innocent, released, and three months later killed his wife, and committed suicide. The pressures of being on Death Row destroyed his marriage, his life, and he ended up dead, his wife ended up dead, and his three small children ended up orphans! Another friend of mine, Robert Domer, of Canton, Ohio, who is now a college professor and teacher and also a consultant for criminal justice, spent five years on Ohio's Death Row for a murder that never happened, and it took him five years to prove that the victim died of a heart attack!

Also, in Texas, Clarence Lee Brandley, has just been found innocent after 9 years on Texas's Death Row. His case is perhaps the most racially biased case in the history of the United States.

Audrey my friend, I could tell you story after story for weeks, even months, and still not exhaust the supply I have . . . I have each and every case known in the United States, up to date, memorized in my head in case *anything* ever happened to my master files. If I were to tell you some of the macabre stories of how they have executed "Innocents" it would make you sick . . . absolutely sick!

This theme is picked up by an inmate in Texas:

What I've just told you about my case is not a particularly unique story. I'd love to tell you that my case was especially egregious, but it's not. In almost every case you might be able to get the "inside story" on, you'd find similar tactics used by the authorities. It's true that a lot of the guys really are guilty as charged, but invariably the tactics used to indict and try the guys are just as abusive and illegal as they are in my case—as they were in Brandley's case.

The thing is, if the police, Rangers and prosecutors have this malevolent and corrupt system in place to use against the guys who did commit crimes, there is nothing to stop them from using it against innocent people. And they are using it against them. What makes it particularly hard to fight is that it comes across that you're trying to defend the real, hard-core and guilty guys. And, as with me, a lot of the guys who might be guilty of the crime they're charged with, well, they happen to be people who don't exactly command respect and admiration from the general public. The result is that this corrupt system, though mostly hidden by apathy and complexity, is completely resistent to being amended. It's immune to attack.

What happened to me and to Brandley and to Randall Adams was not the result of a mistake, a single malicious act, an isolated incident. What happened to us is the typical product of a well oiled machine. It was "standard operating procedure." It's been going for years, is continuing as you read these words, and will continue for a long time. There will be many people victimized by this system.

I talk to the old timers here, the ones who have been in the prison system on and off for years. They tell me that cops and prosecutors have always been capable of this, but in the old days, say from '72 on back, the authorities would bend the rules and use bogus tactics only when the person was particularly obvious or dangerous and had a long history and they'd been unable to get him in any other way. They tell me that they themselves understood why it would sometimes happen.

But it seems to me that the need to prosecute, the need to win at any cost *every* time, in other words, the politics of crime and prosecution, have changed things so that the dirty old system used only occasionally has become the rule.

In the old days, things were usually moderated by the fact that the prosecutor couldn't used the bogus system on just anyone. The victim had to be particularly evil. Now, with the public's willingness to buy anything they're told, the prosecutors can and do do it to most people they can get capital charges against.

It's almost as if this machine, the corrupt system, has gained a life of its own like some malevolent god that everyone is terrified of, afraid to defy. And like some ancient cult, the masses sacrifice lies to that god in the hope of appeasing it and averting evil, harm and ruin.

3

Society's Debt—
and Society's Response

They say a man ain't supposed to cry
No matter what, no matter why.
Well I am a man an I hope you understand
Quite Often
Like the rain falls from the sky
Many a tear has fallen from my eyes
Mainly because I'm not afraid to show
How I feel inside.
You see Mama taught me to live
On love
An not some foolish Pride.

—Willie Reddix, Mississippi

The childhood pattern of those on Death Row is all too familiar: an unhappy home, lack of love and affection, violence, sexual abuse, poverty, lack of education, lack of self-esteem and self-identity, and, in many cases, racial discrimination. Clive Stafford Smith estimates that 90 percent of his Death Row clients were sexually abused as children. One prisoner wrote that he was introduced to alcohol at the age of six, another that he was forced into male prostitution at the age of eight.

The question does, of course, arise as to why some men respond so violently to their upbringing and circumstances while others do not.

Apart from that, not all the men on Death Row had deprived childhoods.

But many did. The following is a remarkable account of the childhood and introduction to crime of an inmate in Georgia:

Perhaps to help you understand me a little better and give some kind of explanation as to why I'm here on DR I should tell you about my life. Also, this information about myself should explain why I don't and haven't had any form of support since I've been on Death Row.

I often wonder what my life would have been like if I had been raised in a home with caring and nurturing parents. I received very little emotional support or sustenance from either of my parents. I instead was subjected to indifference and comments aimed at belittling me.

I was raised in a home where violence was a ready solution to family problems. My mother often beat me, usually with extension cords or whips. My father's beatings were usually more severe. Both of my parents physically and mentally abused me. At the age of ten, my father beat me so severely that I had to be treated for a broken leg. As a result of my introspection and alienation from my family, at a very young age, I developed a pattern of running away from home. My first episode of running away from home occurred when I was in the third grade, and this continued through my adolescence. I ran away from home at least 15 times. It was often that I walked away from a beating with bruises all over my face and head.

At the age of 12, I was taken by my mother to Georgia Regional Hospital where I spent several weeks. My mother's complaint was that I exhibited antisocial behavior patterns, and that I ran away from home repeatedly. This admission followed shortly after an incident when I reported both of my parents to the police for growing marijuana. While I took some of the marijuana to the police station and while others of my family silently supported my account, neither the police nor my psychiatric social worker believed my story. I told them I had reported my parents because I wanted to be placed into a foster home. During my stay at Georgia Regional, when I told the social workers and psychiatrist I was being beaten and that my parents were involved in drugs, I was reprimanded for lying.

Despite a notation on my physical exam report about scars from beatings and a burn on my chest, my treatment team sent me back home. The stay at Georgia Regional assumed I was overstating my bad home environment because of their failure to consult with any other family member except my mother. It was at this point and time that my home life was not only intolerable, but was also very dangerous. I think after this incident I gave up all hope of trying to find someone that would help me because I never tried again.

While many children become very introverted when raised in the type of environment in which I was raised and are rendered so immobile that they fail to seek help, I attempted to find a better environment for myself.

These efforts first began when I was in the third grade when I would run away from home. I needed some rest from being beaten because my parents felt I had been bad or for something I didn't know about or do. This effort also took the extreme form of reporting my parents to the police for growing marijuana when I was 11, so that I could be placed in a foster home. While I recognized I needed a different home setting than the one I found while residing with either parent, I was repeatedly thwarted in my efforts. With each run away, I would return because I had no place else to go. And when I asked the staff at Georgia Regional not to send me back to my parents because I could not live with them without being beaten, they, after performing no investigation above speaking to my mother, chose, for whatever reason, not to believe me and sent me home. I was thus unable, despite my efforts, to find a more nurturing and caring environment.

Throughout my adolescent years I would run away from home and live on the streets, steal food out of stores, until I learned about detention centers. I then would break into a school or store and set off the alarm intentionally and wait for the police so I could be placed in a detention center when I got tired, as a child, of living like a wino. After a month or two they would send me back home and I would immediately do the same thing again, spending very little, if any, time at home or with family members.

At the age of 19, my criminal life began to develop and take form. I no longer would steal or burglarize to be arrested, but I started doing it for money. This continued until I was arrested for this crime that I'm on Death Row for now. I was in the process of committing a burglary when this happened. There's evidence in my case to support the fact that the killing was an accident. The victim wasn't beaten or raped. She had a bruise on her hand that she got when we were struggling for the gun. She was shot once in the right side of her chest but in the angle of her heart. She died instantly. I didn't know she had died because when the gun went off we both let go of it and I ran.

Yes, I accept the responsibility for this crime happening, although I didn't intentionally take another human being's life. But I will never accept the indoctrination that I'm a heartless, cold-blooded murderer. If for whatever reason I must be executed—"God forbid I will"—then I will meet death with a smile on my face and nothing but love in my heart for all mankind, and, yes, even for my oppressors.

One of the most agonizing and frustrating things about being alone in life and in my situation in particular, is watching the guys here who receive mail and visits from their family and friends. They are fortunate in the sense that they have someone in their life who is expressing their love and care for them and see to it that they are able to go to the institution store to get the things they need so they don't have to eat the slop the institution feeds. But, what's amazing about it all is watching them take it all for granted.

Between now and the time I meet death I will never stop seeking or desiring to find or have that special someone in my life and I'll never stop looking. If I meet this special someone only a split second before my death, then all of my wishes would be delivered and it would be then that I become the richest man in the world. I guess for me, and maybe because I've never received it, love is everything!

When I was in Mississippi in December 1988, one of the men I met was Leo Edwards, who was executed seven months later. Leo told me at one point that he "thanked God for being where he was." For the best part of an hour, I listened as he told me the story of his childhood. He came from an unhappy home and had been abused by his alcoholic father. He did not obtain much education and drifted into petty crime at an early age. A spell in prison introduced him to drugs, and it was while under the influence of drugs that he committed the crimes for which he was eventually executed in June 1989. He wrote about his childhood as follows:

I had turned to drugs because there was no feeling of love or happiness in my family for as far back as I can remember. There was always tension and fear in the atmosphere because of my father. It seemed he wanted to beat me whenever he saw me. I used to think I was running away from home when I was 9, 10, and 11 years old and I hid underneath the house.

Look, I hope you can forgive me if I don't go any further with this; it brings back memories that still seem to find a way of hurting my heart. But I still have my boyhood dreams deep down inside and one day, God willing, I will be able to live it.

Walter Correll provided the following account of his formative years to his pen-friend Paul Allison:

As far back as I can remember, my dad was a heavy drinker and every time he would drink, he would hit my mom and me. Of course this caused me to have trouble so I started running with the wrong people and getting into trouble. Well, it got so bad that my parents had me put in a foster home where I stayed for seven years. At first, it was all right, but then I started getting into trouble at school and at the home.

When I turned 15, I was moved to another foster home where I stayed for four months. While there I learned about skipping school and about pot. At first, I didn't do a lot of these things, but when I got back home it got even worse. But, I'm getting a little ahead of myself. In the foster home, we went to church every Sunday, but the problem was that we were forced to go by the lady who ran the home. As you can guess, that made me rebel against church and God. I was forever sneaking out of Sunday school, or I would play sick so that I wouldn't have to go.

Then, I got to go home and that's when I really got into drugs and alcohol. At first, it wasn't bad, but my dad was still drinking and beating on my mom. I started staying away from home as much as I could and my drug habit got even worse. Everyday, I had to have something to drink or some kind of drug. As everyone knows, after so long you get used to a drag, you need something stronger to take its place. Only someone who has taken drugs knows what I'm talking about.

Well, one thing led to another and I quit school at the age of fifteen and that's when I really started getting into trouble. I started stealing bikes and other things out of stores until I got caught. The judge was very fair and put me on probation, but I wasn't happy. I wanted my parents to suffer for putting me into a foster home. So, I kept taking drugs and getting into trouble. At the age of 18, I got my first taste of what jail was like. I got eight months, but before going to court, I prayed and made a lot of promises to God if He would help keep me out of prison. And He did. Well, I did my time and got out, but went back to the same way of life. I didn't have any way to pay for my drugs, so I talked my dad into getting me a job where he worked, but it didn't last long. I worked long enough to get my first paycheck and then quit.

As you can guess, it wasn't long before I was in trouble with the law again. Me and a couple of friends stole a jeep and went to the beach and had fun until we came back. We got caught, and since I was the oldest, I was the one the blame was put on. Once again, I was praying to God and making a lot of promises if He would keep me out of prison, which He did. But after I got out it was the same old thing all over again. Over the years it was the same thing time after time.

Then one day while I was working my boss said the cops came by his house and said they wanted to ask me some questions. I couldn't think of anything I had done, so I called them and told them where I was. When they picked me up they said I was under arrest for capital murder and I just froze. They had to carry me to the car. For three days I was questioned about this and no matter how many times I said I didn't do it they kept pushing and finally I couldn't take any more and said I did it.

Walter, white, was convicted in 1985 in his early twenties. Although in close touch with his parents, he had not seen them for three years in 1990, for his father had retired and could not afford the journey. Walter's former wife had nothing to do with him and, he said, lost their

*child to welfare. He began writing to Paul Allison, a journalist in Liv-
erpool, in June 1990. In his first letter, he writes of his former confusion "because of the drugs I was taking. But the lawyers I have now
say they have evidence to prove I am innocent."*

*In his second letter, he writes that his "very good lawyers have
already proven I'm not guilty, but our court system just isn't fair. From
what I have seen after you are sent to prison they don't like to admit
they made a mistake."*

In his third letter he pursues the point:

This may sound stupid, but I don't want a new sentencing because I
don't want to spend the rest of my life in prison. It has been proven
that I'm not guilty and for that reason I want a new trial. A lot of
people can't understand this way of thinking, but that's because they
never had to face anything like this. See, spending the rest of my life
in a prison is the same as being dead. Oh, I would give anything if the
pain and suffering would stop for me and my family, but until someone
admits their mistake it will go on.

In August he writes somewhat more positively about prison life:

Being in prison isn't so bad itself, it's just what this place stands for.
If it wasn't for the death penalty I really don't think it would be so
bad. The good part is this prison isn't as bad as some of the others in
the U.S.

I have learned the more you call and treat a person like an animal
the more they become one. If you want someone to learn from their
mistakes you can't just throw them into a hole and expect the impossible to happen. When you open that door and let them out they are
going to be worse than before. That's why a lot of people end up going
back to prison after they have been released. No one took time to try
and really help them.

How can killing someone show that killing is wrong? The funny
thing is that the state says executing someone isn't murder, but if you
look up the dictionary it says something like "to have someone trapped
where they can't leave and the taking of a life.

Later in August matters begin to take an ominous turn.

There are times when I get so mad that I can't stand myself, and the reason for this is because my lawyers have evidence to prove I'm innocent, but so far none of the judges have done anything. Three weeks ago the State Supreme Court turned down another of my appeals. Well, since that happened I only have three appeals left and if something isn't done soon it will be too late. If they go as fast as the rest of them have gone in two years or less I will be gone.

At the end of October 1990, Walter writes,

Yes, I'm sure there are a lot of people in prison who aren't guilty and I don't want to sound uncaring, but all of them can't be facing death the way I am. It's really scary to think that men can treat others this way, but we must keep praying for them.

I have found out something last week that I think you would like to know about. Would you believe the courts have said that it doesn't matter if a person isn't guilty or not. What matters is that they got a fair trial to begin with, but that doesn't make any sense to me.

Then, in December, danger lights really begin to flash.

Well, my case is really going bad right now, because another of my appeals was turned down and that leaves me with only two appeals to go. If you ask me there's not much hope, because the courts have had every chance in the world to do what's right but they haven't. Well, guess I will close. Remember you are in my prayers.

Again in December 1990:

To be honest if the next court doesn't give me a new trial there will be no hope of ever getting one. Of course the lawyers can go before the Governor, but he isn't going to do anything. Before he got into office he said he was against the death penalty, but when he found out he couldn't win that way he started saying he was for it.

In late January 1991 Walter wrote:

I pray every day to get a new trial and I truly believe God is going to answer my prayers. But at the same time I have to get ready for what can happen even if it scares me so much that I have nightmares about it. Yes, I have had dreams, about going to the chair and when I woke up I was so scared that I didn't sleep for two days after that. As I told you before it is very hard being here, because if you manage to keep your mind off it during the day, you dream about it at night.

In late February:

To be honest I am so scared that I don't know what to do, but there is no way I will ever give up.

In March he writes:

I have never felt so helpless as I do now. If the Federal Courts don't give me a new trial I'm not sure I will be able to hang on any more. See, in the past I have tried to take my own life and that was before I came here. It scares me to think of doing this, but I just don't want to die in the chair for something I didn't do.

In May:

I used to write to a guy in Mississippi who told me they would test the chair with rats and then throw them in front of the cells and say, "This is what your black ass is going to look like." The guards would test the chair and the guy in the cell could smell the wood burning and hear it too.

Walter's mother, who was in poor health, wrote at that time:

I have to take two depression pills every night to keep from having nightmares. I have been taking them since Walter has been in prison and he has been in there going on six years. People tell me I will have to try and not think about him being there, but they don't know what it feels like having a son in prison and who has been proven innocent. I have had enough heartache by losing three members of my family in 17 months and I don't know if I can take it if Walter is given the chair. We are going to have his body brought back and have him cremated and buried between my husband and myself. It is going to be really hard for me to do that, but I will have to because I don't want him buried down there. I just hope I can get through it when the time comes.

Walter Correll was executed on January 4, 1996.

Toby Williams, a black prisoner in Huntsville, Texas, convicted in 1985 at the age of twenty-one, describes his feelings about the way in which society has responded to those on Death Row:

As I look out the window into the free world (a window we call a television set), I often hear many misguided voices speaking out about people being convicted of murder who should never be released no matter what, because it is impossible to rehabilitate a person after they've committed murder. Firstly, how do you rehabilitate "heat of the moment"?

We're portrayed as animals by many who know nothing about us or our cases, primarily for just being in this position, guilty or not. But since it is possible for an animal to be tamed and trained, we may as well be portrayed as less than an animal since it is impossible to be rehabilitated.

Although I've been enduring this pain for over five years (since 9.27.85 on Death Row), I've learned a lot and I've found new interests such as calligraphy, poetry, writing, collecting stamps, art string, art, and building such crafts as jewelry boxes, crosses and picture frames. And although I'm in this misfortunate position I still have feelings, a heart, I still know how to care, and help others, and most of all, I still know how to love. With the help of God—who I strongly believe in— I'm able to pull up a smile even in my most depressing moments.

Since I'm stripped of so much, I often wonder how long before I'm stripped of even those things God has allowed me to maintain.

The following account of society's response to those on Death Row comes from John ("Mali") Irving, while still on Death Row in Mississippi:

To make a human being a slave or to enslave a group you have to do something criminal to those people, you have to cripple their humanity. In a purely spiritual sense you have to darken their minds over a calculated period of time, you have to render their reasoning faculties inoperable and you have to weaken their wills.

To keep their humanity in this weakened state you have to keep the gas chamber, electric chairs and other methods of terrorization in operation. Fear weakens the others with the sounds of gasping choking and dying slaves. This is what the death penalty is all about; keeping the oppressed down through an extra-legal method of terrorization.

What do you suppose the average black living in the state of Mississippi felt about the killing of Earl? This is the insight: they felt themselves "being terrorized" and while the average one of them could not verbally articulate what they felt you could ask the overwhelming majority of them if they thought it possible for black men to innocently be put to death in that fashion, and they would answer yes. Why? Because black men as a group have never been free from that particular form of terror.

Part of the reason I have chosen to remain in the church is because I see the problem as fundamentally a spiritual one. My religion is one of involvement. I believe the church ought to become more involved with its "resources" and from within the Anglican communion I will "challenge" the church leadership. This is part of my hope for the future; within the souls of our people (God bless their oppressed hearts) there is a "deep river of love" and enthusiasm for human rights and social justice.

This love and enthusiasm is at present being "misdirected." It must be given leadership and be redirected to legislate away the death penalty at the state levels to abolish it in this country.

Vic Roberts in Georgia writes of the isolation as follows:

Think constantly of us, as if chained with us.

Death Row is not just fences, bars and steel doors, bad guys and bad food. No, Death Row can be and should be compared with existing not living. It is filled with people with isolated hearts and suppressed minds; with loneliness that leaves one with an internal and external need for love and affection—and ideas, desires and feelings that we should be doing something constructive and positive. But the dreary anxiety pushes and swells, uncertainty smothers, suffocates, until it finally absorbs the imagination. Death Row is agonizing frustration, fruitless despair and unfamiliar indifference.

I am on Death Row. Why does my heart ache? Why will correspondence, caring, love and affection give much needed pleasure and satisfaction? All around me is suppressed and dead. It crushes in on me. Even the walls of my conscience seem to close in on me. It makes me inelastic. It is life without meaning, life without purpose. It is, indeed, no life at all.

I can easily stand criticism, correction, incarceration, even punishment. But the silence, the isolation, the unforgivingness from society— even from the churches, the pastors, the Christians—is terrifying and debilitating. Does anyone care? Does anyone care to know who I am or to know of the love I hold within my being?

Death Row is a place where many of us struggle to find answers in our own debilitated, enfeebled self, because there is no one to listen or to try to understand. It is a place of endless routines, where Time itself is a dreadful task. It is the Pit of Hopelessness. But the most heartbreaking thing about Death Row is watching as society goes to church, kneels before the "Father" and asks Him to bless their lives with peace, happiness and joy, watching as society pays its tithes, but seeing that they are still very much in debt because their debt lies unpaid for years, lurking in their souls.

It is not the freezing winter cold nor the heat and humidity of summer that depresses and spiritually disrupts, but the waiting in anxious anticipation for the letter, the card that never arrives; the waiting in pure faith for the visit from a loved one who never comes. No one comes because no one cares.

Two prisoners on Alabama's Death Row, Wallace Thomas and Jesse Morrison, made the following plea to society:

We, the inmates of Alabama's Death Row, have been portrayed as animals unfit for society. We have loved ones and families who have suffered as much as anyone. We have sat here for years, praying and hoping for positive results. The only time we are heard is during our trials and hours before we are electrocuted. However, we are human beings also. We have mothers, fathers, sisters, brothers, daughters, sons, nieces and nephews who are affected as much as those of us who sit here on Death Row. The death penalty has destroyed family members, caused many to lose jobs, and caused others to relocate and begin life again. It has caused our children to be singled out and humiliated in school. The death penalty has caused legal, economic, social and psychological problems for us and our families which can never be resolved.

Many of us have made mistakes as humans will err; many of us regret these mistakes, and many of us have learned from these mistakes. All of us want and need the opportunity to prove to society that we can be productive citizens who can contribute to this society in a positive fashion.

We wonder how much hate and vengefulness the American nation will endure before its citizens stand up and say that enough is enough. We are the only civilized and free country in the world which says that if a person makes a mistake at the tender age of 16, he must die for it. We are the only civilized and free country in the world which says that we will stop murder by murdering in the name of justice, and we are the only free country which says that if a person is not the right color and has no money, the chances are that he will never encounter justice.

The death penalty cannot cure ills that won't go away. We must seek lasting solutions that will make us a better people. We must start by abolishing the death penalty.

We ask you in the name of love, peace and true justice to lift every voice and demand an end to the death penalty in the United States of America.

Wallace Thomas was executed in July 1990.

A white prisoner in one of the Deep South states has written to his pen-friend in Cambridge, England, about the abandonment and isolation of those incarcerated on Death Row, and the way in which families and friends often shun them or slowly drift away:

My family aren't all that far away but they could be on the other side of the world and it would be the same. The reason I don't talk about them is because of the way they have treated me since I have been here. It hurts me deeply for I love them so much and that will never stop.

If I let my lawyers take care of things the way they want to do it, then I would get off Death Row. So why don't I let them have their own way? We both know why I am here, yet maybe if I had not been on drugs and drinking that night I am sure I would not have hurt anyone. But what happened happened and I can't turn the clock back! And if I were to get off Death Row I would have to go to a camp and sooner or later I would run into someone from my home town and they are the people who really want me dead. It has been made clear to me in more ways than one! None of my family members are able to live any where near my home town, and they blame me for that and that is why they turned from me. My (ex) wife has made it clear that she doesn't want me seeing my (our) little girl! And she goes out of her way to make it as hard on me as she can! For every now and then she will write to me and tell me if I will get someone to bring her up she will let M. come, but then when I find someone that will do that for me, she backs out and I fall for it every time. I have to because she could be for real at any time and if I didn't go for it, and she was going to let her come, then I would have lost the chance! So I keep on letting myself get hurt time after time!!

I wish there was a way to do away with this Death P stuff. But for now we have to live with it! You said you didn't know how I was able to deal with it! Well at times I can't but I don't let it show, when you don't have all that much to live for it kinda gets hard to find reasons to fight! But we keep trying to find those reasons to go on! . . . How do I cope? Everyone has their own way of doing it, you have to find a way that works for you and the way I do it is by never letting myself get close to anyone that would hurt too much when it comes my time if that in fact happens! This I guess is one of the reasons why I don't get close with my family for I know they are going to hurt but they are only going to hurt that much more if we were a lot closer and I can't stand to see anyone hurt, I would gladly take the hurt for anyone, I have always been that way, well that is unless I was on drugs at the time, as it was the night that got me put here.

Sam Johnson in Mississippi describes his feelings upon the impending visit of his father and sister in 1988, the first time they had been able to afford the journey from Rochester, New York, in the six years Sam had been on Death Row:

I know that you know that my father and sister will soon be here to see me and I've been hit with a double dose of happiness (smile). I pray this will find you, our family and everyone fine and in the very best of health. My love and best wishes to everyone. I am doing much better now that I can look forward to seeing my father and sister again. In my prayers I've asked to be allowed to see my father and sister again in this life—I've also asked to be free to see them again—and know that I will soon see them again is an answer to my prayers. I can't really explain the feelings that course through me but I feel GOOD!"
  I feel like I did as a child in the summertime when school was out and I used to rush home from play to wait for my father to get home from work. The minutes would seem like hours and I thought my heart would burst from beating so fast if he didn't hurry up and come home. When he did come home I used to "jump him": he would swing me into the air and I was the happiest person in the world! Knowing that I will soon see him again gives me similar feelings that I had as a child. A part of me still believes a little bit that he can come here and make things all right for me in the way he used to do when I was a child. There wasn't a hurt he couldn't stop from hurting when I was a child. The child in me still believes that he will come and stop my pain and the adult in me is patting the child on the head and telling him not to worry because soon this will be behind us and happiness will be ours again. My sister, I love all of you for loving me, for renewing my hopes and beliefs in my existence and all that surrounds me and and/or that I surround. I feel in harmony with everything and I feel wonderful.

In the December 1989 issue of the Texas Death Row newspaper Endeavor, *the editor, Gary "T" Graham, wrote:*

Texas is one of the few states which does not classify 17-year-olds as juveniles. As a result, seven other youngsters and myself are facing execution in Texas after being convicted of capital murder while under the age 18.

Before my arrest in 1981, I was one of many juvenile delinquents roaming around the streets without a sense of direction or purpose in life. Today I am confined on Death Row, but I feel good about myself, for indeed I have taken many steps in the way of self-betterment. I have obtained my GED, assisted in the founding of Endeavor publication and am constantly seeking out ways to atone for my wrongs and to better myself.

I am not sure where the road will lead me from here, but I will continue to protest the execution of juveniles, which is clearly an unnecessary punishment, and unquestionably inappropriate retribution!

My religious and moral convictions lead me to stand against *all* executions, but when I hear about juvenile executions, I realize our country is not moving forward in step with the evolving standards of decency that mark the progress of a maturing and civilized society.

I wonder how many misinformed Americans honestly believe my execution or the execution of anyone makes society safer? Be for real, America! It is time for this nation to stand up and address the true causes of crime (poverty, drugs, unemployment, entertainment through violence, etc.), instead of murdering our citizens in the wee hours of the morning and calling it Justice!

4

An Evil Place

Many prisoners sum up Death Row simply in one word: hell. *It is a word that recurs again and again in their letters. The following is typical:*

I have spent 21 years in continuous incarceration. I am 40 years old. I have no desire to foresee hell in any other form; for I have already discovered it. This is a literal "hell-hole." It is a *LIVING HELL.* If the fires do not consume me, I hope to someday be free; to tell of my terrifying experience. That such a HELL, under no circumstances, can be the answer. *Not ever.* This is my hope. An aspiration for which I live.

Michael Sharpe writes in Endeavor, *the Texas Death Row newspaper:*

When a man first comes to death row, the first thing he experiences is the loneliness. You are locked up in a five-foot by eight-foot cell all of your own. It comes complete with a toilet, a sink, and a bunk that is always too short for you. No one really knows what loneliness is until they come to the row. No matter how many letters you get or write; no matter how many friends you make, from day one there is a big compartment in your heart that is labeled loneliness. On the row a person feels lost in deep despair. You feel no one will ever be able to help you. All is lost.

Another Texas inmate:

Many, many books have been written about prison life, but there is no way that you can ever know what this place is like unless you have been in this cage. You cannot describe the misery and despair in a place like this—one has to feel it.

Or a man in Louisiana:

A man without hope is a man without a dream . . . for if I try to think of a tomorrow it only comes down to one thing, sad, lonely and without a purpose.

Judy Haney in Alabama:

I like to have went crazy when I first got lock up, I had work and took care of my kids since I was 16 and I got lock up when I was 36, so it was hard. I started reading more and doing cross-stitches that took a lot of time, and I got into soaps real big, so I learn to cope with all the extra time.

Bobby Brown in New Jersey writes:

Prison life isn't easy nor is it a smooth ride for anyone. It's more easy to die here without the help of the state or anyone else. The mind seems to die slowly with the mere frustration and mental pain, if only you know! That alone is the death penalty.

Christopher Burger, age thirty-three, wrote from Georgia in 1993:

Yes, these past 16 years have been hell. No one really "lives" in here, we just do our best to survive. You asked me if during those times I had dates on me if I had anyone with me to help me get through those awful times. During the first one—March 1984—I did. I had a close friend who was here. It tore her heart out, it was so painful for her that not long after, she ended our friendship.

Edward B. Fitzgerald, in Virginia, executed in 1992, wrote as follows about his experience on Death Row:

I live in a world I hope no reader ever experiences. My house is 52 square feet in size and doubles as my yard. I receive room service for everything. Not because I want to, but because I cannot leave my house. My house is, in fact, my entire world. I have nothing beyond my 52 square feet of floor space, smaller than many bathrooms. My house is so small that my toilet is also my washbasin and dinner table.

My room service consists of cold food on paper plates and a dirty mop twice a week to clean my concrete floor, which I sleep on. I must yell to my neighbor in order to talk to anyone. Air conditioning is an open window in the winter time and heating is by the sun during the summer.

I am not a vicious dog or any other type of violent animal. I am a prisoner. I live in a world many of you believe I deserve. But mainly because you don't know me or just what kind of conditions I truly live under. The things you take for granted I don't even dream of getting: hot food, medical services, education, sunlight, fresh air, clean bed, clean room, and many other normal things. All I get is threatened by a riot squad if I take more than eight minutes in the shower.

I admit I'm no candidate for citizen of the year. But does that automatically make me runner up for vicious animal of the year?

Much has been said about prisoners as a group. But to explain is futile, because a prisoner's world is beyond a nonprisoner's comprehension. As I am, you'll never know unless you become like me. And I hope you never do, you won't like what you see. Any human can become an animal in prison.

How do the men on Death Row cope? Much depends on whether they are guilty or innocent, on the support they receive from family and friends, and on their mental resources.

Some prisoners manage to keep fairly busy, what with correspon-

dence, legal work, writing articles and even books, craftwork, and various other things such as martial arts, yoga, and meditation. The ones who suffer most are those lacking mental resources. Above all, remorse can eat people up. In their minds they will go over and over the events that landed them on Death Row. They persuade themselves they are innocent, or they blank everything out. This may take the form of drugs (either prescribed or smuggled in) or escapism into endless TV soaps.

On this question Stephen Nethery, a white prisoner convicted in 1981 at the age of twenty-one, wrote:

In my experience here I have noticed two extremes that many men go to. Some men will feel so terrible about their crimes that they will give up on life, and have such hatred of self that it is dangerous; to the point of suicide, extreme depression, etc. In fact, just two nights ago a man on another tank (not the Work Program) began to cut himself on his male organ, and this is not the first time for him to do this. I have to think that he is so burdened and weighed down with his guilt feelings that he despairs of life. Then on the other hand, some men convince themselves that they didn't do anything wrong, and they have absolutely no remorse or guilt at all because they are convinced that there is no sin, or something to this effect. Some men have this karma attitude, believing that everything that happens just happened, and we have no control over any event. And, since we have no control over the events, how can I be guilty of something I could not help but do? So, we have some that go overboard with guilt and self-hatred, and others that go to the opposite extreme.

Sam Johnson in Mississippi has summed up the feelings of those who are innocent:

For the first year or so I was filled to the brim with pure hatred over what had happened to me. Losing all that I had and everyone who I loved filled me so full of hatred I almost did go crazy. All of it drained out of me when it dawned upon me that I had to stop thinking about all I had lost and start thinking about what I could gain even from the worst of situations a person could be in.

To be wronged, as I've been, by an experience such as this would be for you, as it is for me, an affront to your dignity, integrity, and all else that you hold sacred and you would know, as I do, that to crack would be to never be able to prove your innocence and your mind would never allow itself to degenerate into a state where it couldn't strive to bring your innocence to the light and regain your freedom. I didn't harm or kill anyone and I can't allow myself to deteriorate to a state of being where I can no longer strive to prove my innocence.

Jan, children, in their innocence, at times are more perceptive than adults and I say this in response to what one of them said concerning innocence acting as a sort of a buffer to the intense feelings of guilt and remorse that most of the others here have. Whichever one of them said that certainly hit the nail right on the head (smile). I've witnessed guilt and remorse literally destroy people in here and my innocence is what, I'm sure, preserves what little sanity I have left (smile).

Of another inmate he wrote:

At one point in time I was in a cell next to a guy who had killed his half-brother, raped and killed his half-niece who was 12 years old and killed his half-niece's schoolmate who was also 12. His case certainly is a tragedy and at one point I felt deep hostility toward him and I felt it more because he raped and killed those children than because he killed his half-brother. It took time for those hostilities to leave me but when they did leave an understanding I've never had came to me: I have no right to judge anyone and he did what he did because, at that exact moment, he felt right in doing it. He has an IQ that's slightly above freezing temperature Fahrenheit but he knows that he was wrong and he is not as dumb as he wants people to believe. I've spent hours and hours and MORE hours helping him learn to read. He is not a person who I would trust around anyone outside of this environment but he is a person and I can't and/or won't mistreat him. I watched each new day bring a brand new death to him through his feelings of guilt and remorse and I've seen this place destroy him.

Similarly another inmate has written:

While I wait for my decision I sit daily and watch the harassment, torment, hate, anger, physical abuse, verbal abuse, loneliness and even love at its utmost. I see people driven to the point of seeming insanity; I see people who lose themselves inside.

A black man convicted in 1981 in his early twenties echoes the feelings of many when he writes:

This place is really catch up with me. I think about dropping my appeal at times just to keep from thinking about the future and how old I be if I ever get out. But my lawyer help keep my spirit up because I believe he doing everything to save my life. And you and R. are very very supported to.

But in his next letter he writes:

About me giving up my appeal I said that out of serious depression and mostly the stress I am going through. And I fell like a fool for saying such thing. But at time I really do fell that I be better of dead but I don't think I have enough courage to sign alway my own life. I'm to big of a coward but it seen like thing are getting so bad that a time I dont believe my little mind could take another year but each day I some how find the will-power to keep me going. Mostly it the wood work it realax me and help keep my mind off alot of thing and the encouraging from my lawyer and you and my grandma really are elevate when I'am felling low.

Willie Reddix, who has moved off Death Row in Mississippi, has vividly described the pressures:

It's been a somewhat tough six months for me, though nothing I won't overcome. I believe there is a madness going on in this prison. I'm beginning to see all the reasons one can and will die for in here. Right now officers and guards are going around taking people out of their cells, cutting their hair for no good reason. They don't have anything better to do. The ones who don't want a haircut, the guards beat them down with four-foot sticks after handcuffing and leg-shackling them. Then they cut their hair anyway. God knows what they are doing but it doesn't make any sense. I'm sick of seeing and hearing all the madness. I don't think I will forget any of this time soon.

And more times than I can remember I've ached beyond imagination to see the children, any children, at play. Very seldom around here do we get the chance to see a child. In more ways than one I live to behold a child's smile face to face out from this man-made hell I am forced to dwell in. Please don't misconstrue. I am not at all bitter or hateful toward those who hold me in captivity. In fact I am often grateful to be where I am, considering the children who are starving and dying all over the world needlessly.

Jack Potts in Georgia is one of the longest-serving men on Death Row in the United States:

I have been on death row since 1974. I am the last of the original 15 who began death row in 1974. There were 15 more to begin with back in 74. Everyone has been executed except me of that 15. I am sure you know Georgia has executed, murdered 14 men as of last year.

In order to survive, the prisoners are forced to adopt a tough veneer, both to other prisoners and to the guards. The following letter provides a powerful impression of the stresses the prisoners face, compounded by the, in many ways natural, reaction of the guards:

At no time during these past two months, even though I've not written, have you or any of our family been out of my thoughts, heart, and prayers. Now, as always, I pray that this day finds all of you fine and in all that's good and of God. All my love to all of you.

Before I entered into these past two months I had felt certain I'd reached the absolute nadir in the depressive depths that could be reached and withstood by any human being. I was wrong. I've gone below the below and while there I couldn't write. I'm ashamed to admit it now, but I came very close to giving up and hanging it all up. I can't, not in a few words, explain all I've gone through and I ask that you please bear with me while I talk. Somewhere within what I say will be an understanding that will let you know what I've been through.

With this I'm sending copies of papers that will let you see some of what I'm having to contend with. They have taken my word-processor and this is why I'm forced to punish your eyes with my handwriting. They, also, have taken all of my books, legal material, personal property, and just about everything else. Before doing this they started back to beating us again. So far it's only been the one brother I mention in my complaint but his beating has everyone else living/existing in terror while wondering who will be next?

Since I've last spoken with you three other brothers have arrived. One of these is the guy I told you about who killed one of the guards here. The other two were charged with robbing, killing, raping and burning the bodies of a whole family. This tragedy happened near here and most of the guards who work here know the family who was murdered.

The hostilities and hatred the guards feel toward the new arrivals spill over upon all of us here and, although subtle, we are being mistreated worse than ever. Several white inmates here on the row have elevated racial tension by trying to kill one of them over what he did, or supposedly did.

This doesn't even come close to my saying all of the things I want and need to talk with you about. I'm not feeling at all well right now. I'll write again as soon as I can. Things aren't going well for me at all right now. I'll write again as soon as I can. I love you with all my heart and soul and know this always. Please pray for me as I pray for all of you.

Sam Johnson, Mississippi:

This experience had almost caused me to forget that "real people" still existed and it does my whole being good just to be able to talk with you. You know what suffering and injustice is all about and I feel comfortable with you more so than I would with someone who had experienced neither. I'm able to feel and understand your feelings as I hope that you are able to feel and understand what I feel.

What I experience is not dissimilar to what you experienced growing up and living in Belfast. Over the years I've kept up as best I could with what has been happening in Ireland and, like this, there aren't "proper" words for what it is.

"Equality" doesn't mean that the next person is "equal" to you but you are "equal" to the next person. In my heart I know that you know what equality means as well as I do and are against inequality and injustice as much as I am. I often ask myself, "When will it end?" I don't have the answer but I pray that I live and have the strength to help bring about its end. I don't believe that "everything" that always was always has to be. God is the only "constant" and humans can change inequality and injustice into justice and equality. Into "real love."

In spite of this I still believe in mankind. These people and this experience has taken me so low until I have had to "reach up" to touch the bottom but I still believe in mankind.

A lot of the guys in here have stopped believing in anything at all. So far I've been able to resist the temptation of this. I hope that you don't mind that I let some of them read your letter. I let them read it to try and show them that there really are people who care left in this world today. You are "hope" to more than just me, E.

Another inmate in Mississippi:

You don't have friends when you come in here. When I was free I had lots of so-called friends. Since I been here I haven't heard or seen them. What kind of friends are they?

I am tired of being in here. I don't know how much more I can take. Thank you for being my friend. Your caring helps me so much.

I just feel very alone, if anyone can make it through this they can make it through anything. How can any of us prepare ourselves to die? I have been here eight years now. I don't want to be so old when I get out I can't play with my son. Sometimes I want to give up, but I can't. I will fight them till I can't go anymore. I don't like my son to see me here like this. When we get a visit, no contact any, we have on handcuffs and behind bars.

We all feel down sometimes and ain't but one man can bring you back up and that is God. When the state take someone's life, yes it hurts, not only Leo but everybody. He don't talk that much anymore. I am trying to hang in here for a little while longer but its getting harder and harder.

Also from Mississippi:

We go outside sometimes whenever they let us. There's no trees up here. Everything is flat. I want to go home so bad. I want to be free to do what I want, to go as I please. They give us a visit two times a month but I don't get one. In the winter here you freeze and in summer you cook and the bugs will eat you up. You can't see the sun set. I have almost forgotten how a sunset looks. Sometimes I want to run away and keep running, running, running for ever. People here are so full of hate. It is an evil place.

I like to go outside and look up at the sky and thank God my father for letting me come outside. I like looking up and seeing the birds flying over because its a great joy to know that there's still some things in this world that's still free.

But even though the prisoners see Death Row as hell, some, at least, are able to place their privation in some kind of perspective:

Quite frankly, I'm quite amazed that there is an interest in any of what I write. I mean, I'm just one person out of millions in this world going through their own individual nightmares. I'm constantly aware that whatever I face in here, every day people watch their children starve to death, their families die of disease that could have been avoided, or they have their whole world blown to pieces by rich, arrogant foreigners. This place might be Hell, but it's only a relative purgatory compared to a lot of other places.

In their struggle to maintain a modicum of sanity and to survive, some prisoners turn to religion, while others dig deep into black consciousness and see things primarily in political and racist terms. John

B. Irving, on Death Row in Mississippi from 1976 to 1995—his entire adult life—wrote to his pen-friend:

The thing about racism, against which I have and do continue consciously to struggle the most, is the evil of depriving the other (the victim) of characteristics most identifiably human. While struggling to retain my humanity here on Death Row, there was a period of time when I suffered from what I would describe as an "identity crisis." In other words I didn't know who I was in relation to the American system. Since existing on Death Row involves isolation and alienation from all supportive relations, unless there are those who reach out to embrace one (humanly) there is no other except God to affirm one's existence and humanity. To resolve my "identity crisis" I had to understand its causes—i.e. that it was that I had to act against—to retain my humanity.

Racism has been a factor depreciating the God-given value of black life and amputating black humanity (by its artificial social and economic construction of reality) from the very beginning of the organization of the judicial system in this country. The victim in the crime for which I am condemned was white, and in such a case the state's courts, as presently constituted, cannot be impartial and fair. I had a white resentencing court and an all-white jury in an area of the state where blacks still have no rights in the minds of the whites. If I was a white man I would be free and certainly not on Death Row. To know what equal justice under the law means and the value of it to all human beings, one only has to experience being deprived of it when the defense of one's liberty and the protection of one's life was dependent on it.

In any event, to study the history of the white legal system in this country, seeking to understand one's present relation to it as a black person, is to uncover how laws were devised, interpreted and applied to cripple (to enslave) and strip African Americans of their humanity, even the characteristic use of their original names. Therefore, in struggling to retain my humanity in this Death Row experience I have tried to recover my African identity through the adoption of an African name. Every time a friend calls me by my African name it triggers, in a genuine way, "feelings of love" for the other, by me.

You asked me if I could describe the way we are treated on Death Row, the routine and the surroundings. I fear it would take a book to do justice to this subject. You are absolutely correct: "They do set out to de-humanize us in any way they can." The treatment would amount to torture even without the death sentence being a factor. We wear no watches or rings or other jewelry. The only furnishing in our cells are a wall locker and a television. Apart from these, our cells are stripped and we are not allowed to personalize them. Generally we are only let out of our cells for one hour five days a week. There are no recreational programs with the exception of an occasional basketball game. We spend 22 hours and 45 minutes each day locked down in our 8 × 7 cells. There are no education programs and no work details for Death Row inmates. We have no windows to look outside. The overwhelming number of inmates, in this kind of forced idleness, live to watch TV. They go to sleep turning off their sets, and wake turning it on. Originally conceived to provide entertainment, televisions have become tools to aid other brain-washing techniques.

The environment is rigid and unrelaxed, geared to be restrictive and to punish all who exist within it. Your observation, "that they deny us contact (physical touch) by our loved ones" is also correct. In fact, our visits are, in a twisted way, used to undermine the self-respect and emotional health of those who participate. We are so restricted and punished that we are deprived of all the normal benefits (under the law) granted to incarcerated persons serving sentences involving time [i.e., nondeath sentences].

There is a death camp in the state of Mississippi. The majority of its residents are black. I've lived within its walls for all but a few months of the past 13 years of my life. Within these walls, not unlike the Jews, I have been terrorized and traumatized by this experience. All of those who have been executed here were close to me. Along with them I have felt the betrayal of our humanity in my heart and in my soul. I know that no segment of society should have to bear the brutalization of this humanity and that it should be halted.

I grew up with a love for the wide open spaces, the hills, the lakes, channels and springs, being true to the spirit of the outdoors. I used to enjoy hunting and fishing and camping out, being under the moon and stars at night with nature's sounds entertaining me and feeling at one with the darkness and all of creation. To be sure, today, hunting and fishing do not appeal to me anymore. I am the hunted, the caught, the prey, the victim of the crafty, the cunning, the powerful. I can identify with all hunted, captured, preyed-upon life forms in a way that I can see myself at one with creation, being senselessly destroyed for sport or materialistic profits.

Another prisoner in Mississippi wrote to his pen-friend:

I knew Sam [Johnson]; we were side by side for over two years, we are very close. He taught me most of what I know about the law of mankind. I was moved for no good reason, just another ploy of these people to keep us separated and keep us from unifying ourselves in this man-made hell they keep us in!

I stay pretty much to myself. It's very easy to get misled or killed in this place hanging about with the wrong people.

I don't allow the noise to affect me. Yes, I do get cold sometimes, mostly when I'm walking around in the morning time. I don't have a sweater so I try to walk up and down my cell doin' a little callisthenics till I warm up . . . there's no heat in our cells when it gets too cold and the heaters at each end of the halls isn't working. I sometimes burn the milk carton or newspapers that I have, most of the time it ain't so bad.

A female prisoner writes of the deprivations—and how some respond:

The food is so bad we have to buy something good to eat off the store or to starve onself. It is mostly junk food, but it fills the spot. So in other words we are really paying to stay here, if you don't have any one to help you, you are mess up real bad. We have to buy everything from the store here, even prison is a racket for money and some of these women don't have anyone to help them, and they have to do without or sell their body. They use to give us tea, coffee, salt, tolit paper, sugar, stuff like that, but as the first of the year they cut it out. You either buy or do without.

Conditions in Parchman Penitentiary, Mississippi, have sometimes brought the inmates on Death Row out on hunger strike. One such strike occurred around the time that Leo Edwards was executed in June 1989. John Irving wrote of this time:

Today marks the 22nd day that I've been on the strike. I talked to Leo months ago about this action. The last time we organized a strike here the prison authorities repressed it, blocked out media coverage and punished the strikers and our families with denials of visits, calls, mail and other rights and privileges until the strike was broken. This was fully participated in by a majority of prisoners (1983).

A few days later he wrote:

Today marks the 31st [day] of the hunger strike. I can't write much for long sittings.

Eight days later he came off the hunger strike. Five days later he wrote:

I'm still on a spiritual high. The experience had enormous value to me, not just the political statement I was able to make but a spiritually empowering experience as well. I lost a lot of weight. I'm still going through a process of regaining my physical strength.

Another inmate wrote of this experience:

They are still treating us worse than animals but, other than this, things are fairly quiet. The hunger strike, as you already know, has ended. I'm trying to get this old body back into shape (smile). Not eating as I did took more out of me than I knew it would. Oh, I'm in good health, it's just that I'm not as I was before I stopped eating.

A further strike was held in July 1991 in protest at the conditions in the block where the prisoners were being temporarily housed while Unit 17—Death Row—was being renovated.

Mark Allen "Wiseguy" Wisehart in Indiana writes of a prison riot:

It began as a sort of "nuisance protest" whereas you throw cereal boxes and paper and orange peels etc. on the range to ensure that the police on duty has to do some work that day, and must sweep the range. Then when some police would mumble and moan it became a game to *really* get to them, so the mess changed to wet and sticky items to ensure that you had to sweep and scrub. Then it turned into burning— burning paper, cups of styrofoam, bowls and even chemically treated fire-retardant pillows that *do* smoke and smolder. At that time they (the administration) shut us down. So they (the inmates) started throwing "assorted nasty things" on the police as they walked by. It's tense right now, there are a lot of broken windows, it's cold, but at least, for now, it's quiet.

A twenty-five-year-old man in Huntsville, Texas, writes bleakly about the point he has reached:

I'm a fatalist and believe that my destiny is predetermined. I'm at a point in my life, that I've almost lost my will to live. I have nothing to look forward to, no prospect of ever getting out. This might sound like a comment made out of desperation but the awful realization of this is, that if I had someone that cared about me, someone that was close to me, and perhaps came to visit me, someone other than my mom, I'd have an incentive, the motivation, to go on in this environment.

A Georgia inmate, Victor Roberts, has written:

The real prison is agonizing frustration, fruitless despair and unfamiliar indifference. The real prison is where too many people struggle to find the answers in their own enfeebled illusioned self, because there is no one else who will listen or even try to understand.

It is a place of endless routines, where time itself is a dreadful task. How much more longer must we wait, how much longer must we knock at the gates of the righteous, before the outcasting of hate and unworthiness cease, and become an expression of love and affection?

Does anyone care to know who I am or to know of the love and affection I hold within my being?

Death Row is much more than a place filled with despair, uncertainty, sordidness, indifference and futility. It is the dungeon of hell that awaits all individuals sentenced to death and, for many, to unrest for the remainder of their lives. Too many of our dreams, ideas, feelings and thoughts have been replaced with the monstrous burden of regret . . .

In Alabama, Billy Kuenzel gained some relief when he was given an official task:

I have another job, it is what we call hall runner. What it means is I am out of my cell so I can take ice or hot water to the other guys who are locked down. So I am out of my cell every day one week and four days the next week and please believe I do like this. It enables me to help someone plus get some exercise. The officers in charge told me I would be good for the job since I cause no trouble. We don't get paid for it, but it is OK as long as I can lend a helping hand.

The way I see it is I am at the lowest point of my life now, so I only have one choice and that is to better myself and pick my life up. If I don't help myself, how can I expect anyone else to want to help?

A man in Texas expresses a similar determination:

I am not under any circumstances going to let these people deter me from my work and writing. I know that they will never stop trying. They must also know that I will never allow them to succeed. I guess that it is a game that must be played but it makes no difference that I am in their ball park and playing by their rules. I shall win.

It is very demeaning to me to know that I was so stupid as to let myself get in such a position that I can only sit and wait for someone else to rule my life. How totally stupid of me! I wish I could get the proper angle so I could kick myself real hard.

Edward Fitzgerald in Virginia wrote as follows to his pen-friend in Ireland, Dr. Liam O'Gorman, about the effect of being on Death Row:

There are many things, both mental and physical, that happen to those on death rows. And different things can occur during different stages of their appeals. It probably covers the entire scope of human actions. Abandonment is an overwhelming feeling in this kind of situation. For many we are zoo animals, for others we are monsters right out of fairy tales. And those are just the ones who never knew us. For those who did it is shame. They don't want to be known as knowing someone on the row. Knowing someone on the row is as much a shameful thing to many as it is to be here. Some will tell their friends that you are in jail for some minor crime, they'd never tell their friends that they know someone on the row.

But most just act as if they never knew you at all. I think it starts with the shock that they knew you and all of a sudden you are in a place like this, by the time the shock wears off all they knew is the shame. You no longer become a human even to those who knew you. It's a bad feeling to have known someone for years and then all of a sudden they act as if you were the monster that ate New York. Most of the time you never hear from them, other times they write back and tell you not to write to them any more. And for some that even includes family members. So you are cut off from the things you remember, it's a solid case of being abandoned. Then you have to pick up the pieces and start all over, often times with no one by your side. Sometimes you get friendly with someone in here and they have a friend who has a friend who might write, other times you take out "personals" ads in magazines and just hope that through all the other ads someone will write. Usually if you do it this way you don't dare mention you are on the row. You just make up some reason you won't be getting out. Then if things work out you may tell them. But then they feel as though you lied to them so they abandon you as well. It's a no win situation.

I think anyone in any institution has a death of personality to some extent. Everyone has certain things they are good at and they enjoy. In an institution your choices of what you are allowed to do are strictly limited. Partly due to the security and also because there are so many people there. Often times you have to find new ways to have a personality. I used to act like a little kid around my kids and the animals. I just love dogs and cats and would play with them all the time. I used to love it when my daughter would say, "daddy, you silly." But it made her feel good and I'd have fun. But you can't have that kind of fun with a roach, which is the only animal you can have. And don't try to play with one of the other guys like he's a three year old.

So you suppress yourself knowing you'd love to have a kitten or a puppy to play with or you know your child will be grown up the next time you see them and you aren't silly any more. Many of the guys lose themselves completely and take on a completely different personality, usually acting like a gangster. You can usually tell the ones that spent time in foster homes and the like, they mouth off the most and for the simplest of reasons. They ended up in what is nothing but a prison to many before they even had a personality. Some are lucky and channel their personalities in different directions but good directions rather than hurtful ones.

Depression is a biggy. Most of the guys, me included, want to get executed the moment the judge says die. They don't care about any appeals, just get it over with. By the time the first appeal has run its course, even though it's denied, you want to fight the appeals process till there is no hope at all. But every day you feel at least a moment of depression over something. It could be the smell of the morning air, looking out the window and seeing the barbed wire, getting handcuffs put on, having to ask for a meal through a set of bars, or the memory of what once was and of those you've hurt just by being here. Sometimes it may last a moment then you put it out of your mind, other times it stays with you for days. Sometimes you try to remember something, but just can't, you've forgotten what food really tastes like, what it felt like to walk further than 10 feet without having to turn, all kinds of things. And then the biggy itself, to read your appeal was turned down yesterday. You feel one court closer to the chair. But even though, the depression of forgetting and not knowing is worse than remembering. To know your child is out there but don't know how they are is worse than the memories of the fun you used to have together.

Many people avoid telling you things because they don't want to depress you. What's depressing, is not knowing. When you don't know what's going on around you it's the same as being abandoned because you are still cut off from what is going on around you even though you aren't able to be there. It is like the old question about if a tree falls in a forest and no one hears, does it really make a sound? Well, I don't know if it made a sound, but if you happen across that fallen tree let me know it fell or I'll forever have only the past memory of it standing. My daughter isn't three any more, she's 13. I have memories of her being three, now I need to know what she's like at 13. So depression is a trade-off. Some handle it one way, others another, some dwell on it, some ignore it, but it's all around every day.

Jo Payne (Virginia) wrote in 1992:

It is to me, like being on a small merry-go-round and life is limited to doing whatever I can without getting off the merry-go-round. There are times when the routine becomes a stranglehold that I can feel trying to dehumanize me each day. It kind of reminds me of the many days and nights I used to have to remain locked in my bedroom when I was a kid. I guess we all feel it in our own way, just as the condemned's family and friends do in their own way each day until the executioner ends the stranglehold for the condemned and leaves the family and friends with sorrow.

This repetitious life on death row, where each day brings a person closer to violent death, makes it hard to think sometimes. (Makes it hard to feel like thinking.) It tends to make it hard to feel motivated. During the better than 5 years I've been here so far, I've found the past two to be the hardest both physically and mentally. As each year passes the stranglehold routine of the row has had me struggling to remain thinking of life, future, and continuing to better myself as a living, caring human being.

There are times when I feel so apart from life that reading, watching TV, listening to the radio or conversating seem useless, meaningless and at times irritating. It is not something easily explained. Maybe it has to be felt and experienced to really understand. The only way I know how to explain it is that life does not have the same joy and interest when death seems to overwhelm one and one so clearly feels . . . or knows that he isn't really a part of life, and the small way he is will soon be deliberately ended.

I know that there are many who will say "good, I'm glad they feel like that for they made my loved one or another human being feel this way when they took their life." For myself, and I'm sure others, this too stagnates and saddens my thoughts. It saddens me to steal from my hopes because: (1) it is the same cruel reasoning used by one who murders. It says I don't care how this human being feels, or how his family and loved ones feels. And, (2) when an innocent person, or someone who really didn't intend to or who if not mentally deranged or highly intoxicated would not have killed, is placed on death row, their chances of getting fair justice is lessened by such cruel reasoning, because people of this attitude don't care or want to believe that the judicial process isn't perfect and those who are innocent and able to change by incarceration, treatment and maturity will be killed.

Prisoners in many states comment how the type of people coming onto Death Row has changed. In particular, they comment on the gangs. A black prisoner in a Deep South state who has been on Death Row for fourteen years writes (February 1996):

Now as for the gangs. I will never as long as I live understand their way of thinking. Their coming to DR is the biggest (if not the only) reason for the problems we now have here on DR and I know they are the reasons for the prison treating us like dog shit! Sorry for writing that down, but it was in my thoughts . . .

Getting the death penalty didn't change them at all. That's something I can't understand. How can someone know they have people trying to kill them every day and not give a damn? Life to them is but a game and what happens to them after they leave this world is not a part of their small brain. They wonder how and why I could become a Muslim when their gangs are all they need in this world. I just tell them the reason: because life has meaning for me. And the taking of life is not something I take as a piece of cake. I've done some things in my past that I look back on and I can't believe that face can be the same face I see today. (Why can't they see the light?)

His views echo those of a white prisoner in Texas, writing in October 1995:

Another thing that has been weighing heavily on me are the changes I've seen on the Row the last few months. I've not wanted to talk about it, hoping things would maybe mellow out. I hoped I was wrong. For years now I've talked about how we seemed to be a refuge away from the hostility and racism that typifies the prison system. This is changing, and I fear for this place. America is undergoing a nasty series of social changes. Kids these days are becoming more and more hostile.

When I first wrote to you, I was on lock-down awaiting an execution date. Two friends on lock-down had recently returned from court hearings in some of the larger counties. The stories they told me about the kids in jail there were shocking and frightening. An entire generation, I was told, was being turned loose on the world without the slightest hint of conscience, social concern or the slightest evidence of normal human compassion. I didn't want to believe it, hoping that my friends here were falling prey to the same biases that influence the media these days. But I kept hearing it again and again from people I trusted. Eventually, they told me, these insane kids would be making their way to the Row and we'd have to face them ourselves.

Since the beginning of the summer the level of violence on the Row has risen. I kept thinking this was an aberration. But they really are that bad. It's not all of the new kids coming, or even half, but nearly half. They're mostly black, though a lot of them are Hispanic, and the level of racial hatred they harbor astounds me. The old-timers, the black and Mexican men they should have respected for their years here, are as freaked out by them as I am. They don't listen to the old-timers. Many of them place no value on life, anybody else's or their own. It's not only the Row has changed, but rather that the streets have changed and the kids coming in now merely reflect that. The solidarity that characterized the Row is fast dying, and for the first time in my life I feel the tension and feel the need to watch my back.

The surprise is not that it's becoming this way, but rather the surprise is that it hasn't been that way all these years. For me, and for most people I've known over the years, there's been this surprise that the people in here were as mature and respectful toward one another as they have been. I came expecting the worst of the worst, as would most people outside. Instead I found a higher quality than I found when I was free. Now they're becoming the worst of the worst, just as the public would like for us to be. Though I often describe this place as a Hell, I more often make reference to a relative purgatory to what it could be. The purgatory is passing and now it is truly a welcoming to Hell I'm facing. Again, there are some good people coming in. It's the others who are taking control, however.

5

Welcome to Hell

The following excerpts are drawn from the letters of a white prisoner who must, of necessity, remain anonymous. For legal reasons other names have also been omitted or changed.

Before the cold spell hit the other day I went out to the rec yard and walked around. Somehow some leaves had blown into the yard. I and the other guy out there noticed that right off because leaves are sort of nonexistent where we are. These obviously had to have blown over a building and through two fences to be in our rec yard. They were pin oak leaves and I remember thinking it was kind of late in the season for pin oak leaves to be dropping. And then it occurred to me that I really didn't know what had or hadn't dropped off—or what shape the grass was in or how moist the soil was. Or where the stars were for the season. Once upon a time, Ruth, I knew by the feel of the air and the changing of the clouds when the phases of the seasons' changes came—I knew the faces of the seasons' changes. I knew the cycles of the moon and the positions of the stars by equinox. And the order of the leaves dropping and which animals came and went with those changes. I used to go to the orchards when the pecan leaves fell (they all fall at once in almost a single day, ya know) and I was always ready for the night(s) of the Perseid meteor showers. A blue moon would have been cause for a party with my friends (the next one after this one won't happen until after 2000). I hate to come across sounding like Running Wolf of the tribe or Jim-bob o' the Pines, but it really struck me just how separated from the reality of the earth I am any more. All those rule changes and subtleties which were intimate aspects of my day-to-day reality are alien to me and have been replaced by the subcultural rules of behavior, the subleties and changes of this prison that one has to have in order to make it best in here. It just hadn't occurred to me until I was hit with those leaves how much of that part of my reality was gone. I've thought about it before, but for some reason the reality just hit me particularly hard that day. I guess that might be because I don't see any trees at all where I am now. Prison walls surround three sides of the rec yard and the other side faces the side of the garment factory which is itself seen through two fences, one with sheet metal covering it. The only sky I see has to be during the day and it's through "xxxxxx"s of chainlink fencing. When I was on the other wing my cell was on the third row and I could see the horizon and some trees in the distance—that was something. Now, nothing. Except what blows over the buildings and the fence, and those leaves are dead. I was truly in tune with nature (god, that sounds so damn corny), which was my environment. Now I'm in tune with this environment. Kind of a shitty trade off, really. All that because of a leaf.

I went out to the rec yard yesterday morning when nobody else was out there and lay down on the warm concrete while a cool breeze was blowing over my body. And from there, I could look up at the sky and after I stared long enough I could just about ignore the chainlink fencing that blocks the sky from coming down to where I am. Then I could close my eyes and pretend I was lying on the ground in the early spring under the cool breeze of the fields we used to gather in when I was younger and free. There were all these great places on the warm concrete. One place called Sandy Sherry Lane with its fireplace/chimney megalithic monument on Bradford Mountain, had white poppies and dewberries growing. And there was a place called Sunset Hill where we all used to go every evening to watch the sun set. Another place called Strawberry Fields, cliché as it was, actually had native wild strawberries growing which, though not very edible, smelled delicious. One place I thought about that I hadn't remembered in years was the old Indian altar. Lying on the concrete made me think of that because there was this huge flat slab of iron ore and big boulders around it to sit on that the natives put there a long, long time ago. I used to lie on that slab and stare at the sky on days and on nights. We used to fantasize that the Indians had at one time sacrificed humans there, though we all knew that wasn't the case. Actually, the "altar" was more than likely used as a convenient place to smash nuts and acorns. I've made love many times out there. Anyway, I thought about all those places out on the recreation yard yesterday while I had the whole yard to myself.

Death really is changed for me now. It used to be that death was like a familiar to me, a part of nature and part of life. When you got old, death was there to take you on out of this hackneyed life and give you your rest. "Ah Death sweet sister of Morpheus . . ." I was with some of my relatives when they were old and finally passing and I never thought of death as anything other than part of life. I rode a bike for a long time, and I rode it pretty hard and extremely fast—you can't be ignoring or fearing death when you do that.

And then all the drugs, like testing limits. With the drugs someone somewhere had to set limits since it's often the limits you're testing. Death was kind enough to do that for me. It gave me the edge needed to keep the thrill (both with the drugs and the bike), maintain the diversion. For some people seeking the "redline" is almost a religion. Redline! It's the redline, Ruth. The redline tells you when the wattage in the amplifier is high enough. You know when you're going fast enough when the tach hits redline on the bike. Put enough shit in the spike and you'll actually see the redline before your eyes when you pull the needle out. Do it enough times and you carry a permanent reminder in the redline down your arm—and in the scars the stitches leave after you crash your machine. Inspiration, ecstasy and madness are all there on the redline. It's the edge, the border between life and death and when you get on that line, when you stand on it you're close enough to see death as it is.

I've been there so damn many times, Ruth. It made life interesting and it was always there for me when and if things got too boring in this world. That is as death should be, Ruth. Unfortunately, that's all changed now. They've stolen Death, Ruth. Death, a perfectly natural thing, has been taken and used as a tool by the people who want to run our lives. No one has the right to do that, to take death and use it for their own purposes. It suddenly becomes perverted, and evil—a sick thing. Now that the government owns it and controls the use at will, I hate it. They've changed it. Or maybe they've always owned it. I don't know any more. I see it as a tool of a twisted government trying to get me as it's already gotten my friends down here—and all the other friends who were shot by policemen on the streets years ago, now that I realize who owns it. And even with this Persian Gulf thing, it's the use of the tool, Death, that all the trouble rides on. It's theirs, to dispense, to mete in controlled doses, so much for our guys (a willing sacrifice) in order to pass some of it on to the other guys, all in order to force will upon someone somewhere. Like a tool, it's a transfer of force, energy. Send our guys in and let so many die so that the death will be multiplied many times over to the other side, transferred so that they are moved to bend our way.

With me and the others down here it's a tool to apply to get re-elected, to make people do things they might not have done otherwise (like vote for whoever is tougher on crime). They can't leave it alone now. Leave death alone, let it ride its own waves and come and go naturally, it's no longer a tool. It's just a part of nature. But true to modern man's addiction, they always try to conquer, to control and own nature—even the part of nature that death is. Now I find it hard to separate the two, separate real and natural death from the mutant version. They all bother me now. And I sometimes can't be sure which is which. Did Jack fall prey to this sorry goddamned prison system—or did the rogue, feral beautiful thing that natural death is finally give Jack a way out of here? Would it have happened anyway, even if he were free? He knew it was coming, I think—but he also knew this wasn't any place to try to face it. Sometimes, in fact quite often, I think I'd welcome it, especially after last week and after the days of the dreams (more on that later).

And I remember the old days. But then I think about the other side of it now, the perverse mutant it's become. And in that sense, giving in would be to cooperate with the system, to let their use of the tool happen and in doing so some way validate it. I think in that I see the reason R. could fight so damn hard and never give in like I've wanted to do so many times. I've got that insight now and I see what he meant.

At the same time, however, I have the old memories, the old image and familiarity from seeing it so close so many times in the past when it was a friend. Sometimes I think that doing it myself is the way to take it out of their hands, that inviting it my own self with my own hand makes it mine and not their tool any more. Sometimes I wish I had someone to talk to.

God I gotta get out of here, Ruth. Yesterday was the six year anniversary of being arrested. Think back for a minute to where you were six years ago as you read this letter—where were you and what was your life then? Now try to think how much life has gone by for you from then until now, how much life you've lived, how many changes you've gone through. No doubt that's a lot of life, Ruth. It should have been a lot of life for me and every day I think about how much has been taken away from me. I shouldn't, but I do. Every month that goes by makes more important the weighing of the consideration whether there is enough left to keep fighting for. Don't take that wrong—I'm not going to give up any time in the near future, but it is a relationship I do think about. It's kind of like with a car or something. I mean, if it gets a dent, it's still a good car. A big dent can be fixed, the car can recover so to speak. But at some point the car is damaged enough that it's not worth recovering anything from—it's totaled. I often wonder how much one has to lose of life, how much loss and damage it takes to push the situation over the edge so that life is "totaled." I really wish I didn't think these things. I just keep thinking, wow, six years and still going. Even if, IF, I get out of here ever it'll still be a lot of years away. Will I reach the "totaled" ratio sometime during that time?

I had a dream about my children the other night. I hate those dreams worse than anything in the world, Ruth. In one of the Camus plays, *Caligula*, Caligula says that everybody we touch in our lives, we carry with us the rest of our lives, but that the dead we knew are no problem because they weigh nothing—it's the living we drag with us who weigh so much to carry. That's so true. Sometimes I wish I could forget the children, in a way. They, or their memory, is like being haunted by the most painful of ghosts. At the same time those memories—and those dreams—are all I have left of them. They're *all* and I can't let those go. If I could do that it would be the final and ultimate betrayal of the center of my universe. Painful or not (boy, that's an understatement!), I have to embrace those memories, which are all I have left. Even if it means embracing the pain. I guess that sounds pretty self-destructive, and it is truly an obsession. What else can I do, though?

Every so often I dream about them, and that's bad. But there are some dreams other times which are not just dreams. You know how when you wake up after even an intense dream, the type of dream you wake up from with the feeling of a touch still on your skin or a taste still in your mouth, over the course of the day the dream slowly fades from memory and becomes less real like a dream should? Sometimes these other dreams don't do that like they should. They become just as real, intense and tangible as the memory of what I ate today at lunch or the card I read from you last week. I know in my mind they aren't true, they're just a dream, but that doesn't save me from the feelings the memory brings with it. In the bad ones, the really hard ones, like the one the other night, I find my babies. The dreams always have certain surreal aspects, the circumstances in which I find my kids perhaps. Like this last one I just happened to accidentally move into a house that just happened to be near where my ex lived. More surreal yet is that my ex was just a common, normal person and she was mellow enough to let me start seeing my kids. But the kids they were so real. Sonia remembered me but didn't quite feel comfortable with me. Billy didn't remember me but he trusted me because Sonia did. And I can remember holding them and talking to them and playing with them. And I remember my ex agreeing to start letting me see them, being a fantasy real person. I can remember the color and texture of the carpet, the layout of both houses—everything in such exacting detail. And then they woke me up—and it felt just like them being taken away from me all over again and that hurt. I tried to go back to sleep but I couldn't. I couldn't find them again. They were there just a minute before, just as real as this typewriter is right now. And then they were gone, like stepping through a door and not being able to step back through where you came from again. Then the dream never faded away during the day to being just that, a phantom memory, a dream.

I remember talking to Ann a little over a week ago and I remember looking at leaves in the rec yard a couple weeks ago. And I remember holding Sonia and Billy a couple days ago. I wish I could forget and I hate myself so damn much for wishing that or even thinking it. Those are the times when I really do wish I could die so I wouldn't have to go through that again, to make them real in a dream only to lose them again. It happens every few weeks to me like that. One time I woke up holding a dead Sonia and that was the worst time. Those dreams, like this last one or the one with a dead baby, are the worst times in here. That's when the razor blades really start looking good to me. Like, have you ever noticed how the double edged ones, or the craft ones, look like carnival tickets? I have. Or bus tickets or train tickets, tickets out of this place.

The other day I saw that door again. I know this is going to sound crazy, but please bear with me. You know the tracers or darters you sometimes see out of the corner of your eye, the little dark things running by just at the edge of your peripheral vision, but when you turn to see them they aren't there and you never quite make it out? Just like that I see this big hole, like a door or entrance to a cave, sometimes out of the corner of my eye, usually when I'm tired or when the stress and edgies are getting out of hand. If I don't look at it I can just make some of it out. I know that little Ann went through and others have gone through, the one that fascinates and scares the Hell out of me so bad. Sometimes it looks like some Lovecraftian formless dark evil to me. At other times it's bright and beautiful to me. Often it's only dark until I get a little peek at what is behind it, like through the crack of a door, and I see the bright. At times like that, it's beautiful though I don't trust it. I wonder what happens if I go through, Ruth. I can still never see it directly. It's like the act of focusing directly centers the psyche again in this reality—the door is always there just waiting but I can't see it usually. And like when it's there, if I don't refocus on this world again by accident or intent, I'll go through. If it is madness that is waiting on the other side, is it dark like the door or is it bright and beautiful like I think it is? And if I go through it, are Sonia and Billy there like in the dreams, so real and tactile, where I'll be forever and don't have to worry about being woke up and lost again? Or is it so bizarre and extreme that I won't remember them to feel guilty about betraying them by forgetting them? Sometimes I want to find out.

The door was there when I was free too. But I always had something to make me look at it so it'd go away. Or something to get my attention and center me and love me. And Jeanette would need to be picked up and loved. It's like love was the antidote to madness then. Before Karen and Jeanette there was the fuckin' redline. The door would get close and wide, but the intensity of the redline and making it through redline alive would always force a focus. When it wouldn't there was always speed (both uses of the word) to augment, like using pain or other neuro-stimulation to divert your attention. Sometimes there was the acid. Sonia and Billy never came there to haunt me, which is one of the things that makes me think the bright aspect of the door might provide that escape. For a long time it was the codeine. I had a rather intense romance with her for a long while. It never stopped the dreaming or the memories—but they didn't hurt. She kills more pain than just the physical. When I gave her up, the codeine (ah sweet Morpheus, sweet sister of death—that's from polymorphously perverse Genet), it was only when I had Karen and Jeanette to love me instead. And before codeine, it was the redline. In here, though, I've got nothing to distract or center me. In here it's just me alone in this cell with the memories, the ghosts and the black hole out of the corner of my eye.

Imagine trying to discuss that with family in the visiting room or with strangers from the University of Texas!

Saturday morning I guess I wasn't in the best mood. At goddamn 6:30 in the morning they bring a maintenance crew into the wing to recaulk a couple of windows. And they just happen to have to park their tool-box-on-wheels in front of my cell—by banging it into the bars. Cool, I can always go back to sleep. I even overlooked them having to rummage through the box for their tools. But when they started literally "hooping," yelling at the door to the wing (about 70 feet away) to guys passing in the central hallway, I started getting a little pissed. What really blew it was when one of the stupid son-of-a-bitches, using a screwdriver and a putty knife, started using my fucking bars for a practice drum set. I came up out of my bunk ready to destroy someone or something, and, well, I sort of called them every kind of stupid dog-fucker in the world. This inmate actually acted offended that I'd get mad. His partner told him to relax because I was "*just* a death row convict." So they started running on about "yeah, they jus' fuckin' def ro convicks, fuck them, man . . ." And then the guard escorting them came and told me to leave *his* inmates alone. Then the bastard had the audacity to tell me I couldn't go back to sleep, that I had to get off my bunk and go stand at the back of the cell because they didn't want me that close to the tool box. This cracked the inmate workers up and they had a good laugh with the guard, who kept going on about "who the Hell does he think he is getting mad? Stupid goddamn death row con, hell, he ain't gonna be 'round much longer anyway." This sort of pushed my adjoining neighbors over the edge too, and they started telling the guard and inmates to bring their asses close enough to the bars and then say that shit. And I'll be damned if the wing officer didn't come down and tell *us* to shut up. I asked for a sergeant and, unfortunately, the only one who was on that morning is a real scumbag. His only reaction was to tell me I shouldn't be yelling at other inmates or talking that loud that early in the morning. That's how I spent my Saturday morning from 6:30 until 8:00. I fucking hate this place!

This morning didn't seem to be much of a change for the last few days. Do you remember the new population inmate porter/floorboy I told you about? The one who got my last two neighbors moved and who has been telling everyone to dump their leftovers in the toilet so he wouldn't have to rake the trays out after meals? This is the guy I tried to explain the "prison law" about snitching. And the guy I tried to explain the problem to about toilets backing up. Well, this morning I awoke to the sound of a waterfall, the sound of my toilet flooding and the water cascading gently down the sides of the toilet and across the floor, soaking my boxes and a stack of paperwork I'd stupidly left on the floor from the night before (two weeks worth of paperwork ruined!) and a stack of xeroxes. Standard drill, Ruth. Jump up and throw everything onto the bunk and sit with your feet off the floor. I hate starting days like that here (R. can tell you what a nightmare toilet floods are in here). Eventually they got the toilets unstopped (surprise-surprise—they found a logjam of chicken bones!). Turns out that the new floorboy has decided that since we won't flush our leftovers down the toilet, he'll do it instead by taking the leftovers to one of the empty cells on each row and dumping them himself. Just to prove to us that the toilets wouldn't flood, he said. Yeah.

After the flood the next step for me was to get some disinfectant (something about a soup of feces, rotting food and shower drainings drying on my floor makes me a bit edgy—plus I am a true "bacterio-phobe"). The officer on our wing this morning was Ms N., who is a true mutant. Really, the lady looks like something of a genetic mix with a frog or something. I don't mean that maliciously—she isn't responsible for that—but it does give her an attitude problem. Officers and inmates making cracks to her don't help. This lady gets all bent out of shape because I ask for the disinfectant. She actually acts surprised that I am concerned. "What's the problem?" "Hey, it's the sewage drying on my floor. Ever hear of fecalform bacteria? Or hepatitis being spread through raw sewage?" "Why are you worrying about it? Nobody else is." "I'm not them. A lot of them heat food in their toilets because they don't know anything about disease control." "Well, you're not any better than they are and they aren't asking for any disinfectant." "I'd bet they'd be really tickled to get some if you offered it to them. Besides, why does it bug you that I'm asking for any? What does it hurt and why should it get on your nerves?" "What is it to you? You expect me to cry about your problems?" "I'm not asking you to cry to get worried about me. I just want some disinfectant and don't understand why you're getting so cocky about it." (I made extra sure I didn't use any profanity because this lady has a reputation for writing a guy up in a heartbeart for cussing.)

"If you think your cell is bad, wait until you see the shower you're fixing to get into. There are still toilet paper and bones floating in there." "Why can't you get it cleaned before you start showering the wing?" "Because I don't give a shit. And I don't know what makes you think you're any better than anyone else." "I don't think I'm better than anyone. I just don't like the idea of having hepatitis or diarrhea. And I really don't appreciate you cussing at me when you're so quick to write everyone else up." "Well, like I said, I don't give a shit about that either. And I don't know what you're worrying for about your stupid diseases when you're just going to get executed anyway."

Ruth, that's the second day in a row I've had someone throw my death row status in my face as an excuse for talking to me like I'm shit. Not much I can do about it, really. For what it was worth, I did ask to talk to the sergeant. Sgt. B. was on—he's a pretty decent guy, really. I explained to him what I was so hot about, both the problem trying to get some disinfectant and the problem with Officer N. He said that as far as he knew, we were *supposed* to use disinfectant every time the toilets flooded and he'd see to it we all got some. He also said he'd check into the problem with Ms N. and see what had really been said. He checked with the other officer, who doesn't like her, and he confirmed what I said. Sgt. B. came back a few minutes later and said he'd spoken with Ms N. and he could tell me for sure she wouldn't say anything like that again. That was a surprise. A minor moral victory, really—but even a minor one means a lot in here, especially after the last few days I've had.

You know, at one time it was almost the "curse of God" for anyone, officer or inmate, to throw up someone's death row status in an inmate's face. And in the last couple of years I can remember it only happening *one* other time (a rather memorable encounter I had with a night shift guard, the origins having been in a dispute I had with her concerning a bogus write-up against my cell partner). But then twice in two days. It's like they're trying to make me act like what I'm accused of being. Sometimes I think they do that by intent.

Today is the sixth anniversary of my arrest. Please, please, hold the applause, no congratulations please . . . My seventh Oct. 16th in captivity. It was on a Sunday morning just such as this, a cooler, damp one following an unseasonable warm and humid previous evening, that I found myself sitting on the toilet as the State local Gestapo burst through my front and back doors, leaving them splintered (pretty intense, considering that neither was locked). I'd gone to a late Halloween party the evening before dressed as, of all things, a biker (pretty original, eh?) and spent the evening trying to redirect the advances of a cute airhead from me to my friend, Dave, who had a bad case of lust for her. Silly me, hung up on fidelity and all that. It was a nice party. My girlfriend Betty didn't go.

The next morning my mother came by and told me that someone had called her house and my brother's house a number of times during the night before but would leave no name or message, other than asking if I were home or about. Someone had also pulled into her and my brother's driveways a few times but had backed out and left without stopping. We just assumed that it was the cops. They'd been steadily harassing me since the murder investigation had begun and this wasn't anything new. Naturally I was paranoid about it—but I'd been living in paranoia since the night of the murders. Would the cops try to arrest me and/or plant something, on me? Would N. try to kill me to make sure I didn't talk? Would the police kill me if they couldn't make a case? Yeah, I was paranoid, Ruth. I also sort of had a feeling inside that whatever was supposed to happen was about to, that fate had finally boiled over.

I remember thinking about what I'd do if they tried to arrest me. I'd talked to an old friend the afternoon before after work about that inevitability and had pretty much decided that rather than try to risk the criminal injustice system and the years they'd put me through even if I did win the case, I'd rather just flinch when they said "Freeze!" and not have to worry about it any more. But my friend assured me that they couldn't arrest me if I were innocent, and that even if they did that Betty would wait for me and that if Betty didn't, she and my other friends would never abandon me so I had better not let the cops shoot me. That conversation from the previous afternoon was on my mind the next morning when Mom had left after warning me.

So there I was, sitting on the toilet reading Suetonius Tranquillus's *The Twelve Caesars* (ain't that a kick in the rubber parts?) when I heard footsteps running past the window and then "CRASH!" through both the front and back unlocked doors. Three seconds later the bathroom door comes crashing open, just as I'm standing up to get my robe (I was completely naked preparing to take a bath) and there is Warren Lane crouched, gun in position ready to blow me away if I move one more step toward that robe. I almost got my wish anyway. Lane, that son of a bitch, just smiled and said "I got you now, motherfucker" as he pulled the hammer back on his gun and moved the aim from my chest to my head. That was when Bill Howard and Taylor came up behind him and told him to hold off because the "locals" were coming in the back door. Lane uncocked the gun and told me that I was one lucky motherfucker. Howard was holding a small pistol in a piece of cloth in his hand and he asked Lane what he wanted to do with it now, to which Lane answered that there wasn't any use in putting it down now since Stephen Groves, the sheriff, had fucked up and let the locals in the house before he'd "finished with" me ("I thought I told Groves to keep them outside until I finished with him in here"—"Well, that fat sonofabitch couldn't piss straight without someone holding his dick"). So it looks like I've got Stephen Grove's incompetence and the local cops to blame for me being alive to endure this Hell. Anyway, Lane barked at Howard and told him to put "that damn thing" (the pistol) in his pocket. They came in, kicked me in the nuts and dragged me into the bedroom and kicked me a couple more times while one of them stood on my neck and Lane stuck his gun barrel in my mouth and read me my rights, mixed with various statements threatening me, cursing me and telling me I would confess before he was finished. Meanwhile, all the other cops were busy tearing the house up, and I remember Lane and Howard complaining that with the locals there they couldn't do much (I think they had other things they wanted to plant). They finally let me up and took me to the bedroom in handcuffs and kept asking me stuff and telling me about how they were ready to kill me for not having told them what had happened when the investigation first got started a month before, that I was going to die for that, for having lied to them. They also told me how angry they were for having slept all night in their cars the night before and for me having got past them the night before. They had arrested N. the afternoon before and had then gotten a warrant for me. They didn't know where I was (I was at the party) and had staked out my house, my mother's house and my brother's house. Their worry was that I'd gotten word of N.'s arrest and had split the country. Apparently they'd had the highways watched too. They told me they'd decided that since I'd gotten away they were going to, or had decided to, kill me when they did catch me but that I'd fucked it up by showing up back in T-ville, having gotten in right under their noses. They kept ranting on and on about that, kept telling me that I'd die for N.'s murders because I'd lied for him. Howard had the audacity to get in my face and spit in my face and tell me how he's almost messed up his marriage because of all the time he'd spent on the case and that I was to blame because I didn't tell them the truth from the first day. And every three or four minutes Lane would whirl around (if he was facing away) or look me in the face and call me a motherfucker or sonofabitch or cocksucker or whatever and palm the Hell out of me, up side the head so to speak. And so on and so it went, Ruth, hey hey my my our boys in blue will protect you too Ruth if you let 'em, and I was silently cursing the local cops and the sheriff for having talked me into letting 'em.

Eventually they decided I had to be taken away but the locals said I had to have some clothes on to go outside (believe it when they tell you nakedness is a great multiplier of humiliation when both are forced on you), so someone found a pair of jeans, of all things my last pair of vintage Levis "big bell" bell bottoms (true collector items) and someone held them while I stepped into them and they pulled them up. I couldn't see who had done me that service but it was Bill Howard who said "let me do that" and zipped them up. I, thinking he was being for a second human, soon learned the game when he zipped up my dick in them and all got a really royal laugh out of that, Lane still palming me up side the head in regular periods. I don't remember speaking at all the whole time. When they took me outside I could see all the people leaving the church down the street but I couldn't see Betty among them. The only time I struggled was when I was going out and I saw Lane stop, tense up and start around with that hand again and I'd had about enough of that shit and I jerked back. Which caused Lane to grab me by the throat and throw me down, drop with his knee to my chest and stick his gun to my throat and push it so I couldn't breath. Again with the cocking of the arms and really horrible grin and saying "I'm going to love this," but it was Sheriff Groves who grabbed his shoulder and whispered where he could hear "Goddammit, Warren, the locals are watching—don't do it here." And for the second time that morning Lane said to me (the first time being when he couldn't shoot me in the bathroom), "damn, you're one lucky motherfucker—that's twice now." So they picked me up and I couldn't breathe for a minute because he'd fucked up my throat (I wore around a huge bruise for days after that) by jamming the gun into it.

And so, Ruth, that was the last time I saw my home and the last time I got to breath clean, free air six October 16ths ago. I think I died that day. Again, it would seem. The first death was the night of the murders. When N. pulled the first trigger, he didn't just kill his family, he essentially killed me too. So maybe it'll be the third time that's the charm, only this third death is being such a long, painful process.

I was taken to a justice of the peace in T-ville for some preliminary paperwork, about five minutes worth. I tried to talk to one of the only cops I ever trusted in my life while I was there but they wouldn't let me. When they took me back outside my mother and Betty were there, but the W. County people were very rude and called my mother a bitch and threatened to lock her and Betty up too if they made a scene. Sheriff Groves and Taylor drove me back in the car to W. County and all the time amazed at how mad Lane and Howard were and they groused about the local boys having been "breathing down (their) necks." When I got there to the W. Co jail I was arraigned by some old lady. Then Groves called his wife on the phone while I was sitting there and invited her to come see what he'd "caught" just in time for the election. And the fat old cow did come to see. After the excitement of showing me off they took me into the sheriff's private office and handcuffed me to the chair, though they took my ankle chains off and later put them back on. Lane then came in and told me I was fixing to confess, rather sign the paper they had typed up. He had this little burlap bag about three inches in diameter and about a foot long and he had a two-by-four about three feet long. He put one end of the board on the floor and held the other one and smashed it with the burlap bag (I later heard it had bird shot in it) and told me that the next one would be my shin.

Then they put the bag on the desk in front of me and started walking around and talking to me, telling me what they had on the paper they wanted signed and telling me I'd have a chance to live if I signed it immediately, Lane slapping his hand with a nightstick he'd picked up off the shelf by the desk. I told them to fuck off, that I wanted a lawyer. Lane was kind of off to the side and behind me but I felt the nightstick on the ol' elbow trick. I think I hollered then. Anyway, the deputy from the next room knocked and opened the door and stuck his head in and told them they'd better be cool, that someone had just called from T-ville and a lawyer was on his way right then and he'd already gotten a statement from the locals that I didn't have any marks when I left T-ville and had better not have anything wrong when the lawyer got there. Lane chuckled and shook his head and leaned over into my face and said, "Looks like you just got lucky again, cocksucker. You are the luckiest sonofabitch I have ever seen. Well, you won't stay lucky for ever—there ain't gonna be a fourth time."

From there I was taken to a very cold and very, very dark cell. They let me have light in it a few days later. Do you have any idea what absolute darkness can do to you, Ruth? You see things and time gets weird. And you consider signing anything they hand you if they'll just turn the lights on again. I don't know why they turned the lights on again, but I think they gave up on trying to get me to sign the papers after they'd beat N. into changing his statement to what they wanted. The real bitch of it is that N. told them the truth at first—but I think they already knew what happened. The thing was that that wasn't a capital murder and it was only one conviction. Anyway, that first October 16th was the first night of total darkness. In more ways than one. And the lights aren't on completely.

And that, Ruth, is what October the 16th means to me. And remember, our boys in blue will protect you too if you let 'em.

Not all my friends are alien to me, though those that aren't are the ones I've made since I've been here (who are all a lot more solid and worthy than *any* of my old circle of friends). The big thing is the loss of my children. It's too late for that. I don't think I'll ever get out of here, Ruth. I'm not being pessimistic in that. Look at the stats on my chances. Still, the idea of being free is wonderful and I could take a lot of shit if I thought that was in any way a realistic expectation. I just can't let myself even fantasize about that—I know better and can't afford the disappointment. That hard core wall of reality is what pretty much dictates my attitudes now. It's what makes me not worry about what happens to me in the media, why I risk the exposure so much (and make my attorney have high blood pressure) and why I'm so damn desperate to do everything I can to fight the death penalty. It's like I've got to make my dent in the thing before I'm gone. That's a lot of pressure but I'm also not worrying about whether I burn myself out or not. That's something I worry about with a lot of people outside.

I occasionally go through these bouts of confusion, fatigue, terminal nervousness and inability to focus a single thought. Serious or not, I'm afraid I'm letting these execution dates I've hanging over my head get to me. Which is pretty stupid. Like so many people down here, sometimes I think I'd rather have it carried out and over with than keep facing it again and again and again.

The important thing for me is that my *need* to do something, anything! to fight the death penalty is more important to me than whatever marginal risk (and the risk is marginal, believe me) I bring upon myself. In fact, taking or being part of any action I can against the death penalty is about the only reason I can justify my existence any more. It's the only damn reason I haven't dropped the appeal or cashed in my own chips. So let me know more and I'll let you know. Either way, I'm sure I'm not the only February date.

Also, I hope I didn't come across sounding too negative about my situation here. I sincerely want out of this place. I just don't know what I'd have to face. And I, justifiably I believe, fear what's my option. I'm not institutionalized. It's just that, well, there's something I didn't exactly explain well last letter. I'm scared to death that efforts to save my life will result in me getting a life sentence. There is the popular opinion that being alive, even in here, is better than being dead. This is a mistaken idea, at least for me and a lot of guys in here. It's very much an error to think of existing in here as being alive. People outside who are dedicated to abolishing the death penalty are usually dedicated to the sanctity of life, period. When fighting the death penalty they're too often satisfied with just keeping someone alive, even if they're locked in Hell for all of eternity. And lawyers are the world's worst about that. That's what my first appeal attorney did to me. He refused to touch any reversal or acquittal arguments in any way. All he thought he should do is just get me a life sentence. He actually thought that was the best compromise for both sides. I wouldn't die and the courts wouldn't have to let me out on the streets. I actually think he was operating from the assumption that I was guilty. Anyway, he was satisfied and his actions didn't even get me a life sentence, and he blew off my best arguments, probably beyond recovery.

What I am getting at is that I fear a life sentence worse than anything in this entire universe or any alternative universes. Death isn't such a big deal, not compared to that. The State hates turning cases around worse than being sodomized by oxen. But when it comes between the idea of trying someone who might actually win a trial or giving someone a life sentence, well, they'll drop that life on them quicker'n shit. One of the worries I didn't voice very well in the last letter is that I worry that outside help/spotlighting will be too easily taken for a life sentence plea. So even if the help offered from Ireland or anywhere else is a valid and safe concept, not a hindrance to my appeal, how do I say "thanks" but reject the help if it looks like a life sentence might result? How do you sound not like an asshole if you have to say, "sure, thanks for the help but only if you try to fight for my freedom and not just keeping me alive" when the people involved value life, even more than freedom? I guess I'm saying I don't know how to look at the offer of outside help. And I realize also that I overstated my case about what I have to face out there. Oh, the facts are right—I just have to think about how I'll handle that and ask if it's fair to accept any help to get me there (especially when I worry that other people might be more deserving or "next up" for help). But even with the facts like that, rest assured that I'd still relish the chance to get out and face the world, even without my children or a job or safety. Extinction like that is a lot more respectable than being snuffed in here whether it's by execution or the slow smothering of a life sentence.

So I guess what I'm saying, I don't like what I'd have to face out there but I'd still enjoy the challenge of facing it—I think of myself as somewhat of a gonzo-balls kinda guy. But I'm also saying, as ungrateful as it sounds, that I'd appreciate any help I can get *but* if the best it can get me is life in Hell, well, not to be rude but "thanks, but no thanks—give the help to someone else." As corny as it sounds, the old "liberty or death" gig still rings true.

My decision would be so much easier if I thought the outside pressure would actually have the chance of forcing the state to do what it should do, rather than compromising to appease. That would depend, of course, upon the attitude of the outside group(s) and their skill in making their exact desires known. Aaaaarrgh! I just don't know what to make of it and I've no doubt I'm freaking myself out, tilting at windmills, seeing beacons *and* demons in the dark when neither actually exist. And I hate being like this. But Hell, just what sort of experience does anyone have for basing decisions in dealing with this type of intention? Can't really remember past experience with rules that might generalize into this situation.

Sometimes I feel like a ghost in here, Ruth. I'm caught between two worlds and I'm "ill at rest." I don't know what I think right now. And I find myself caught between the world of the living and the dead. Sometimes I find myself jealous of those who've completed the cross over, the friends in here and out there who are already officially dead, and Goddamn, there are way too many of both. And sometimes I'm envious of the living who still can move in the real world with new life and sunlight and touching. Like a memory, my old friends either remember me with kind affection or they try to block me out and forget having known me—maybe my name comes up in conversation sometimes. There are pictures of me "back home," and everybody goes on with life and they tell their kids who that guy is (was?— certainly I'm not that person any more) in the old photographs. Some- times people come to visit the concrete and brick monument where I'm interred, each of us in our little plot in here (like niches in the walls of a catacomb or mausoleum?), coming I suspect to perhaps honor my memory. Too often the dead I'm jealous of actually have it better. My own brother visits the grave of his wife's dead brother more often than he visits me. My aunts and uncles and cousins and others visit the grave of my father and grandparents more than they visit or write to me. But what do they visit when they come to see me? They do the ritual at the gate and sit and wait and sometime soon I'm brought to appear. From there they can see and hear me, even talk to me—but they can't touch me and I can't touch them. And because I'm not really of their world any more, my time is limited and when it's up, I've got to go back to my little crypt where the other ghosts in white walk too. And wait to finish the crossing or be let back in the real world again. Am I a ghost, Ruth?

Or am I a vampire? No doubt, I'm undead—but I'm also still flesh. I even find myself sleeping during the day and waking at night. God knows, there are as many stories, legends and myths about us down here as Dracula and Nosferatu ever had told about them. Nobody knows us, but we're still feared and reviled by those good people out- side. And even locked in this crypt, dead and away for all practical purposes they still want to drive the point further—so many out there would relish the chance to be the ones to drive the final stake and get it over once and for all. Sometimes I'd like to let them too. We're the new vampires and ghosts. We're the people who've been completely transformed by the legends and myths. We're now the replacements, the ones they warn their children about, the ones who're supposed to come from nowhere and get you in the dark if you're not good and ever vigilant and ever ready to kill. Welcome to Hell, Ruth.

6

Prison Life

This is an experience that I care not to remember. Whether that's good
or bad, I don't know. But the result of this attitude is that my yesterdays are all jumbled.
                    —Harvey Earvin, Death Row, Texas, 1991

*Vic Roberts describes how he spent his twenty-ninth birthday in the
Georgia Diagnostic and Classification Center on June 28, 1991:*

Just a short note to thank you for sending me a birthday card. It were
a very enjoyed and pleasant surprise. I had a pretty nice birthday considering my situation and etc. I spent my birthday playing chess and I
just basically tried to enjoy myself! I also spent alot of the day just
listening to the radio. Then at 9 P.M. on my birthday I had myself a
party. I had candles (I made), soda, and sweet cakes, and I even tried
to sing "Happy Birthday" to myself, which didn't sound too good to
the inmates in the cell-block. But, I sounded OK to myself! I guess
they thought I was going crazy trying to sing happy birthday to myself
out loud, but I didn't care.

*In a letter written in May 1991, Toby Williams, on Death Row in
Texas, summed up his view of prison life. Toby is black and was convicted in 1985 at the age of twenty-one.*

Can you imagine being surrounded by others who endure your pain? I
only thought this type of cruelty to another human being existed in

concentration camps. Boy! Was I sadly mistaken: this is one fellow American to another, sadistic American to sacrificed American.

Everywhere you turn you feel that everyone around you is against you; some you actually know are against you when in fact they know nothing about you.

Imagine spending twenty-one hours a day and twenty-four hours on weekends in a tiny cell being annoyed by others complaining about unnecessary things that have nothing to do with the cruelty or unnecessary rules. To recreate, shower, visit, etc. you are stripped of your clothing in front of either males or females who open your mouth as you maneuver your tongue, run their fingers through your hairs, raise your arms, lift your testicles, or run their fingers through your pubic hair, turn around to lift your feet, and bend over to spread your cheeks, while the guards search your clothing. When going to recreate or shower, you're only allowed to proceed in your underwear, shorts only—no matter the condition of the weather. The same situation applies when a guard has you stand in front of your cell while another one goes through your personal belongings looking for nothing. Each time you step outside of your tiny cell, you are handcuffed. What's it all for? There's already a thin line between sanity and insanity, no matter who or where you are—so much more when you have the threat of death hanging over you. You try to avoid the thought of it all by doing something to keep your mind occupied, but there's always some guard around to make sure you keep the death threat on your mind; at the same time the guards use other things to bring you down mentally.

Imagine receiving a disciplinary report for something small, or for no reason, from a guard who perhaps had a bad day before arriving to work. No matter the circumstance, it's automatically a major disciplinary report. In a disciplinary hearing you are in the majority of cases "guilty." No matter how much proof you have to prove your innocence, you'll receive either commissary, cell or property restriction, or all three running concurrently. Commissary restriction means you cannot purchase anything from the store. Cell restriction means you aren't allowed outside activity. Property restriction means you are only allowed writing materials in your cell, sometimes nothing. All restrictions are for a certain amount of days, usually beginning at seven. Too much protesting alone concerning the disciplinary action or anything else you are dissatisfied with could result in the use of force against you while your hands are cuffed behind you as you are grabbed by the neck and legs. If you're uncomfortable—live with it. The slightest movement will result in a knee in your back or neck, while your face is hard pressed into the cold cement.

Imagine being very sick, and the only way you can see a doctor is to fill out a sick call request, which takes approximately three days to receive back stating if you have an appointment or not, and approximately five more days if you have the appointment. The only way other than the appointment you are allowed to see a doctor for a medical problem is that you must be bleeding badly, be having a heart attack, or have broken something.

Imagine having to eat mostly half-cooked cold meals that cause you sickness most times. In some you may taste grit, or find some kind of insect. For breakfast you must have your light on in your cell around 3:00 A.M. in order to be served. Either cold pancakes, watered down gravy, stuck together grits, or oatmeal, or half-cooked green eggs.

Imagine having to greet your loved ones for a visit in handcuffs. After you are relieved of your handcuffs, you are locked in a small cage (like an animal) in the visiting room where other prisoners visit their loved ones. Not only are you deprived of your privacy, you aren't allowed human contact—you are separated by a metal screen and wire in the middle of glass when visiting.

You can avoid the cage and handcuffs by working in the death row garment factory. In order to do so, you must keep a clean record for at least six months to convince a classification committee of your sincerity in working, sewing sheets, pillow cases, aprons, hats, pajamas, undershorts, towels, pants, shirts or different types of officers' clothing. To work there, though, is like administering your own poison as well as administering poison to the other death row prisoners, because you are helping the state to make and save money to pay your own and other death row prisoners' way to death.

Every morning I awake I have to reach down into the abyss of my being to pull up the strength I need to face another day.

As I look out the window at the playful action of a couple of birds, I realize it's not the large or expensive things that we miss, it's the very small things we miss the most. I used to love to watch the sun as it descended beyond the horizon to take the warmth and beauty of her ageless flow to another people across the world. Now I can no longer see even that. I keep telling myself day after day, tomorrow will be a brighter day, but as each day approaches the light seems to get a little dimmer.

Sometimes I wonder if it's all an illusion being played out on the stage of my consciousness, and that at any minute someone is going to snap me back into reality. But then I ask myself, is not what we call reality an illusion? Does anything last forever? When that ends, will it end in death?

Can you imagine so much pain?

Again from Texas, Jonathan Wayne Nobles (white, born 1961, convicted 1987) gives his account:

You've often asked that I describe prison to you, I shall make an honest effort to do that today.

To use an adage "variety is the spice of life." I believe that the blandness of this place is one of its chief injustices. Here there is no life only an existence, "a carrousel of time and rollar coaster of emotion."

My cell is most likely smaller than your bathroom 9 ft. × 5 ft. In what was once my home my closet was larger! Yet for the most part this is now my world. I can if I am a "good boy" come out and shower once a day. Allso the "good boy" merits three hours a day of recreation, Mon.–Fri. This 9 × 5 space is my bathroom, my kitchen, my dining room, my closet, my bedroom, my study—my all! I am given clean sheets once a week along with a clean towel, my bed is my sofa, my only place to sit other than the tolite, if I am not here or not awake to exchange sheets at 6 A.M. I get to keep mine for another week. In the summer months it stay's above 100° on the wing—such sweet sheets! During the summer I sleep on the bare concrete floor—its cooler and I can daily wash it and somewhat reduce the smell.

Smell is one of the first things you notice about prison. In the real world you often smell the love and joy of someone's home. Spices in the kitchens, sachet in the linens, pipe tobacco in the den, woodsmoke from the fire, and the leather of a favorite chair. There is no polite way to describe the aroma of prison. Fear, anger, rancid sweat, blood, stale urine, and wasted seamen.

There is no disinfectant to clean up a cell with, maybe once every 6 weeks you can get a little scouring powder to wash out your bowl (tolliet) and very little ventalation.

There are some here, without exaggeration, who have not showered in MONTHS! During the summer there is one person who will save his milk from breakfast, lets it sour and will only bathe in sour milk! No he does *not* rinse it off!

Sex; you get a punk, or you be a punk, or you masterbate; or yours is a life of celibacy. If sex is part of a normal healthy lifestyle, this is a very unhealthy place. Deviant (homophile) men pretty much keep their distance from me. I supposse my feelings and attitudes towards them are probably, most likely, rooted from the abuse I experienced as a child. I can and have let it be known that it is best to keep your distance.

Noise; it never ends, 63 people are kept on a wing, 21 to a row, they 24 hours a day yell back and forth to conversate, and those who have radios constantly blast them, of course each on a different station.

Vermin, rats, mice, roaches, cricketts, ants, lice and fleas. Don't worry if they steal a little taste of your food, most likely they should be upset at you, if you look closely now and again you find that one of their family members has been served to you. Extra protein rations.

Last night before laying down my pen I was trying to give you some insight as to what prison is. I guess I'll continue along this line for now.

The eye sees rust, and grime, stains of yesterdays world. The walls that are painted are white, all clothes except an inmate's shoes are white, but nothing stays white. Prison is a place of dirt, filth and stains. And always the same, "Prison is a carrousel of time and rollar coaster of emotion." These words best describe this existence.

The worst part is what transpires within the slow death of the human heart and mind. There are no real dreams here, no plans of a wanted future. And as dreams are the sap of life, your roots soon dry, your structure decays and rots, your leaves fall, your limb whither and crack, and constantly you are blown thither in the wind.

So if I should choose to let my time on earth be taken from me, it would not be because I do not value life, but rather because I love life and respect the dignity which represents life, and beyond all else I understand that this existence is not life.

Judy Haney, on Death Row in Alabama since 1988, describes her living conditions:

The unit I am in has two rooms, Anne in one and I am in the other. We have our own rooms but we share the yard. We get along great together. She's been on Death Row now 13 years. She is in the last stage right now. I have been housed by her off and on, for six years.

She and Anne also mixed with other women in the prison:

Last week they told everybody they had to send out all blow dryers and curling irons, hot rollers, and that everybody had to have their hair cut up to their ears. Margaret these white girls was crying all up and down these halls. Some of them had never cut their hair, it was so pretty. It was just another way for this place to control these girls. I am thankful I wear mine short.

Judy, married at the age of sixteen, wrote in 1993, at the age of forty-two:

I got a letter from my daughter and she told me she was four and half months pregnant and she is going to carry it. So I am going to be Miss Young Grand-Maw. I am thrill to death.

An inmate in Texas describes conditions as follows:

We have one shelf that is four feet long and 1 feet wide. There are people who have been here 17 to 18 years, and they have accumulated many items such as typewriters, fans, radios, many law books, enor-mous amounts of piddling equipment, and all sorts of things. [Recently] they have changed many rules. And one is, you have to put all your equipment, the items I named, all on the one shelf. Anything on the floor or anywhere else is considered contraband, and is taken and destroyed. And there is nothing we can do. We can't even have a picture of family members on the wall or anywhere else. It's hard Ann, very hard. But I'm going to make it.

Again from Texas:

The bunks we have to sleep on are solid metal . . . They are exactly 6 ft. in length and 26″ wide. We have a plastic covered mattress that is 2″ thick. The pillow is also covered with plastic. Now you can imagine the heat from this combination. So that is why I sleep on the floor. It is cement and somewhat cooler. I have slept in worse places before. At least there are no snakes or leeches. So you see, there is a good side to everything after all. I do admit however that one has to look rather hard at times to find it.

There may be no snakes or leeches, but there are plenty of vermin. The same inmate describes the other inmates staging cockroach races and betting on the outcome, even though anyone caught betting on anything is sent to "lockdown."

Without exception, the prisons suffer from inadequate heating in winter and poor ventilation in summer. Sam Johnson from Mississippi:

I've not written in a while and this has been due to it being HOT, HOT, HOT here! This heat has been sickening and I've not felt up to doing anything until now. It hasn't been below 116 degrees in the last two weeks! This building isn't air-conditioned—or any "conditioned"— and it's always hotter in here than it is in normal places by at least 20 degrees. It's been rough in here, Bro! In addition to the heat, the position I have to get in (chest on knees with arms extended their full length—which puts me at least two feet away from it) to use the typewriter didn't make my writing as much of a pleasurable experience as it normally is when we're together. It rained briefly today [August 30] and that brought the temperature down to about 100 degrees and I can truly enjoy being with you again and holding a conversation.

The following is an account of events during one week in August at Huntsville, Texas, when temperatures were higher than 100 degrees:

Now the following things I will say to you are not meant to upset you, nor to try for sympathy from you. They are simply some things that I think might help you to have a better knowledge of this place.

On the 24th on a lockdown wing an inmate attempted to (I should say did) emasculate himself. He is now in a critical condition at the prison hospital in Galveston, Texas. (This was his second attempt at this.) On the 26th the kitchen caught fire and destroyed quite a bit of equipment and food. The inmates on the 2nd and 3rd tiers could see the flames coming through the roof. It also damaged the laundry next door. No one knows yet if it was arson or an accident. You guess! On the 25th an inmate was found hanging in the recreation area of a lockdown wing. I knew him. Nothing has been released on this yet, but I understand it was suicide with an assist from another inmate.

On a fight between inmates:

This was a direct result of placing the wrong inmates together on the same wing. Quite often this is done on purpose, though this will be denied by the officials. What better way to get an inmate to lock down than to place him in a position where he has to defend himself. Not only this but it also gives them a legal excuse to tear the cells up— supposedly looking for weapons.

We do have a library here but Death Row inmates are only allowed one book at a time. The process we have to go through to get one and the fact that all the volumes are outdated and the selection is very limited makes it not worth the effort.

On an inspection:

They are getting ready for some sort of federal inspection here. They call and tell them when they are coming—instead of arriving unannounced. That really makes sense doesn't it? They run around painting over all the rust and dirt and anything else that doesn't move. I find this rather amusing since I have seen quite a few of these inspections. The only things these so called inspectors look at when they come on these wings is the inmates. If we are going to be put on display the least we could do is let them throw us some peanuts. Heck, I like peanuts.

On racism:

You do know that racism is very prevalent in here. It dictates the way a lot of these inmates live. It also might surprise you to know that this system likes it this way and they do try their best to keep it going. (It works for their benefit.) They deny this on a regular basis—but believe me—it is the truth. I see it constantly. I have no part in it. If someone is decent with me—then he gets the same treatment. If not then I simply have absolutely nothing to do with him. So far I have had no trouble in that respect since I have been in here. What troubles I have had with other inmates has been with members of my own race, and only minor stuff at that. It has been my observation, since being here, that the two most difficult things for most of these inmates to learn is (1) to act as a human being with some degree of dignity, and (2) to mind their own business. In their defense I must say that to learn anything positive in here is extremely difficult.

On guards:

This might surprise you but there are times when I do feel sorry for these guards. It must be terrible to enjoy working in a place such as this. We have a very young and new guard on duty in the wing now and I feel sad for him. He really has an attitude problem, if only he knew how much he had to learn and how far he had to travel I think he would change . . . at times one feels like an animal on display.

Also from Huntsville, Texas:

Here in prison the prison guards are ice cold toward you. To them we, prisoners, are deserving of our lot. Eighty per cent of society supports the death penalty. Legislators are pushing to expand the death penalty and to impose life without parole. All around there is so much hatred and negativity. Sometimes I can't help but wondering if the people who wish me dead is trying to convince themselves that I am an animal, or if they are trying to convince me that I am an animal. Then here you come showing me love. Showing me friendship, and placing value on my life. It's enough to make you cry. Out of all of the people in the world who are so deserving of love, I sometimes want to ask: why me? But I never do. I just accept your love and friendship, and thank God for it.

There is, however, another, radically different view of prison life in Texas. The following account highlights the differences between the Work Program and Segregation—the latter sounding very much like the other Death Rows in the southern states.

You asked about the Work Program. All on Death Row can qualify if they want to work, and if they can stay out of trouble. There are some who are so dangerous, and have been in so much trouble, that they can never qualify. Plus, many have associated themselves with illegal gangs, such as the Aryan Brotherhood, Texas Mafia, Texas Syndicate, etc., and these men cannot qualify either. Many men just don't want to work for "the man." Sometimes I have an inner struggle myself, when I think about working for the very people that will execute me if it comes down to that. But, being on the Program gives me more opportunities to meet and fellowship with my Christian friends, and this helps me very much. If we can grow strong together in the Word, prayer, and love, then surely we will be in a much better position to help others when opportunities arise. We all draw strength from each other when we are together like this.

The work isn't hard at all, and it is air conditioned in the factory; which is great now because it gets to 98 every day, with high humidity. But, in the US we have many people that just hate work; any kind of work. I used to be quite shiftless and lazy myself, so I speak from experience.

You asked about the "mood" of the men, and I can only tell you about the 29 or so men that I live around; and I have contact frequently with a few others. But I believe the moods vary from tank to tank. For instance, here on the Work Program we have more things to do with our time, but on the Segregated tank they are locked in their cells most of the time. So, many of them get bored and find things to do; make noise, create disturbances, curse and argue with guards and inmates alike, etc. So, if a person is not strong-minded to begin with, and doesn't occupy his time with reading, craft work, etc., then the mood can easily swing from bad to worse.

It is in these situations that some men just decide to give up on life, and others are influenced to drop their appeals by others that do it. The Work Program would be just the right thing for many of them, and it would help them as it would give them more to do, more out-of-cell time, etc. But, many are influenced by the others when they hear such things as "they are working for the man that is trying to kill them," or, "only a bunch of snitches and homosexuals are on the Work Program." So many of these men aren't willing to live their own life and do what they feel is best, while they let the others dominate and influence them.

We do not get paid on the Work Program. They say our pay is the extra privileges we get for working, so I guess it is in that sense. The work we do is sewing in a small building they built adjacent to Death Row called the Garment Factory. For a long time we sewed underwear for the prison population, but just last week they began a change, and now we are going to start sewing officer's pants for their uniforms; other inmates somewhere in the system will probably sew their shirts. When they first started the Program they had two shifts, but now they have three and I'm on the third shift; which usually goes from 3 P.M. until 6:30 or so; though we come in early at times. That means I am free to do all my letter-writing, craft work, exercise, Bible study, etc. either before we go to work, or after we get back in.

As for freely mixing with others, I can mix as much and as often as I want with the 29 men on this tank; we can meet in the dayroom, or in the yard, which is connected to the dayroom itself. Also, the tank next to our tank doesn't have a recreation yard, so if they want outside recreation, they have to come to our tank; so I can mix freely with those 29 men; 29 if they are full to capacity. There are two other tanks

that hold people on the Program, one tank holding another 29 or so
men, but the other holding close to 60. I can't go visit them whenever
I want, but any of them can come to our Sunday church services, and
we can talk and fellowship then. Plus, I work with some of them also.
There are also services held for Catholic and Islamic people; but I
never attend these myself.

Now you asked about "chains and shackles," and "body searches."
Remember, the Program is much different than Segregation. On Segregation the men are stripped, searched, and handcuffed with their hands
behind their backs before they come out of their cell for anything; to
go to the shower and back, to the recreation yard and back, visiting
room, dentist, infirmary, etc. But on the Program we never wear handcuffs, though we have to have an officer escort before we can leave our
wing to go to work, visit, dentist, etc. We are searched (kind of lightly)
coming and going from work, mainly because we work with scissors
and other objects, and they don't want any of them being turned into
weapons. And, we are usually searched fairly good after a visit, because some have been caught trying to get drugs and other contraband
in from visitors. Also our cells are searched fairly often, usually when
we are gone to work, or out for another reason. But usually we aren't
searched coming and going to our dayroom and yard, mainly because
they are all right here together on the tank, and they would have to
search a lot of people, and often.

We have our group Bible studies on the yard or in the dayroom;
usually depending on the time of day. Well, let me just tell you my
usual routine, and that way you can see what I usually do. Every morning around 5 or so we eat breakfast, and most of the men get their trays
and go back to their cell, with most of them going back to bed. But I
stay out in the dayroom with my Bible and other study materials, and
usually three other brothers join me; often one or two of them will
sleep in, but lately we've been real constant and regular, all four of us.
We eat, brush our teeth, etc., and we usually get started by 5:30 or a
little after. We pray, read the Word, and get into our study books. We
most always study until 7, many times 8, then we can either stay out to
talk, play some ball (they open our recreation yard at 7), or go back to
the cell to cross stitch, read, etc.

Sometimes I come back and take a nap, but lately I've been making bookmarkers. In fact, I can take my stuff out with me and sit around in the yard or dayroom cross stitching while I talk. Anyway, it is the evenings when we also have Bible studies, and they are always on the yard because the dayroom gets noisy after the men turn on the TV and start slamming dominoes; do you have dominoes in England? So with all the time I have left before or after work, I can read, write letters, do crafts, watch TV, play basketball, handball, volleyball, etc., or other things. It varies from day to day, but we always meet and pray in the mornings, and often one of the brothers will say, "Why don't we get together tonight and sing praises to God?" Or, "let's get together to-night to pray and study the Word." Then, when I know we have a meeting planned, I'll work with more fervor during the day so I can get done what needs to be done, then I'll be ready to meet the brothers on the yard; usually at 6 or 7 P.M. The yard is closed at 9 P.M., and I most always come in to my cell, pray, then hit the sack.

The dayroom stays open until 11, except on Friday and Saturday nights, then it stays open until 1:30. I very, very seldom stay up that late, and if I do it is even more seldom that I'll stay up that late in the dayroom, but in my cell. I guess I need to admit that I don't use my time as wisely as I could, or as I should. I should have been finished with the bookmarkers for instance. And, I should have finished my history course by now, though I still have two or three months left on my one-year expiration date. Plus I have letters that I should have an-swered weeks ago, and stuff like that. Perhaps I can get my act together and get busy, at least to do the things I know I should be doing.

Here in Texas it isn't so bad, as far as prison goes. We often complain about the food, and sometimes it is really awful, but most of the time it is good to decent, and many times real good. We get clean clothes and a shower each day, we have cable TV, though we don't have per-sonal TVs, and we all take a vote and the majority wins. We have access to the law library books, regular library books, educational programs, good dental and medical care, we can purchase fans to help in the heat, radios to hear music and news programs, electric razors, alarm clocks, food items, drinks, and much, much more. In many ways, we have it much better than some people in the free-world, especially when you see how people suffer in India, Africa, etc. Some of the guys here sound like a bunch of sissies by the way they moan and groan all the time.

Well as you no doubt have learned by now, I have my own particular way of looking at things. Maybe I'm way off base, but I can't find many valid reasons to cry and complain like so many do; and, to my shame, like I do much more than I should. Here are men that are demanding that the public give them respect and decency as human beings. They hardly seem to care about the things they done to get on Death Row, nor do they seem to care about the victim's families. All they want is mercy and respect as human beings. Yet, many of these same people will not give much (if any) respect or decent treatment to their fellow inmates. How dare we want respect and decent treatment from the free-world, when we treat each other (and the officers) like animals? To me it sounds like the old American motto: "Look Out For Number 1." It seems like so many don't want to change their rotten attitudes and way of living, they don't want to take advantage of the educational programs or other opportunities, they don't even want to find these beautiful friendships that bring hope and joy into the life. But, they are always on the prowl to get, get, get, and if they can't get everything to their own advantage, then they're not interested.

There is, however, a very different view of the Work Program, expressed in a letter by David Herman (January 1996):

Contrary to published reports in the papers, the food here is generally not fit for human consumption. The meats served are 50–75% fat, undercooked or burnt, and frequently cause diarrhea or other more serious problems. Recently they started adding a chemical filler called Vita-Pro to many dishes, with severe stomach cramps and gas afflicting most everyone. The rare times we do get good food are limited to holidays and when inspectors are scheduled to visit. And for "security" purposes, health inspectors may not visit unannounced. They must inform the prison of their intentions well ahead of time, so no surprise inspections ever occur. Of course, the kitchens are cleaned and menus changed for such visits.

The Work Program is not some idyllic environment where volunteers labor blissfully for the state while awaiting execution, and then thank the administration when they're strapped into the gurney. If an inmate decides not to "volunteer" for the program, they are forced to live in a cell half the size of Work Program cells, recreation is limited, visitation must be done in a cramped cage, and handcuffs are used whenever out of the tiny cell. And that's even if the inmate has *no* disciplinary cases whatsoever! Population inmates get "paid" for working by earning good time to shorten their sentences, better visitation privileges, and other prison "freedoms." Death Row's best conditions are worse than population's worst nonsolitary conditions. The only real incentive most people on the Work Program have—myself included—is to avoid subjecting our loved ones to the stress of delays in getting a visitation cage and seeing us in handcuffs while being treated like an animal.

Of course, the administration has decades of experience in such matters and uses the leverage of Work Program "incentives" to take away many of the basic privileges and dignities afforded even the incorrigibles in the rest of the prison system. If I get locked down for objecting to some admin injustice, then my mother will suffer for it. She has to drive three hours to get down here, and three hours to get back; and she's night blind, so she must leave home after sunrise, and arrive home before sundown. If she is forced to wait a few hours for a cage to come open, then she cannot stay to visit. And seeing me being brought to that phone booth–size cage in handcuffs makes her cry. The thought of the prison torturing my mother like that makes me pause. Which also leads admin to put the worst of their guards on Death Row, knowing they are actually safer here than in the population! That means that we are constantly threatened by unscrupulous guards who are trying to make a name for themselves, and some even blatantly lie to get inmates locked down—with the approval and support of the higher-ranking officers.

I have confined myself to fairly general areas, without names, dates, or details of specific instances. I could fill dozens of pages with personal experiences alone, but I won't. I can't afford to be locked down for some mail censor's idea of "sedition." I may be in jeopardy for the little that I've said already. But you need to go beneath the whitewash being splashed around, so you too won't be used by this system to perpetuate the lies about this dismal place. No, Death Row is not a medieval dungeon, or a Russian gulag; but it is also not some country club pampering us until we're put to sleep by the humane and benevolent state.

From Virginia, Edward Fitzgerald wrote:

For the most part you learn to block out the noise in prison. You know certain sounds and respond to them no matter how much other noises there are. When I sleep you can turn the TV or radio up and not bother me, but if my cell door opens I'll wake up. You can stand outside the cell door yelling, but as soon as you mention my name I'll hear it. In prison you never enter someone's cell when you think they are asleep, no matter who they are. Much of the time people make noise trying to get a guard's attention. I think being deaf is a qualification to be a guard. Sometimes someone is just being an ass. But mostly it's just unavoidable noise because the place is mainly empty of noise absorbing material and the place is made out of concrete. Walk down a sidewalk, you won't hear your footsteps, walk into a warehouse, you can't help but hear your footsteps. It doesn't take long and you get used to it. It's only when someone's being an ass that makes you mad. Around here you know every now and then everyone will act like an ass out of depression, so you live with it and don't give it a second thought 'cause you never know, next week it might be you.

Jonathan Nobles temporarily left Ellis Unit 1 at Huntsville, Texas, for an operation on his foot. He describes his brief glimpse of the normal world:

My trip and stay in Galveston was wonderful, I guess one could say that it was my own little holiday. I don't remember how much I said in the letter I wrote from there as it was rushed. I wanted you to know that at last something had gone right in this pitiful hell. My room faced east looking out over the Gulf of Mexico, which was less than a mile away. Though I was unable to see beach goers, I could see the whitecaps as they came rolling into the shore. And the sunrises were beautiful. A great golden disc lifting up out of a deep blue horizon. I would spend hours on end at the window looking out at everything I could see. There was also a grocery store a few blocks away, and there I could make out the forms of the people going in and out. At night there were neon lights, traffic lights and the tail-lights of cars to look at. I felt like some alien being sitting up in a spaceship looking down at, and analyzing strange life forms. It is no longer my world, all of these years away have taken me from it.

I also had a very enlightening experience while waiting in pre-op there was a young girl maybe six or seven years old, her mother was there beside her holding her hand and pushing the hair of her forehead to and fro. It looked so comforting and loving, but at the same time seemed so forgiving to me. To comfort or be comforted is a basic quality of human nature, but looking on at that and realizing that it was not a scene from a TV movie seemed so far from me, so unnatural. Maybe I have become more institutionalized than I realized before now. It seemed like I was off in a dream or on some fantasy ride at the amusement park.

The following, remarkable letter was written by a prisoner on Death Row in one of the southern states to a psychiatrist concerned with the case of a fellow-prisoner well known to the writer.

Dear Dr. L.,

I am a friend of J.J. You have an interest in his case, I understand. In whatever way I can be of help I am willing. So please do not hesitate to call on me.

I received a post card from L.M. yesterday. She thinks that you may be interested in hearing about how J. and I became friends and the way that he influenced my life.

Actually, Dr. L., there is not very much that I can say about J. per se, as my experience with him amounts to a couple or three brush strokes in a very large painting. In fact, the positive influence that he had on me cannot be fully appreciated without going back long before we met.

I came to death row in the latter part of 1977 with basically one problem. I was uneducated—virtually illiterate. But because of the environment in which I was placed I developed other problems that were more harmful.

In only a year's time of having been placed in a hostile prison environment I had become desensitized, uncaring, untrusting, and—with much shame, I confess—dangerous. But, the good news is, I got my life back on track. And J. deserves much of the credit.

Here's the story beginning with the day I came to prison.

When I arrived the old Building Tender system was still in place. Under this system prison guard brutality was a way of life. Exploitation, manipulation, violence, and homosexuality were widespread. Manhood was measured by one's ability to impose one's will on others. Surely this is a distorted conception of manhood, but the fact is irrationality becomes rationality in an irrational world.

Generally speaking, there were three classes of prisoners: predators, preys, and crazies. The predators were often paid shakedown (extortion) to let live. The preys often paid shakedown to live. The crazies were generally left alone. But by no means were they exempt from the ever present threat of violence and cruelty. Unlike the so-called weaklings (preys) who were singled out daily, the crazies had to first stick their hands into the fire, so to speak. For this reason, some guys pretended to be crazy. Faking split personalities, inflicting self-mutilation, claiming to be haunted by demons from hell, or to be someone other than themselves.

I never gave much thought to playing crazy. If I had any fear, playing that role was it. The rumor was once those prison doctors begin treating you, you won't be faking for long. So I decided to take my chances, trusting that I could stay out of harm's way by being sensible.

I managed to avoid a lot of trouble but, even so, I had my share of run-ins with would-be predators and oppressive guards. I also served my share of time in solitary. Mainly from trusting inmates who I thought were friends, but were actually undercover snitches.

It was there, in solitary, where I made up my mind that no one was to be trusted. Prison was indeed a jungle, and it was necessary to live by the rules of the jungle if you wanted to survive. Trying to avoid trouble was senseless. There were no hiding places. Trouble had to be met head-on. Perhaps even invited.

This is who I was when I first heard the name J.J. The word was floating around that some new guy was trying to starve himself to death. I didn't know if he were a militant, crazy, or pretender. Didn't really care at the time, to tell the truth.

About a year or so later, I guess, I ended up next door to J. At the same time I had no idea that this was the guy who I had heard about earlier. Remember, prison is no social club. No one is enthusiastic about meeting anyone. Especially back then. The rule was you do your time and let the next man do his. Unless, of course, you had a hidden, selfish motive for being sociable.

Commissary was delivered the next day, I believe. I didn't make it. I seldom did. Shortly after it was delivered I heard this metallic tap on the bars. I looked up and saw this hand reaching a coke round.

Right off an alarm went off in my head. According to my experience, nobody gave away anything free. The coke became a live worm, squirming and twisting in his hand. It was bait. Surely, this guy was a weakling, want-to-be-predator, or a real homo.

Reminding myself that trouble had to be met halfway, I accepted the worm and waited for him to make his play.

Surprisingly, J. never approached me with any funny business. Nor did he stop sharing with me. Cokes, sandwiches, etc. In fact, he even offered to buy me a fan one summer.

He seldom recreated because he was always busy. So I stopped in front of his cell one day to check him out. In stature he was very frail looking: easily breakable. But his eyes held no fear. He was quite composed; completely undaunted. His voice tone, facial expression, and total mannerism exhibited a friendliness that I had not known since I were on the outside.

Gradually—I am talking long months—I began relaxing with J., and investing trust in him. I later learned that he was sharing with me because he was sympathetic to my state of poverty. It was sad just to be on death row, he thought, but to not have anything was just too much.

By nature or nurture I can't say, but I can say, and quite honestly, that J. is a sensitive and giving person. His sensitivity and freehearted-ness did not impress me in and of themselves. What did impress me, though, and very profoundly, is that he stayed true to his constitution in an environment that did not allow kindness.

This was a turning point in my life. I realized that it was okay to be myself. It wasn't necessary to become one with the jungle to survive. Prior to this realization, I was totally unaware of how far my surroundings had pushed me out of character. Getting back to myself was like a long, happy journey back home.

Based on what I have shared with you it is clear that prison life is not conducive to self-betterment. This is also true in the area of education. Most prisoners have very little, if any, education. And the sad thing is no one will admit it. Why? Because just as "manhood" is misdefined, "ignorance," too, is misdefined. It is equated with stupidity. No one wants to appear stupid, so guys try to hide their shortcomings in this area.

If you were to ask someone a question you would be played off with—excuse my description, but for lack of a better one allow me to say—a form of child psychology. "You mean to tell me that you don't know the answer to that, man?" or "You dummy," are common answers.

This way the guy not only covers his ignorance, but he builds himself up while putting you down.

As you well know, there are exceptions to all rules. There were a few guys who had their minds on getting an education and wasn't going to be shamed out of it. A couple of these guys came to J. for help. Seeing that he was sincere in helping these men, and that he had no need to use them as stepping stones to make himself taller, I felt comfortable in asking him to help me.

I was probably his biggest job. I wasn't able to pick up a newspaper article and comprehend it. Excepting adding and subtracting, I knew absolutely nothing about numbers. To make a long story short, J. educated me on every subject that the General Education Diploma test entailed. But we were separated before I was ready to take the GED test.

In 1984 the general prison population was opened to death row. I decided that it was to my best interest to go. This way I could learn in an actual classroom setting.

The class that I was assigned to was scheduled for GED testing in three weeks, but I wasn't included because I did not enroll in time. But I nevertheless got wired up in the pre-test talk and the overall atmosphere itself. Surprisingly, some of the guys were taking the test for the third, fourth, fifth, and sixth time. In fun they were teased, but quite obviously respected for their stick-to-itiveness.

The next time that the test was given I passed. It was my first time experiencing a real sense of accomplishment. I went on to successfully complete a paralegal correspondence course from Blackstone School of Law.

Thankful for the help that J. had given me, I began helping others get their GED's. After successfully helping three or four guys I wanted to do something on a mass scale. Unfortunately, the warden made it perfectly clear that organizing would not be tolerated.

Well, Dr. L., this about sums it up, I guess. If you have any questions write me, okay?

Sincerely,

R.

To convey the atmosphere of prison visits, Martin Draughon (Texas) sent his pen-friend the following reflection he wrote in 1988. At that point he was twenty-five and had been on Death Row for a year and a half.

Never Say Goodbye—Deathrow Visit

I walk in and step into the tiny steel mesh cage. You're already sitting, waiting on the other side. I stand facing you while the escort uncuffs me.

Arriving with shackles on no longer embarrasses me. Sometimes I think they would have us on leashes too, if they could get away with it. I never thought that wearing handcuffs would become a way of life.

You're looking so pretty and loving, as usual. I look into your eyes and become entranced in your love and beauty, forgetting all that I'd planned to say—yet what's left to say? Can't we touch? "Just one little touch, Warden?" Yeah . . . I'm dreaming again.

There's only two hours we're allowed to share together, although we're separated by reinforced glass and steel wire mesh and aren't really "together." Still, when I look into your loving eyes I see no reason for words. Your eyes say it all.

I see in your sparkling eyes the secrets we've shared. I see in them a reflection of me and I follow it trickling down your cheek in each tear of loving, frustrated passion. The liquid treasure is wiped away by delicate hands, to be stored somewhere deep within for some far away day.

We talk a little but the conversation seems strained and unimportant. I want to keep you entertained well for the short two hours but I know how to stretch only so far. How much could I talk about, living my life in a 5' × 9' barred room? Once again we end up sharing our dreams, fantasies and desires.

"You've got ten more minutes, Draughon!" the guard says. The bright, sparkling, reflective eyes immediately turn sad and blurry, yet my image seems to become more pronounced as your eyes grow dimmer and sadder. The overwhelming realization of reality becomes manifested again—the liquid love is flowing once more.

The first five—wondering what to say, to do. The last five—trying to prepare ourselves for that excruciating moment of walking out different doors, in different directions. It's only a door, a fence, a reinforced glass window and steel mesh, yet it's a world between us.

I often wish you could relate to what I feel, understand my emotions—and loss of emotions. The sadness and regrets never depart.

You look past me sitting there. The guard comes and unlocks the door on the steel mesh cage. We say our "I Love Yous," but never a good-bye. Just the word, good-bye, seems to carry a bad omen on deathrow. I stand to get cuffed, backing out still looking at you. You try to leave with grace, but I doubt there could ever be any.

In the back room while undressing to be strip-searched, I am silent. Happy but sad. Cuffed once more, I am escorted back to my 5' by 9', where so many thoughts are racing through my mind. Now I remember all the things I wanted to say and ask.

I sit on my bunk and look at myself in my tiny mirror, and it's like I'm looking at you again. It's the same reflection I see in your eyes and in your tears. The thought crosses my mind, that each of your shimmering tears are drops of medicine; the only medicine I know of that's capable of healing my wounded heart.

Next visit probably won't be much different.

A prisoner in California writes about his wife's visits:

There are many times I realize I've ruined a visit because she feels the same pain I feel. Such as sex, I'm a healthy man with normal desires. It's so hard to go years and years having to hold such desires at bay. Sometimes I'll get one of the "magazines men read" and go through it. Well, that's about like a starving person reading a cookbook! Then there I go, out to a visit and I ruin it. Now I realize that she is dying inside because of her own desires. We are both getting older, it's so hard to know there are things, good things we'll never feel or do again. Or at least I know I won't and she isn't now. Her way is to block it all out. I don't know, she must be much stronger because I feel like I'm about to explode at times. I hope you know I'm not just talking about sex; I'm talking about death, my death, execution, freedom . . . I mean everything going on in the world. It's passing me by and I'm having a hard time accepting it.

Harvey Earvin in Texas describes his experience with visits:

When my nieces and nephews come to visit—particularly the very young ones who have no idea they are inside of prison, and who carry on as if the place is an amusement park—it is an experience within itself. Their innocence, in a strange way, brings to life a part of you that is otherwise dormant outside of their presence. Watching them interact with other children in the visiting area, whom they've never seen before, never ceases to amaze me. In a single glance, young children with spirits pure, simultaneously have the same thought, one would think. "Wow! another kid to play with," is the thought, apparently. And without effort they come together, giving no regard to color, sex, or any other social barrier: running, laughing, skipping high with light shoulders free of burden. As if they have a secret unknown to the adult world—the secret to universal peace and harmony. And that inner part of you which only they can awaken aches to be in their midst.

Without being called, intuitively, they sometimes come running, perceiving that it is time to go. They climb first into the big, wooden chairs, then on to the board running along the glass partition. "Goodbye, Uncle Tee," they usually say. "We love you and we gonna come see you again, okay?" Then, as always, they press their little palms up against the glass and wait for me to do the same, then, we kiss.

On their way out they never look ahead; always back, waving cease-lessly, wearing sincere, but forced smiles. There's an ambience about them—a telling ambience. Innately they know, but they don't *know*. They feel it. They taste it. They smell it. Something is approaching. Something far away. Something foreboding.

My curiosity led me to conduct a survey. I asked forty-two of the men here how they felt about having to visit their loved ones with a partition between them, and not being able to touch, kiss or embrace them. The result was startling. Thirty-eight per cent said they disliked the setup but wasn't particularly bothered by it. (Another way of saying "I can deal with it.") Thirty-two per cent said they have been here long enough until they have become accustomed to it. Fifteen per cent said that they never really thought about it because of other matters of more importance, such as the outcome of their appeals, or finding good law-yers. The majority of the remaining fifteen per cent expressed outrage.

There are also visits in Huntsville of a different kind:

At least for the time being we don't have to put up with the tour groups. Until a month ago, they were bringing in tour groups two and three times a week. I always hate this, as do most of the guys here. It's like we're on display or something, like we're animals in a zoo. That's exactly the way the people in the tour groups look at us. What they don't know is that we're not permitted to speak to them. I don't think that anyone should be required to talk to them. In fact, I don't think the tour groups have any place in the system under any conditions—just as we shouldn't be forced to talk to them, we shouldn't be forced to be gawked at by them.

But since we don't have a choice, we should have some reciprocal rights. We should at the very least be given the right to not be exposed, followed by the right to know who the group is. Beyond that, we should be able to speak to the group if we want to without fear of punishment. As it stands we will be written for either creating a disturbance or being out of place. The problem is that when one of these groups comes through all they see is steel-eyed silent convicts. I can surmise that they think we're either too ashamed to talk or we're too mean. In fact,

I've heard people in the groups ask why we didn't talk to them and heard the Warden tell them, "Would you have the guts to face the public if you'd done what they have?" He didn't say, "They're told not to, prevented by threat of disciplinary action, removal of privileges and basic rights." I think that if there is any pretense that there is something to be gained, some illumination or education, an essential part of that experience would be the opportunity to talk to the men you're viewing. Anything that excludes that opportunity is simply freak-show gawking. And what part of our sentence says that we're also supposed to be subjected to the added humiliation of that?

David Holland in Huntsville (later executed in 1993) retained his sense of humor:

I received a travel brochure in the mail today—from Princess Cruise Lines—they offered me a 40% discount on an Alaskan cruise if I book 3 months in advance. Do you think I should take them up on it?

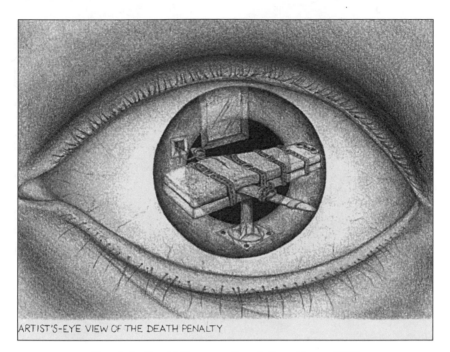

ARTIST'S-EYE VIEW OF THE DEATH PENALTY

Sketch by David Herman, Death Row, Texas, 1995.

Edward Earl Johnson (Mississippi), photographed days before he was executed, May 1987.

Edward Earl Johnson (right) *playing chess with Sam Johnson at the Maximum Security Unit in Parchman Penitentiary, Mississippi, May 1987.*

Edward Earl Johnson with members of his family, taken May 19, 1987, shortly before his execution.

19ᵗʰ July 1989

Hi! Bro!!

These are only a few quick lines to share the GOOD NEWS of today!

I've just, a few moments ago, got off the phone speaking with Tony.

Bro, the State Supreme Court has ruled that it won't take it upon themselves to re-sentence me to death! They've ordered that I be taken before a jury so that a jury can determine whether I should be re-sentenced to death or not!! Great News this is! I'll send you their decision as soon as I get it!

Also, Bro, the Court has ruled that Our Willie MUST BE SENTENCED to LIFE! His life has been spared and he'll not walk the same path as Leo. The GOOD NEWS CONTINUES!

The Court ordered that Our Woodrow's ENTIRE SENTENCE & CONVICTION MUST BE OVERTURNED! He must have a complete new Trial! I'll write more in detail about all of this later tonight. I love you My Brother and know this ALWAYS. Sam

Letter from Sam Johnson.

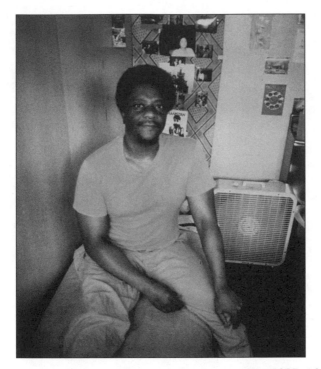

Sam Johnson while still on Death Row in Mississippi, May 1987. After eleven years on Death Row, his sentence was overturned in 1992.

Sam Johnson after he had come off Death Row, taken in December 1994.

*Leo Edwards (Mississippi), photographed in the Death Cell the day before
his execution on June 21, 1989. Edwards spent eight years on Death Row
and survived four death warrants.*

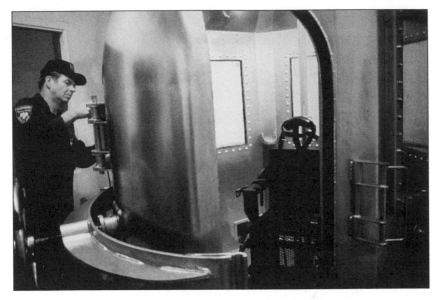

The gas chamber at Parchman Penitentiary, Mississippi.

Clive Stafford Smith in his office at the Southern Prisoners Defense Committee in Atlanta, December 1988.

IN THE SUPERIOR COURT OF WAYNE COUNTY
STATE OF GEORGIA

THE STATE OF GEORGIA)
)
VS.   )   INDICTMENT NO.: 77-1641
)
CHRISTOPHER ALLEN BURGER,)
     Defendant.   )

O R D E R

The Court having sentenced the defendant, CHRISTOPHER ALLEN BURGER on the 19th day of July, 1979, to be executed by the Department of Corrections at such penal institution as may be designated by said Department, in accordance with the laws of Georgia, and;

The date for the execution of the said CHRISTOPHER ALLEN BURGER having passed by reason of post-conviction proceedings;

IT IS CONSIDERED, ORDERED AND ADJUDGED by this Court that within a time period commencing at noon on the 7th day of December, 1993, and ending seven days later at noon on the 14th day of December, 1993, the defendant, CHRISTOPHER ALLEN BURGER, shall be executed by the Department of Corrections at such penal institution and on such a date and time within the aforementioned time period as may be designated by said Department, all in accordance with the laws of Georgia.

The Clerk is directed to serve a copy of this Order upon the Commissioner of the Department of Corrections, the Warden of the Georgia Diagnostic and Classification Center, Jackson, Georgia, the Attorney General for the State of Georgia, the District Attorney for the Brunswick Judicial Circuit, the defendant and last known counsel of record for the defendant.

This 23rd day of _____Nov._____, 1993.

_____
Senior Judge of Superior Courts
of Georgia
Brunswick Judicial Circuit

ROBERT L. SCOGGIN
Senior Judge
GEORGIA SUPERIOR COURTS

Chris Burger's final death warrant. He faced seven in all.

Georgia, Wayne County

      I, Faye B. Graham, Deputy Clerk Superior Court, in and for said county do certify that the foregoing is a true and correct copy of the Order for Execution in the case of The State of Georgia Vs Christopher Allen Burger, Case No. 77-1641, as the same appears of record in the General Records of said county.

      Witness My Official Signature and the Seal of the Court, this 24th day of November, 1993.

Faye B. Graham

Deputy Clerk Superior Court
Wayne County, Georgia

Christopher Burger (Death Row, Virginia, 1977–1993) with his mother, Betty Foster in 1993. This was taken four months before he was executed.

Vick Roberts, Georgia, 1991.

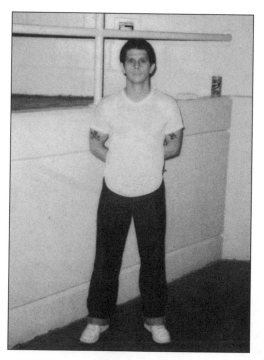

Walter Correll (Death Row, Virginia, 1985–1996), at twenty-nine years old, taken November 1990.

Johnny Lee Gates, Georgia, 1991.

Michael Lambrix, on Death Row in Florida since 1983.

7

Three Blind Mice
and a Cocktail

The letters quoted in this chapter are about survival: the different ways that the men and women find to cope with up to twenty years of waiting for execution or reprieve.

From a prisoner in Texas:

In a prison setting, prisoners—voluntarily and/or involuntarily—attempt to sever the wires that connect their hearts to the people and things they love. It's a method of survival. Real men, according to prison codes, are not suppose to cry, get depressed or display emotions bordering on effeminacy. To show emotions, other than those leaning toward truculence, is to invite unwanted attention. Only scorn and mockery befall those who openly admit that they cannot handle the pressure, the pain is too great. Social order (or lack of it)—outsiders will find it hard to believe; for even I, witnessing it firsthand, can hardly believe it—demands that the weak, the falling, the crumbling find their own quiet corners and quietly come apart. There are no caring ears in which to confide. No friendly shoulders to lean upon. No softness, no tenderness, no gentleness anywhere: only solid things—concrete; steel; stone, cold insensitivity. Such pent up anger, hurt, pain, and frustration often lead to ugly endings: loss of sanity, violence, and even suicide.

And there are signs of coping everywhere you look. In one cell a man sleeps all day, everyday. He never wakes up, except to eat or use the bathroom. He's been here a while, but he knows nobody, nobody knows him. What he's thinking, what he's feeling is known only to him: whenever he's awake. He's like a man in a bar vainly trying to drink his problems away; but here there's no bar, no whiskey. But there's a bunk, there's sleep. Then there's the dancer. On every song he dances; resting on the commercials. In the music, it seems, he has found refuge—a safe haven. Impatiently he waits for the next song; the music. It is his medicine; for it helps him to maintain his integrity. It's his friend; for him it is always there to lean on. And it's his tender love; for it enfolds and caresses him. Then there's the political prisoner, so he believes, who vehemently screams at every passing guard: *"Don't fuck with me! I know who you are you fucking KGB! Don't fuck with me, I'm CIA!"* Then there are those who cope by taking psychiatric drugs. Some of the drugs, the very powerful ones, changes the person entirely: their walk, talk, posture, personality, everything. They're always in a stupor, and their mummy-like walk is popularly known as the "Thorazine Shuffle."

Whenever my lawyer hears about men on Death Row hurting themselves or dropping their appeals out of frustration and hopelessness, he usually praises me for my strength. You, too, I am convinced, see me as a man of strength and integrity. I am afraid that my projected image is much mightier than the actual me. I have not always been strong, nor together. There have been days when I have cursed my keepers, and days when I have pitied them. Days when I have hated them, and days when I have prayed for them. There have been days when I have blamed this country's ethnocentric society for my demeaning predicament, and days when I have blamed myself. There have been days when I was highly religious, then not so religious, then totally uncertain, then back religious again all because of my experience. There have been days when I have viciously pounded on the punching bag, did setups and pushups until I physically collapsed, saying in a whisper for only my inner-man to hear, "Survive, Tee. Man, just survive!" Laying there on the floor too tired to move a finger, and my spirits lower than low, just before I consider giving up, the air about me is electrically charged and energy flows into my body. My once lowly spirits are again strong, they lift my weary body onto my feet, and I say to myself, "God lives!"

Apart from depression, time is a big issue. Writing in 1994, an inmate in Texas wrote to Tori Burbridge, the LifeLines secretary:

It amazes me how time is so lost on me lately. A day or two will turn into a month or two, and it's only in retrospect that I realize it. Time was once my ally. It was a future, potentially a wonderful one, just waiting. Now time is the enemy. Only part of the problem is that it runs out, or is running out. Mostly it is my enemy because it crushes me. Its weight suffocates me and, almost as a paradox, it fills me to the point of bursting. That's something that's hard for people outside to understand. As you live and go through life on the outside, day after day time passes through you like the air you breathe. Time flows and makes things happen. In here, where all reality is confined, the time has nowhere to go, so it accumulates. It builds up and builds up until it (like the most rarefied air) begins to show weight and mass.

Nine years weigh a lot, Tori. Ten weigh even more and it gets harder and harder to breathe. That's one of the worst things about this place. Even for someone "doing time," facing a set sentence, the time is only slowed down before it eventually passes on. But "the Row" is different because there is nowhere for the time to go—it's closed, not open; ended. And something else—when someone dies, their time doesn't just evaporate or go away with them, it stays here as a weight for the rest of us to bear. So here we are, drowning under the weight of our own accumulated years while having to respectfully carry the tonnage of time left to us by the other men who have already died.

When time gets compressed like this, it's no longer easy to untangle, to see the flow. It's all in a huge knot, tangled beyond comprehension so that a day or two can't be told from a month or two—or a year or two—ago. And a letter begun today might be finished tomorrow with tomorrow being indistinguishable from a week or a month. So the letter I began "yesterday," Tori, on your birthday, stings me when I see that it's over a month. And really I can't account for the time since then and that scares me.

One thing I wonder is what would happen if there were really suddenly somewhere for the time to go. Would there be a sudden explosion if the pressure were released? If I were actually to get out, what would happen with all those years compressed? And if the years could be bled off in a controlled manner, how have I been mis-shapened inside by that pressure? I'm actually scared to find out.

I didn't forget your birthday. I began a letter to you about then. I remember writing it (a week or a month ago) while in "my corner" in the rec yard. I didn't send the letter. I didn't send you a card. But I did remember to think about you that day. I only wish I could get past mine.

Mark Allen Wisehart in Indiana has also written of time:

You said it seems I don't distinguish between night and day, as you've seen me writing at all odd hours of the morning. Basically true, for instance right now it's 4:15 A.M., and I just awoke half an hour ago. A real good reason for not respecting the traditional working hours is, I don't work. Sometimes, I *do* sleep from midnight to 8, or 10 P.M. to 5:30, but usually it's goofy "off hours." But, like now, for instance, it is quiet. No one is awake, but me. The noise that exists is the clanging and banging of the heater that is almost musically rhythmic, and someone's radio down the range. I feel most comfortable, writing at this time. Besides, there is nothing on TV.

Mark Allen "Wiseguy" Wisehart was sentenced to death in Indiana in 1983. He came to his pen-pal, Mary Grayson, in 1992, after writing to her about her correspondence with Ray Clark (see Chapter 9, "The Pee-Pee Dance") in the edition of this book first published in Britain.

How did I come across *Welcome to Hell*? Well, it wasn't being *read*, that's for sure. A guy got it from a lady he wrote to, and thought it was a "Prisoner who turned Christian" type of book. And since it had a hard and glossy cover, he used it to crush up pills and snort them. I was in his cell one day and saw it. I asked him what it was and he goes "Ah, some **** Bible book!" I asked him to read it, and he gave it to me. Bless his heart.

I've forged some friendships in here among the "dregs of society" that I would place up against the civilized friendship in the free world.

In here we deal with each other as individuals, not as the headline of some newspaper. We are capable of anything, and violence is only part of that equation. I've seen some people get upset and cry over their favorite sports team loss. In 1984, a guy committed suicide, because his team lost in the Super Bowl. I've also seen a man not sleep for three days because he was desperately trying to get three blind mice (literally, they were newborn) to suck milk from a piece of cloth. He considered it his greatest accomplishment that these mice lived. Last year for my birthday, I got *wrapped* gifts from six different guys. One gift was a giant novelty crossword puzzle that cost $15 to send away for. That was a gift they *knew* I'd get a thrill from, and they were *pleased* that I liked it. These "murdering thugs," imagine that.

Judy Haney (Alabama) acquired a parrot from a church organization:

She is a cocktail. She is light gray with small white spects and a yellow head with orange spots on each side of her head. Her name is Baby and I have had her for seven years. She can say her name and "what" and the wolf call and two or three more words. Pat and Cathy are with a church group. It is called PAWS—"Pets Are Working Saints." They have all kinds of animals and they take them to the children's hospital and put on shows for them and to the old folks home and they wanted to put one on Death Row, so I was pick. So Miss Baby is a prison bird.

We have one long bell they ring over here for lockdown. It rings six times a day, and when it rings the officers yell "lock down, ladies," so when she hears the long bell go off, she will say "lock down, lock um up." She will say it over and over until they are quiet. Anne and I get a real kick out of her.

I have a little mouse in my house. We have set traps but he just eats the food and goes on, he is so small he doesn't even trip the traps. He's about 1 in. long. Last night he got into the bird cage and Baby was scared to death of him. She let the mouse eat her food while she stood back and bitched; I had to get up and run the mouse out. Maybe we will catch him soon.

December 26, 1995:

Thursday of last week I woke up and found her dead in her cage. We believe she had a egg blockess. Cathy, the woman who buys her feed, came and got her Friday and is going to have her cut open to find out for sure. I sure did hate to lose her.

From San Quentin a prisoner writes:

I have names for my pigeons. Yeah, I call one of them "Pretty-Bird" and the other one's "Little-Bird." They won't come by name, but when I make this little kissy noise they come a-runnin'! Of course, that's because they know I'm about to give them sunflower seeds. I always feel so bad on the days I don't go up on the roof. As the fellas come back down, they always come by my cell and tell me how the birds were waiting for me. They say the birds will walk within 10–15 feet of them, and when they realize it's not me, they turn tail and split. I wish I could bring them here with me at night. It would be cool to have them in here to fool with. I doubt anyone would care, I probably could, but I never would. No, it wouldn't be fair on them. Heck, I don't like being cooped up in this cell, just imagine if I had wings and could fly? Boy, I'll tell you one thing, if I did have wings . . . I'd be history!

Humor can be an important way through. Walter Correll (Virginia) wrote:

I remember one day when Fitz Bert and I were sitting at the table and we started throwing food at each other. We were sitting there eating when Fitz screamed out "food fight" and the next thing I knew the food was flying. To some people this may not sound like grown men, but in a place like this you have to do all you can to stay sane. Anyway, Bert started running around the table and Fitz grabbed this milk that had been sitting there ever since that morning. Now you wouldn't think it would have had time to go bad but it did. Fitz opened it up and before he could smell it he threw it at Bert. There were these big chunks of milk on his shirt and boy did it stink. This to most is enough to get them fighting, but we were pretty close so all we could do was laugh about it. We were always doing something like this, but the guard was always saying something to us about it, because there is to be no horse playing. When you are in a place like this you are supposed to be like some kind of robot. I have always been the kind of person that likes to play around and have fun, but when I came here that was to stop, but I just couldn't do it.

We are always coming up with some way to make ourselves laugh. Most of the time we just make fun of each other for one reason or another. I think we do this to keep from going crazy. If you aren't able to laugh at this place there is no way you are to make it. Those who can't do this end up killing themselves or get themselves put on drugs that put them so far out into space that they don't know what their name is.

When you face death every day you will do what ever it takes to stay sane. Most people say we are getting just what we deserve, but not even those people would treat an animal this way. If there was some way you could make an animal understand that you were going to lock it away for years at a time and then kill it there would be some group to stop you.

The inmates in Virgina also had another survival technique.

I started drinking again. We made our own stuff. I knew I should have learned from the past, but with everything that had happened I needed some help to get by. It was either drink or go to the doctor and get him to give me some kind of pills to take. For me the drugs was worse than the drinking. If you ask me I think they would like you to be out in space instead of being able to think for yourself. I know to a lot of people this doesn't sound possible, but all I know is that I have been here for the last years of my life and I have seen the drugs that are given to guys who are having problems. One guy I knew before he was executed was taking so many drugs that he would walk around all day not knowing what he was doing.

One Christmas everyone was drinking and someone turned a radio on and everyone started dancing. You have never seen anything as

funny as a bunch of drunk men trying to dance. I was laughing so hard
I couldn't catch my breath. This was one of the times that nothing
happened, but to be honest there has never been a night when the guys
weren't drinking. It gives them a chance to forget about where they are
and what they are facing. To most people this doesn't mean a lot, but
to us it means more than you think. To be able to put yourself outside
of this place for a short time is the difference between going crazy and
staying sane. We are put here for years at a time and those who are in
charge think that we are just supposed to take what is going to happen
to us. It's bad enough being in a place like this without not being able
to enjoy what's left of your life. For us time is very short and we have
to do what we can to make our life mean something.

When the guys drink they are able to forget where they are and the
pain they have to face each day. People on the outside have people they
can talk to but we only have what we can make for ourselves.

*And on coping with an execution, Walter Correll wrote about Ed-
ward Fitzgerald, executed in 1992:*

I have come to where I don't trust preachers so I only trust what I read
in God's word. I know for sure that there is no way he would ever lie
to me or treat me like I don't even matter. I'm not saying that all
preachers are like this, but a lot of the ones I have met here are. I have
been talking to one of them about a problem I was having and while I
was talking he turned around and started talking to someone else. If
God is willing and I get out of here I am going to make sure those I
talk to know I care about them and what they are going through. With
a lot of prayer and a letter Fitz wrote me before he died I have been
able to go on and keep the fight going.

Fitz was always trying to help those around him, but all you read in
the papers was how bad he was. Nothing was ever written to let people
know that he had changed. To me this is very unfair. If a person
changes I think they should be given another chance, but of course
people don't see it this way.

Well the day finally came when Fitz heard that his last appeal had
been turned down and I think I took it harder than he did. We had a

party for him a few days after that and then they moved him to where the chair was at the time. On the night they were to kill him I had had a little to drink. The preacher came around to see how we were doing and when he found out I had been drinking he told me how wrong I was for doing this and walked away. I just sat there at my cell door asking myself how a man of God could talk to someone like that and then just walk away.

I told myself that I would never get close to anyone like that again, but then this guy named Doug came here and you had to like him. After some time he and I started getting close and he has even started calling my parents mum and dad. We have been in the same pod for the last five years and we watched out for each other if one of us needs something. He was only 18 when he got arrested and when he came here he was only 20. We made fun of him for a long time, because he wasn't able to drink before he came here. To those on the street this may not be funny, but for us it is. I always told him that he was living Johnny Cash's song. I turned 21 in prison doing life without parole. Since he came here after I did I won't have to see him die before I do if the courts don't do something in my case. This really isn't something to be happy about, but if you had to see as many people die as I have you wouldn't want to see any more. Even if they aren't a friend it gets to you the same.

The intense pressures are also described by a man in his early thirties who has spent his entire adult life on Death Row in one of the Deep South states. Writing in 1996, he had been on Death Row since 1983:

I'm no longer complaining about the doctor not doing anything for me, I just lay in bed until I get well then I wait on the doctor to come by (with a bar of soap in my hand) and to try to knock him out. I've told the guards what I am going to do so they can get out the way or they can take the chance of being hit also.

I no longer complain when the heater is blowing cold air and the window is doing the same. I just cover the heater vent and window with the backs of writing tablets. They tell us not to cover the windows or we will be given a Rule Violation Report. I tell them to kiss my ass! I can do that being I have no TV for them to take as punishment for rule violation.

I have come to understand I am in their world and what they want to do to me or toward me, I can do very little to stop them. I have no family to help me fight the prison so I just set back these days and watch the time roll by, only dreaming of what life should be.

This place is full of fools. I see one every day no matter which way I look. I look at gang members every day and thank Allah I never found anything in my heart for that kind of life but hate. They only prove what I say about them every time it takes two or more to fight one.

They will not give anything away for free. They even try to sell aspirins to people who are sick. This fool down the hall just tried to sell me some albuprofen for 25¢ a tablet. I told him the same I tell this prison (go to Hell).

Every time I try to be nice toward someone they take it the wrong way. People here know nothing about love. It's not like it use to be when I first come to D-Row. There is no love for the next man. There is no respect for the next man. There is no friendship among anyone, not even the gang members who belong to the same gangs.

It has gotten so bad here, that I try not to turn my back on anyone. I am not use to living my life this way. Even at 17, I could walk away and not worry about a piece of steel going through my back. There is not a day I don't hear someone say they will kill something, meaning one of us. I no longer go on the yard because there is no respect for the next man's life.

I'm too old for these crazy games. That's why I sometimes wish the state would go ahead and put me out of my misery but I come to my senses real quick.

A prisoner in Texas describes the ingenuity and determination with which simple pleasures are recreated:

Today was very warm and sunny. They've not yet mowed the area just outside the fence surrounding the rec yard, so now the ground cover is quite lush. I mention the wildflowers and everyone else admonishes me to call them weeds. But what are weeds except wildflowers that people haven't looked at closely enough? Tomorrow they will mow the area and my lovely garden will be gone, Tori. Today I decided to gather some of the wildflowers to press and dry. I had planned to send them to you, which no doubt violates a number of federal agricultural laws. I'd intended to pick one of everything that grows out there. There are about six or seven species of flowers in bloom right now, all of them small. There are a couple score other types of small plants, each populating a particular micro-eco-niche (not a real word, I'm certain) in the scheme of things.

Here's how we gather flowers through the fence. We take the handle from a broom and tie a shoestring in a loop at one end. We push the broomhandle through the chain link and lay the loop over which ever group of flowers we're after. Then we carefully roll the stick toward the loop so that it is wound up onto the stick. See, you have to roll the stick, and not pull the loop off the flowers or it won't work. As the stick winds the string, it eventually closes on the flowers/weeds and, if all goes well, it gets tight enough to pull the bunch of greenery up by the roots. We've learned that sometimes it helps to use the stick to try to dig the roots out before trying to loop them. It's sort of like spearing fish, only we're spearing the roots, viciously stabbing the dirt at the base of the plant. Then it's easier to loop them and pull them in. This technique was developed after much practice, with suggestions and experimentation done by my neighbor Bill and another guy named Squeaky (whose voice is actually quite deep and resonant). When I told them what I was doing, they both jumped in to lend a hand.

We actually harvested a fair representative sample, Tori, only we didn't count on just how fast the little boogers would wilt. Most of the flowers were completely shriveled within three minutes after being uprooted. Unfortunately, we had no way to convince the guards to let us carry paper and heavy books to the rec yard to be able to immediately press our harvest. I tried to press some of it, but I don't know how much if any will be usable. Nor do I know what the odds of TDC letting us mail the pressings out. Hey, at least we tried.

The same prisoner started off an entirely different craze.

The juggling story—yep, that's one of the memorable high/low points for me in here. In the interest of being the ever-clown I sometimes let my bragging overload my ability. And then *have* to make good on my claim to save face, or in that case save the expense of many cokes. But it was a great experience. The whole thing was really quite memorably entertaining for a lot of guys in here, which is something of value in an otherwise bleak situation. And hey, I did learn to juggle.

As a matter of fact, it started a bleedin' craze. The whole thing began one day in the day room after supper. They had hard boiled eggs that night, a rather rare treat round here. I picked up three of them and made as if to juggle them and one of the guys cleared out. Playing it up, I asked if they doubted that I could do it and offered to make bets. I even embellished the offer with claims of having taken a class in being a clown at college (true) and learning to juggle then (false). I figured they'd back down. But the thing is, well, I'm really quite a pitiful liar, though I can sometimes pull off a joke or two every once in a while (I hoped this was one of those times but it wasn't). They didn't buy it and, dammit, took me up on the bets. Which meant I had to bluff my way through and hope to god that some sort of unseen skill magically manifested itself, which it did not. Well, the eggs ended up as egg particles all over the table and, alas, I lost face. Darn.

The offer was made that I could save the cost of the cokes and save face if I learned to juggle within a week (that was later extended to a month when they saw just how uncoordinated I was). See, this was billed as merely a way to let me save some money on the cokes. In reality, they just wanted to string me along and make me learn to juggle, which is why they extended the deadline from the first week to the month. Not because of any real generosity. I think they took great pleasure in my frustration. By the way, that very obvious/evident clumsiness in my day to day life is what gave away the falsity of my original claim of juggling ability.

Here's the really magical thing about all this, though. As I tried in vain to juggle items, usually rolled up socks, other guys here would get curious and try, some with more and some with less success. And then other guys would see those two or three trying and they'd just have to try. Pretty soon there were literally a couple of dozen guys trying, learning, succeeding and perfecting for the full month. During those few weeks, it was typical to see eight, nine or ten guys in the recreation yard juggling different items, everything from socks and rocks to basketballs and volley balls. Some guys learned pretty quick, like in about ten or fifteen minutes. Other guys took a week or so, but then would quickly learn three or four variations. I had people coming up to me, like with three or four of my most ardent tormentors, and telling me "I learned in ten minutes—you learned yet?" while everybody laughed their asses off. Other times people would come to quietly whisper they'd been trying in secret all week with no success.

Eventually, I got intimidated, which was also a source of great mirth for the guys here, and my cell partner, Lester, had to set up an hour-a-day schedule as part of the criteria for the deadline extension. So I practiced my hour-a-day with Lester officiating. Again, I think it was a source of entertainment since I did a lot of it in the cell with him watching. Eventually, the month ended and I went out with D.P. and Lester (I thought I had the rec yard to myself to avoid interference/nervousness/stage fright but I later learned that about half the wing was watching from their cells through the windows) and, per the agreement, I got them up for 60 seconds within three tries. Just barely. And with D.P.'s and Lester's indulgent and generous interpretation of the rules.

The really amazing thing about all this wasn't so much that I pulled it off. The magic in this juggling was the way it drew everybody into involvement. People who didn't usually talk to each other were regularly outside joking and clowning, laughing with one another. We even had group juggling, like with six or seven objects between two or three guys. Pretty amazing for what is supposed to be the absolute worst group of antisocial murderers the State of Texas has to offer, wouldn't you say? Anyway, the juggling craze went on for a while after the contest ended and I'm still pretty good.

But eventually the guards here didn't like what they saw and started taking the extra socks and confiscating whatever items we'd manufactured, giving write-ups for having contraband (the six-sided cloth balls I'd made). We tried to get permission to make them, the cloth balls, to keep in the rec room for our wing and other ones since they'd been a smashing success. What they were made from was waste material from the Death Row Garment Factory that normally went in the trash. We even volunteered to make the damn things at the factory in our spare time *for* TDC if they'd let us, but TDC would have none of it. I can only surmise why. Eventually the juggling craze faded with the increased pressure from the administration. But it was truly fun while it lasted.

8

When Someone Deeply Listens

I believe that our friendship has grown into something special because
we never expected anything more of the other than friendship, and
because we never gave anything less.

—Johnny Lee Gates, Jackson, Georgia, September 6, 1990

*Those on Death Row often face abandonment and humiliation. They
are cast aside by society, waiting on due process of law until they are
executed. Families and friends—often for understandable reasons—
desert them. In these circumstances nonjudgmental support can become extraordinarily important. The following low-key, sad passage
from a twenty-eight-year-old Hispanic's first letter is typical:*

My family haven't once written or visited in a few years so I don't
know where they are or live, or if they're even alive. But you can't
force people to care, so I'm on my own now that my wife has divorced
me. She was my only contact with the outside world so things can get
pretty lonely as well as boring, so you find me searching for a friend
to correspond with.

*The general feeling is perhaps summed up by a prisoner in Georgia,
who wrote on hearing that there was a group of people in Britain
writing to Death Row:*

I thought it proper for me to thank you personally for having the rare
and sensitive appreciation for the individual and collective humanity of

men like myself, who are under a sentence of death. Few Americans think of us as human beings. Thank you for recognizing that we are.

Similarly a prisoner in Texas wrote "how good it makes us feel just to have some treat us with kindness and respect." Rickey Roberts in Florida State Prison wrote in 1991: "Your friendship is like a long arm of warmth reaching across skies and oceans to embrace a man on Death Row, bringing an enormous amount of happiness and peace in his life." From Georgia, an inmate wrote that he thought "LifeLines is the right name in that where some have only known the feelings of despair and hopelessness they now know the experience of love, hope and a deep sense of worth."
Sam Johnson's response early on in the correspondence was:

I love all of you, my brother, and your acts of kindness bring tears to my eyes. It has been so long since I've felt real happiness until I had almost forgotten what it feels like to be happy. It truly feels good. I'm almost at a loss for words. Certain things cannot be expressed into words and I can't express what I feel other than to say that I love you.

Rickey Roberts in Florida has written:

Your care, support and dedication to reach out and befriend those in the most adverse situation really means something special, I know from personal experience. Many men and women in the various states that carry the death penalty have found themselves very much alone and completely isolated. We may be many in faces and locations but the stories are similar. It really makes a difference knowing people care about you. We live in a world that has become increasingly heartless and violent.

The following letter is typical of the way many prisoners respond when they receive their first, totally unexpected letter:

I can not begin to tell you how surprised I was receiving a letter from a stranger all the way from England, the letter I got from you was the first letter I'v received in over two years, and the only thing I could say was Praise the Lord. I really don't know where to begin so I'll start by saying I'm 35 years old and I'm black and last but not lease I'm on death row. I don't know how the prison system is ran over there as far as doing time with other inmates, but here its a job just staying alive and being a man. I first came to prison in 1975 and I had 15 years for robbery. I was young and had a lot of problems with other inmates, mainly sexuall problems. In our prison system you either stand stronge or be some guy's punk by force. I came at such a young age and I'm fairly good looking and I had problems, but I came with the feeling that my freedom, my woman, my son, my rights and everything else was tooken and I just wasn't going to stand for some inmate to take my manhood and violate any of my principals cause that was all I had left. After ten years of problems in 1985 I was charged and convicted of killing another inmate and sentence to death. I'v been on death row almost seven years and my appeals are running out, but I'm ready I'm at peace with myself as well as the Lord. I became religious about four years ago because I needed help in dealing with my situation and something to cling to. I am what is called a born again Christian and in prison being a Christian is looked upon as a sign of weakness. Because of the life I'v chose to live on death row its caused me problems with other inmates. On Christmas day of 89 while in church someone set fire to my cell that destroyed my TV and radio as well as all my legal papers.

Since then I spend most of my time studying the Bible and praying because its hard for me not to revert back to my sinfull ways because at one hour someone would've been seriously hurt behind that fire. Here where I'm at we are allowed 45 mins of yard every other day and the rest is spent in your one man cell. I have five brothers and four sisters who I haven't heard from since my mother passed away in 1980. It really hurts knowing that they are out there and I'm here about to be executed and they still don't care. The Chaplain here keeps telling me that the Lord will provide me with another TV and radio, a family and give me the strength to go on, but I find myself questioning him, and it hurts because I know I'm not suppose to question the Lord. I can except being executed, but it hurts that nobody seems to understand that these days I spend on death row might very well be my last, and I just don't want to spend them suffering and longing for the love of a family. I'm sorry about forcing you to shouldering my sorrow, but its been so long sence I'v been able to share any kind of thought I probably got a little carried away. I also would like to say that if from reading my letter for some reason are another you decide not to write back I'll understand. But I want you to know that for one day you made me feel humane and your letter was a blessing and will always be treasured. I'm sorry about any miss-spelled words and my penmant ship, but I don't have a dictionary. Take care and I hope to hear from you again.

In the name of the Lord
Love H.

P.S. If you write back I'll sure answer it!!

From Mecklenberg, Virginia, Joe O'Dell described in his first letter to Audrey Elcombe, of Bury St. Edmunds, how he coped and how much even the initial contact meant to him.

You asked if I had any family to contact. Nobody but my sister and Father, who want *nothing* to do with me! I have some distant cousins, but other than that I have nobody. The only way I am able to write letters and pay for the little bit of postage I'm allowed is I get paid 23¢ an hour for five hours a day, for cleaning up after meals, then I'm locked back up in my cell.

Audrey (smile), you would laugh if you saw this typewriter that I'm using. It was thrown away by the prison, and I asked if I could have it to repair. They laughed and said if I could repair it I could have it. I made the carriage bearings out of plastic that I melted and formed, made the carriage return lever out of an old toothbrush, put a rubber band on the carriage to pull it along because it had no spring, and the caps were missing off of the keys, so I heated up toothpaste tube caps, and pressed them onto the key shanks, and voilà, I had a workable typewriter . . . weird looking, and very unconventional. But it worked, and that is what mattered. Also, it has no ribbon, so I use carbon paper and type on a cover sheet that is blank, onto the carbon, which transfers the ink onto the paper. (smile). You do what you have to do to survive . . . I do all my Legal Briefs, etc., on this typewriter, and have been commended by Judges everywhere for the neatness in which my papers are typed. Please don't let the way this letter is typed be indicative of my neatness in typing. (smile).

Yes, of course I would like to correspond with you. You sound very interesting, [with] a very altruistic and compassionate trait, and that is the kind of friends I want to have. I definitely want you to be my friend! I was really truly impressed by something you said, and I quote: "I'm certainly a fighter (in the sense that I will not give up on any idea or matter of importance)." Unquote. I am exactly the same way, and I believe perseverance is the "key" to *anything*! "Can't" never could do anything! (smile). You get knocked down, you get back up and fight . . . just the loss of a battle doesn't mean the loss of the war! Believe me Audrey, I want a Friend like you very much, for there are not many like you in this world.

Victor Roberts in Georgia wrote to the letter writers in general:

I thank you all, for everyone who is on Death Row, for listening, for caring, for writing. It does matter! It gives us all the infinite, unlimited, internal pleasure, peace, happiness and joy to make it through the emptiness of the day and the dreadful, terrifying nights.

Or another inmate:

Do keep writing please. You are all I have in here. Life and Time is really hard for me and other people here. We do not have really nothing to do in here. I do the same things every day. When I get a letter from you it gives me so much to do and think about.

A prisoner in Texas commented on the impact the correspondence had had on another man:

Her letters and support for him have made a profound change in him, for the better I might add. He is very proud of their friendship as well he should be. She has done a world of good for him.

The following comments come from a black man in one of the southern states with little education and officially classed as retarded. The woman he writes to is older than he is, and the relationship has at no time been disturbed by amorous complications.

I do have thoughts of you each and every day since you came into my life and colored my world so beautifully with your caring, loving friendship. Your friendship is a true precious treasure gift of a lifetime. You mean the world to me J., and our friendship has built love, caring, understanding, trust, faith, support and much more, and I am so very thankful for you coming into my life. I never want to lose our friendship that we have, ever, and I never want you to go a day without knowing you have been thought of, and that you are very dear to someone miles, miles away.

You know I never thought I could ever care about a person or truly trust anyone again in my life. You showed me wrong because I can be with you totally, I'm not afraid to express my hurts to you or my fear nor afraid to tell you who I am. That alone means so much to me when I had closed myself up from everyone, keeping the door to self locked up, I don't have to place masks over the face of my real self. I could never tell you truly how much you mean to me because the scholarly wise ones of this world have not found the right words to express the true heart of humans.

What is friendship? Friendship is having someone to walk with, to talk with, to laugh with, too. Someone as special as you.

In a similar vein, a twenty-seven-year-old man in Alabama wrote to his pen-pal—again, a much older woman—that she had been "adopted" by his family.

Like you I am in the process of sorting out my priorities and long ago I made up my mind that you are a dear friend and I would never want to lose you. You always lend a kind word and to me this means more than gold. What you have given me in our friendship can never be bought.

The correspondence can help prisoners to lead something of a parallel life in the world of imagination. As one prisoner put· it, "you become our eyes and ears on the outside." One man in Mississippi wrote:

When our friends share with us the reality of their lives and travels we learn to put aside the pain of confinement and allow our memories and the child in us out to play, to play free of hurt, to play free of fear. Your sharing is one of the most positive and healthiest things we have here, as well as that of our other friends here.

Another wrote:

Please send me more of those beautiful little flowers. I like them a lot. You could send one in your letters when you write. I'd like that very much. They make me feel so happy. I wish I could send you flowers but the flowers around here are all dead and gone.

Similarly David Holland in Texas wrote:

Do not feel badly when telling me about holidays and good times, I enjoy hearing about them very much. At least someone I know is having a good time and that's enough for me.

The correspondence can also awaken dormant memories. The following was received in summer 1990 from a thirty-two-year-old black prisoner:

I received the beautiful postcard of Sées in France. You have no idea how good receiving it made me feel. Thank you. It brought back memories of my young childhood when during the summer I would go with my grandfather to help him clean the classrooms of the school he worked for. The French classroom was always a special treat for me. That is once my grandfather got me interested in it by leaving one of the recorders on one day and leaving on some pretense, telling me to have the room cleaned by the time he returned. No, the room wasn't cleaned when he returned—between trying to understand the French and English translation of each word I lost all track of time.

He gave me a rough go of it, but I found later as we sat together down in his office (which was the boiler room) sharing lunch together that he was actually pleased with me. He didn't say it in words for he was a man of few words, but it was the way he looked at me with great pride and affection in his eyes; it was in the way he would put half of his favorite food in my little hands after each time I left that classroom and I would try to pronounce a word in French for him. That room was his and my private secret. And I feel good being able to share this. It has helped me understand why I have always been fascinated with France. I still cannot pronounce but two words in French!

From Mississippi John Irving (Mali Lumumba) wrote to Jan Mac-Kenzie of Cambridge, England:

I woke this morning with thoughts of you heavy on my mind. In a way unexplainable, and yet, understood, I can feel your long distance embrace. As I read your vivid description of the Suffolk countryside, it allowed me to share in the peace and tranquillity of the area in a purely spiritual way. As you expressed hope of doing, you did take me out among the open spaces. Thank you!

Similarly, Andrew Lee Jones in Louisiana (executed in July 1991) wrote to Jane Officer, his pen-friend in Birmingham, England:

I must say it again. Your letters is giving me hope. Since I have been writing to you the thought of dying in the electric chair don't cross my mind too much because I have a lot to think about when you write. With your letters and pictures I can put myself on a hill, I can run wild on a Scottish island. I can take my mind completely out of this place.

Pen-friends are often reluctant to write about happy and beautiful aspects of their lives, in case it makes the prisoner feel even more deprived, but these examples show the opposite is often true.

In some cases, the pen-friends can help the prisoner to break through the narrowness, suffocation, and fears of their world. A retired couple in Essex are writing to a twenty-five-year-old man in Texas who had lost contact with his family. Gently, they encouraged him to reestablish links. The result was the following letter:

I seriously contemplated the advice you gave me in your last letter, and determined you were right in one aspect of your letter. I could and would not correspond with anyone until I mended all broken feelings with my family, and left it up to them if they wanted to have anything to do with me. At least I'd have the satisfaction of knowing that I tried.

Thank you for helping me realize that it was up to me to take the first step. I can happily tell you that I've heard from my older brother, he sent me a photo of his new-born baby boy, they named after me. He told me everybody is doing fine and that they send their greetings. I can understand why Mom doesn't write much, because she doesn't know how to read and write very well. I know it must be very painful for her to see me in here. I pray to God to make things a bit more bearable for her.

The importance of correspondence is well summed up in this initial letter received from a prisoner in Huntsville, Texas:

Thanks so much for your warm, friendly letter, I can not begin to tell you how delighted I am. Perhaps you already realize that a letter means so much to a person in my situation. A letter is like a ray of warm sunlight in a cold dark cave. And the idea of us becoming friends adds a feeling of joy into my life that I haven't experienced in quite a number of years. You know something, N., my experience has really taught me the meaning and value of friendship. See there was a time in my life when I felt that I did not need anyone, but I have since learned that people were created and designed to interact with, share, and love one another. This is what makes a civilization. And through fellowshipping in Christ we nourish our divine qualities.

N., know that I speak the truth when I say that I am truly grateful that you have extended your friendship to me. And know that I speak the truth when I say that I will never take your friendship for granted, and nor will I ever betray your love.

In your letter you inquired about my family. Well, I have four sisters, and one brother. I had a younger brother but he was killed in an automobile accident. Even today I have to fight back tears when I think about our special moments together. We were as close as two people could possibly get. Anyway, my family and I are from Houston, Texas, which is about 80 miles south of Huntsville. With the exception of my brother, who now lives in Los Angeles, California, my family still lives in Houston.

Although my family is poor and has experienced hard times, we have always been close and shared what we had. Since day one of my confinement my family has stood by my side and done all they could for me. It was only a couple or three years ago that their letters began to drop off. Naturally my brother can't visit regularly because he lives so far away. But when it comes to my sisters, long stretches of time goes by that I sometimes find hard to accept, although I understand the reason. I haven't seen my dad since I was about five years old. As for my mother she still writes and visits whenever she can, but it is obvious that she, too, is tiring out.

Please do not misunderstand me. My family has not forsakened me nor abandoned me. I do not question their love, for I know that they love me very dearly. The truth of the matter is they are trying to escape some of the hurt and pain. They are trying to take a relaxation spell from all of the long years of mental and spiritual stress and strain. So, if not hearing from or seeing my family for a while is the price that I must pay so that they may find a peace of mind, then I am willing to pay that price. My love is that strong. It's a painful price, I admit, but still I am willing to sacrifice.

N., I am not looking to you to take the place of my family, I just want us to become close friends, that's all. I want to share with you my thoughts, feelings, and emotions. And I would like for you to be able to share and confide in me. Here in prison I have one real close friend. The other prisoners, well, I just associate with them. Most of them, it seems, are lost in their own worlds, or have their own concerns. Relationships here (among prisoners) are for the most part superficial. Maybe it's because so many of the men here have lost faith in people.

They feel if their own families forsake them (their own flesh and blood), then there is no such thing as real commitment. I just try to always keep in mind that just like it is hard on me, it is hard on my family too. An experience such as this has a way of destroying a part of those who love you, in the very same way that it destroys a part of you. Therefore, we all must learn to depend on the almighty strength of God and not depend so much on the strength of our families and ourselves. And pray that God gives us all strength and keep our families together.

Yes, I am getting good legal representation. At first I was receiving very poor representation. When I was first arrested my family gave what little they had to get me a lawyer. He took all of their money and still did not do anything for me. I was tried and convicted in a matter of days. For years I tried to obtain a decent lawyer, and never could. Consequently, I came close to being executed once. Then last year a young lawyer who is in his early twenties took my case free of charge. And he has honestly worked as if he is being paid. Now for the first time I can honestly say that I am a little optimistic about surviving this ordeal.

Well, N., I am going to close for now. Do give your wife, daughter, and granddaughter my love. I hope to hear from you soon. Meantime may God bless you and your family.

Your friend

The following excerpt from a letter from a man in Mississippi also brings out what the correspondence can mean:

Contrary to what you think, E., too much mail could never cause problems for me. *Not getting any mail* is what would cause problems for me. You see, the hatred that these people have for me is real and in a controlled, structured environment such as this they very easily could carry out their evil intentions upon me if they knew that I was without family and friends. They know that I am without family and friends within this state because I don't get any visits. I don't get an abundance of letters but what letters I do get lets them know that I do have people on the outside who care for me even if they cannot visit me. I don't know if they read my incoming and outgoing mail but I do know that they record all my incoming and outgoing mail in a log book. I am certain that if I stopped getting letters and stopped writing these people would then physically end my existence. E., I am hated by these people because of the crime I've been convicted of, because of my color, because of my poverty, and because I won't act as a slave. I'm also hated because I have a little intelligence. My strength lies in writing and receiving letters. I don't tell you this in an attempt to cause you to write more than you normally would. I tell you this so you will know that your letters won't cause me any problems.

James McWilliams in Alabama writes (1994) of his initial contacts with LifeLines:

1985 was the beginning of a series of years that would prove to be the loneliest I had ever had. One by one all the people that I call "Friend" started to become unavailable and uncontactable. After many years of soul searching I now understand the pressures they all were under, and have found a way to be forgiving as well.

I had heard other men talk about the pen-pal programs that allowed death row inmates to start new friendships, but I was so hurt from the previous experiences that I didn't want to have those emotions again so I just passed the list on down the lines and gathered up a good book (when they were accessible) and started to read. Well, the cell walls became closer and the book-listing shorter.

After six years of continuous studies in legal research and becoming a paralegal I noticed that I had no one to share all my achievements with, to share the joy of accomplishment with. Once again, the list came to me and the guy next door said that I really should give Life-Lines a chance. I thought about it and for the first time I placed my name on the list.

Several weeks later I received a letter from the Alabama co-ordinator acknowledging the receipt of my letter and stating I would be given a pen-pal very soon. A few more weeks went by and then came a letter. She was very kind and straightforward about herself. But I was still unsure about all this and moved slowly, thinking that this would not last long at all, and that this was some person that had hurt someone in the past and wanted to make amends by doing this good deed. What a fool I was! I have found a person that doesn't care about the fact I am here or the reasons for my coming here. She has only wanted to know what makes me "James."

I have seen parts of England that I have never been to, I have experienced every day of her life just as she lives it. There is so much I have gained from that one letter and over the past two years I have found someone that I could share all my achievements with. Now there is more to my life than just the court's ruling, attorneys, and the walls that hold me. I have a friendship that transcends all that I thought held me here. I have just one regret, I wish I would have signed the listing the first time, I have lost so many years of happiness because I didn't know any better.

Thank You LifeLines: my walls have spread further apart, I am in the door waiting for the mail person to come, never knowing what the envelope holds for me. I could very easily go on and on about all I have gained. I now encourage others to write and hope they will find the special friendships that I now hold close to my heart. There will never be too many friendships in the world.

Harvey Earvin (Texas) wrote to Nadir Dinshaw in Jersey of what the correspondence meant to him:

I thought about staying in because I was enjoying your letters so much, but then I hadn't been out in five or six days, so I decided to go out and soak up a little sun. While out on the yard, sitting off to myself, I still had your letters in mind. And I found myself, in an absent-minded way, lining up pebbles. A friend walked over and asked what was I doing. At first I was a little startled. I looked up at his big, wide, snaggletooth smile and answer, "Counting my friends." Reaching down, he picked up all my pebbles excepting three or four. Because he had difficulty holding all of the pebbles in one hand, one fell back to the ground. I quickly grabbed it as if it were a precious pearl before he could react.

"You're fantasizing again," he said in fun. "You know that I know that you only have three or four people writing to you."

"You're correct on the actual number of people writing to me. But you're wrong in thinking that I am fantasizing about having lots of friends. For I have one who tells me about all of the others. Now, if you don't mind, take my friends out of your pocket and give them back to me."

At that, we shared a good laugh. Laughter is medicine around this camp.

Chris Burger was sentenced to death in Georgia for a crime committed when he was seventeen—a juvenile—in 1977. In May 1993 he replied to his pen-pal after she wrote about her four-year-old daughter's birthday party.

I wish I could have been there. Do you know that I have never had a birthday party? Nor have I had a cake with candles—if I did, I must have been between one and four years old and don't remember it, I just realized that.

Later that year, his pen-pal, Micheala Conway, organized a birthday party for Chris.

I like the idea of you having the party early (October) so that I will be able to have all the photo's in time for my birthday proper. I would love to send out the invitations myself, I have never sent an invitation to anyone before. I know that you are hosting the party for me, but I would still like to send you, Rob and Gayle an invitation too.

Chris's appeals had by this time reached a critical point. He wrote:

There is something else I would like you to do, all of you. This request will be tougher . . . I want you to have this party for me and yourselves no matter what. If things go bad for me at the beginning of October and I am not around physically by Oct. 26th, I'd like for you to still have my party for me, ok?

October 3:

It's my PARTY DAY!!!!! Doc and I just spent the last hour sitting talking about my birthday party, and laughing and wondering what you were all doing right now.

November 10, 1993:

Man! I can't believe all this mail today, I had to have help carrying it all back to my cell! It has taken me over three hours to read it all. Even longer to enjoy all of my photo's. Wow! . . . that was a party! I'm so touched that you all wrote to me during it, telling me everything that was going on and making me a real part of it. Reading this "progressive letter" really did make me feel like I was physically there with you all. These photo's are wonderful, just look at all of that delicious food. You made everything I asked for.

Thank you all for coming to my party, and for celebrating my life and for the love that you have all surrounded me in. You have touched and honored my soul. I love all of you and you will live in my heart forever.

Less than a month later Christopher Burger was dead.

Rickey Roberts (born in 1954, and on Death Row in Florida since New Year's Eve, 1985) has written as follows about the importance of correspondence:

It's people who extend friendship and love that feed my life; give me energy and peace . . . friendship is precious . . . more than precious— it's invaluable, a treasure.

There's nothing in this world greater than knowing you are loved and cared about unconditionally.

You have to learn to adjust to the situation . . . it is a vital part of any adversity, adjusting and making the necessary steps to stay above the emotional strain . . . correspondence and good friendship allow me to escape and feel like a real human being.

Toby Williams, Texas Death Row:

When someone deeply listen to you, it's like holding out a dented cup you've had since childhood, and watching it fill up with cold fresh water. When it balances on the top of the brim, you are understood. When it overflows and touches your skin, you are loved, someone deeply listen to you.

And the correspondence can have its lighter side. Sam Johnson, Mississippi:

You talked about me making "droll faces"—well, how do you expect me to stop laughing if you continue to do what you tell me not to do? You don't realize this but there has been a break in between the time that I wrote the above and the time that I'm writing this. I had to take a break to stop laughing (smile). It took me over 20 minutes and Willie thought that I had lost what little mind I have left over here. He didn't know what I was laughing about and when I didn't respond to his questions of "what's wrong with you?" but continued to laugh, he started to laughing too! His laughing, and not knowing "what" he was laughing about cracked me up even more.

Bro, the police has just walked by the cell, making his count. I looked at him and busted out laughing! I know that he probably thinks I've gone stark, raving mad in here because he walked a little faster in "going by" this cell than he did in "coming by" it.

The correspondence also has its downside. A number of the men on Death Row are angry, disturbed, manipulative, and unreasonable. Initial charm or plausibility gives way to a host of reactions and attitudes that make a genuine, two-way correspondence all but impossible. In some cases, those on Death Row are there because of deep character flaws; in others, Death Row forces them to play a part and brings out their worst side. One man in Huntsville, Texas, sees it in these terms:

I hope the LifeLines project goes well. Everyone is not alike on D.R. It is a mistake to put us all in one group. Each should be judged by his own actions. I know that many will have bad experiences in their contacts, but tell them that all are not like that and for them please to try someone else if the first is a bad one. This is a cruel and hard place, it takes a strong person to make it here. There are some very evil and vicious people here also. I would be less than honest with you if I did not tell you this. Luckily, it does not take one long to find these things out when writing to an inmate. For these types I apologize to you and to LifeLines—for the others I thank LifeLines and you.

Similarly an inmate in Texas has written:

Money is always hard to come up with in here, yet I'd never ask anyone for anything like that. I detest knowing that some of my fellow inmates use letter writing as simply a way to elicit funds or "kinky" letters. Oh, I understand that for some the only way they can get anything in here at all is to do that, so I'm not too critical. It's just that the dishonesty of the whole thing offends me greatly. And as for the kinky letters, well, the tension from sexual frustration is incredible in here. Most of the guys don't know how to deal with it, divert or rechannel it, and they end up having it become part of their lives in a less than healthy way. I suppose I understand it, though it does bother me because it makes it difficult for others who are attempting to write legitimately.

Certainly amorous or pornographic letters are one of the biggest problems in the letter writing between female pen-friends and male prisoners. In their deprivation, it is not uncommon—or indeed surprising—for the prisoner to develop a strong romantic attachment toward those who have befriended them, as illustrated by this early letter from a prisoner in Florida:

Darling, as one whom have always felt it necessary to speak what my heart feels, it is quite relevant that I aware you of the fact that your presence in my heart continues to grow and is maintaining a certain feeling of warmth, love and beauty. It is no less than true, what I feel for you is radiating throughout my entire body. I'm absolutely helpless against the power you have over me. And darling, I only hope that my claim of love for you will not place our friendship in jeopardy.

My queen. The days between your last letter till today, has been a long, torturing experience. I've awaited the arrival of your "third letter" with vast anticipation of hope and impatient. I'm inclined to believe that the long thanksgivings weekend—from Wednesday night to Monday night without mail-call—is responsible for my miserableness of not hearing from you. Nonetheless, I shall pray that today's mail-call will bring some relief from Essex, England. Oh, how great the pains of waiting can be!

My little angel, I hope you don't mind my saying so, but you've a very sexy face. In fact, I'm completely in love with every segment of your face. Your eyes, they seems to radiant a very powerful beam! Your lips are rather firm and seems to have enough electricity to supply electric lights for the whole world—so lighting my fires would be only a small job; your nose is very cute. Strawberry colored, and could never do a face more justice, and though I couldn't see your ears because of your raving hair—which is also beautiful and is worn in a style much to my likings—I'm inclined to believe they [your ears] are very unique, polite, and should be stimulated with a nibbling kiss each morning before you're allowed to accelerate from you're bed.

The sentiments are not always so charmingly expressed, and female correspondents must then decide whether to join the prisoners in a fantasy world of sex on paper, or to provide straight friendship with firm boundaries.

Apart from unreasonable demands for money and prisoners who fall in love or try to steer the relationship in an amorous or sexual direction, a large number of prisoners stop writing at some point. Sometimes this is merely a gap; at other times it is permanent. On this subject, a prisoner in Mississippi wrote to a pen-friend in response to a question:

I really wish I could give you an explanation for why some inmates start off so enthusiastically with their correspondence and then lose interest. I can only offer an observation that many of the inmates in here may enter into such a relationship with unrealistic expectations. When those expectations are not met, they lose interest. Also, you are dealing with a type of person who for most of their life has never been able to start a project and follow through. They started school and dropped out. They started a family and split up. Their parents started a family and split. They have never been able to maintain a long-term relationship. They have had no intimate example on which to base a continuing relationship. Therefore, how can they be expected to do something different now? Does this make any sense? I may sound like a smart-ass for saying such things but that is my honest opinion. You have a few, mostly older inmates, who have had stable families and have never had drug problems. People who have finished school and have worked long-term toward goals. Those inmates, when they wish, can follow through and allow some type of relationship to develop because they know what it takes to nurture a correspondence. They have life experiences to share with others, something to form a common bond between them and someone on the "outside."

Make any sense? Take me (somebody please take me—anywhere out of this place, ha ha), I was married for 10 years. I spent 8 years in the Army. I was a plant manager of a chemical plant where agricultural chemicals and fertilizers were manufactured. I have made mortgage payments. I have had to stick to a budget and buy groceries and clothes for the children. I know the give and take required for any relationship to flourish. Most of the inmates here have been in criminal activities since their early teens and have never developed what are called "people skills."

Apart from depression, which can give rise to a listlessness and apathy in which even reading letters, let alone writing them, is a major and seemingly futile effort, there are also other pressures. These have been well summed up by a black prisoner in Georgia:

Well, my dear lady, I guess this just about wraps things up for me, but before I go, please understand that I'm not a college grad or someone who were born with a silver spoon in my mouth. I don't even have a high school diploma. I can tell in the reading of your letters you are very articulate and very fun to be around. I'm a bit intimidated with the idea of knowing you, in the sense that you might grow tired of me . . . the bottom line is, you knew that I was on death row, why would you want to waste your time on someone like me? Who doesn't have a high school diploma, doesn't have any money or family and is on death row. Tell me truthfully, what kind of person would want to know someone like that?

As his correspondent perceptively observed, she had some difficulty in answering his letter—"not because I felt there was any truth in his belief that he was beneath me, but because I realized that there must be a certain amount of self-confidence (that I could take on the responsibility) in my supposedly altruistic motives."

One gets the impression that the correspondence can, sometimes, simply become a bit much for the prisoners. Survival, for some, can mean battening down their emotional hatches and cutting off from fellow-prisoners, family, and the outside world in general. Although a number of prisoners have remarked how their pen-friends act as their eyes and ears in the real world, for others contact with "ordinary" people serves to highlight their own deprivation. For a while they eagerly respond to the unexpected interest and support, but after a time their lack of self-esteem makes it very difficult for them to sustain a correspondence on an equal footing and to believe that their pen-friend is genuinely interested in them.

Opening up about what they have done is a tremendous risk for prisoners. One man eventually wrote with details of his crime, and when his pen-friend replied, wrote:

I did want to say, first of all, that I am grateful, beyond belief, that you've read of the single worst day of my life, and you wrote again. I don't take that lightly. I know, from experience, that people will cut you off, quick, to find you were involved in anything so heinous.

A female prisoner was less fortunate:

I had a first cousin who was helping me out some last year, well she wanted me to call and talk to her. I finally broke down and called her one Sunday. Her brother was there when I called. I talked to him too, and he said damn if you got a phone and TV you got it made, you don't need no one to help you. You know after that my cousin made like she wasn't able to help me no more.

How do the British correspondents view the writing? A female teacher has commented:

Writing to my prisoner and receiving letters from him are extremely rewarding and a very important part of my and my family's life. It is more time-consuming and emotionally draining than I had anticipated. I am very lucky to be writing to a remarkable, considerate man, and to be doing so against my own stable family background. I think it essential that potential pen-pals are fully aware of the commitment before writing, to avoid either side being hurt.

An art gallery assistant from Buckinghamshire writes:

It takes a long time to write a letter—it's not just a case of dropping someone a line. You have to think very carefully about the mood and effect the overall letter will have . . . It has affected me in a far stronger way than I'd imagined it would. I find the strength of my emotional reaction quite surprising . . . although I'd realized from the onset it would be a responsibility not to be entered into half-heartedly. I am very surprised by how often I think of him in my day to day life. For example, I will go out somewhere with friends and be enjoying myself, and the thought of the man I am writing to will come into my mind, which provokes quite a complex response.

Ivy Phillips, of Norfolk, describes how letter writers and the prisoners' families can grow close. Her account is reminiscent of the experience of many other writers:

In one of his letters he mentioned that his family was very supportive. When I replied I said how pleased I was that he had their support and told him that I had no family. My husband died three years ago and I have no brothers, sisters, or children. Billy [Kuenzel] was quite upset by this revelation and wrote back immediately to inform me that his family had "adopted" me. I found this very moving. His mother and I correspond regularly and I get all the family news. The "giving" is certainly not all on one side and I await his letters as eagerly as he awaits mine.

One of the most moving introductory letters I have ever received came from a woman in England, asking for the name of a prisoner on Death Row to write to. At the end of her letter she added that it might be helpful to share the information that a young man would be coming to trial shortly for taking the life of her daughter. "I am very relieved that the death penalty does not exist in this country."

Similarly a woman suffering from terminal bone cancer, with perhaps a year to live, sent me a cheerful letter asking if she might write to someone. Despite the obvious difficulties of such a correspondence, she clearly has something very special to give.

9

The Pee-Pee Dance

The following excerpts are from the eleven letters written by Raymond Clark, a forty-nine-year-old white prisoner on Florida's Death Row. Raymond wrote the letters to Mary Grayson of Hungerford, in Berkshire, England. They span a three-month period from late summer 1990 until his execution in November 1990.

Dear Mary,   September 7, 1990

My friend, Harold Lucas, to whom you sent a post card recently, is scheduled to go back to court very soon for a resentencing hearing. Thus, as you requested, he passed your card on to me.

My mother recently passed away and as she was my only correspondent, Harold thought I may be interested in having a caring person to write to.

I assume you are aware we are on death row and any friendships we may establish could be abruptly terminated. With this in mind I find it difficult to understand why anyone would willingly tie themselves to a sinking ship, so to speak. However, in my position I am more than willing to respond to anyone who cares enough to write to me.

A little about myself: I was born July 12, 1941. I am 5' 11" tall and weigh 183 lbs. I have brown hair and green eyes.

I am (was) an avid outdoorsman and I love to go camping and fishing. I also was a fairly accomplished tennis player in my day.

I spend practically all of my wakeful hours now reading books. If you decide to write to me we can pursue books further.

Peace,
Ray

Dear Mary,   September 20, 1990

. . . I have never corresponded with anyone "overseas" before and I can see it will take over twice as long to receive an answer to my letters to you.

Since you are my only correspondent your letters already mean a great deal to me. I must admit I did indeed look like a little boy doing the pee-pee dance last night when the guard hollered down the tier that I had a letter. Since I had not had anything back from you, I was beginning to think perhaps my photo had scared you off, I'm glad it did not.

Our new correspondence could very well be of a short-lived duration. One of my attorneys came by to see me on the 14th. He said my final appeal to the U.S. Supreme Court was filed on the 4th of September. He thinks we have a 50/50 chance of getting a favorable decision. If not, the Governor will sign my fifth death warrant and that will probably be the end of the line for me.

My day to day life here is really quite boring and uneventful. Except for four hours of outside exercise per week, two hours Tuesday morning and two hours Thursday afternoons, and a ten minute shower every other day, I am locked in this 6' × 9' steel and concrete box 24 hours of every day. In two more days it will be exactly thirteen years I have lived/existed under these conditions.

Try to imagine living constantly for thirteen years in a room the size of the average bathroom and you will have some idea of what I have been experiencing.

Peace,
Ray

Dear Mary,   October 3, 1990

. . . What a welcome surprise! Your letter postmarked on September 27 got here to me last night, October 2. I was not expecting an answer to my last letter until later on this week.

Please, do not feel bad about asking me questions. Even though we have been corresponding only for a very short time I already feel very comfortable and relaxed when I write to you. I sense that you are a kind and caring person and this makes it much easier for me to "open up" to you in our letters.

Also, when you ask me questions that will give me something to write about. My existence here on death row is very uneventful and boring and there is very rarely anything that occurs here that would be of any interest to you, or anyone else.

It has been very lonely for me here since my mother passed away and I welcome the opportunity to be able to share my thoughts with someone once again.

Yes, letters coming into the prison are opened and searched for contraband but they are not read. There are approximately 1,500 inmates here at Florida State Prison and they generate a daily outflow of mail at around 5,000 pieces. There is also a like amount of incoming mail. There are only three people who work in the mailroom here so you can see it would be logistically impossible for them to censor all of the incoming and outgoing mail. They do have a "hit list" in the mailroom of inmates whose mail must be read. These are men who have escaped, been caught attempting to escape, found with escape plans, or, have made threats or obscene remarks to someone in their letters. If someone calls or writes to the prison and complains such and such an inmate has done this to them, his name will be placed on the "hit list" and his mail will be censored from that point on. I think there are about 100 men current on the "hit list." I am not one of them. I have not been in any trouble of any kind in the entire 13 years I have been here. I try to keep as low a profile as I possibly can. The only way they know I am even here is when they come around each day to take the count.

My case is being handled by a group of attorney's from C.C.R. [Capital Collateral Representatives] which is a state-funded organization formed to help indigent death row inmates with their appeals. I was at first very skeptical about being represented by this group since they are state-funded and it is the state who is trying to see me executed.

I thought it was a case of the farmer telling the chickens, "Okay, from now on the fox will be in charge of your future well-being." But, I was wrong. The C.C.R. attorneys are all *VERY* anti–capital punishment and do everything possible to get stays for inmates who have had a death warrant signed. They have also gotten about 75 death sentences overturned and got life sentences instead. They have been representing me since they came into existence in 1986. My first death warrant was signed in 1985 and I had a "volunteer attorney" who helped me get that one stayed. Since then, I have had three more death warrants signed within a 12 month period. My second in January of '88, my third in April of '88 and my fourth in January of '89.

Currently I am the only man living on Florida's death row who has survived four death warrants. There have been three others who had a fifth warrant signed, none of them are still living.

My three C.C.R. attorneys (two men and one woman) have done an excellent job of preparing my briefs for me to present to the various courts. If I had been paying an attorney $100.00 per hour I don't think I could have had a better job done in my behalf. They have saved me the last three times but I'm afraid this next warrant will be the one to get me. We have exhausted just about every issue possible and have nothing left to argue.

My case is now before the U.S. Supreme Court and we expect a ruling possibly in the next 30–60 days. We have a 50/50 chance of a favorable decision. If it goes against me our madman governor will sign my 5th warrant and that will be it for me.

My attorneys are my only visitors. I never saw my mam either since I have been here. She lived in Connecticut and had a very bad heart and could not travel so I never saw her. She did write and sent me money to buy food and necessities and I was able to call her on the phone when I was on deathwatch. Those were the periods I had a death warrant signed on me.

Peace,
Ray

Dear Mary,   October 17, 1990

. . . Thank you so much for sending me the two photos. They are great! It is so much nicer to be able to look at you as I write and know what you look like. And, I must say that considering your "maturity" you look very well.

Your letter posted on October 10 was delivered to me last night, the 16th. Yes, I most certainly did the "pee-pee dance." In fact, when I saw that blue envelope with the red and blue piping around the edge of it in the guard's hand as he was walking down the corridor to my cell, my heart started pumping like a triphammer, my knees began to knock and my hand was shaking as I reached to take the letter. The guard looked at me with raised eyebrows and said, "A bit anxious for this one are we?" I couldn't even talk, I just nodded my head in an affirmative manner. So, I guess you can say I appreciate hearing from you.

To answer your questions about what I had been doing for money since my mam passed away, well, the answer to that quite simply is, "without." But I have become quite adept at bartering for the things I really need to have. We occasionally have chicken and hamburgers and these meals can be sold with no trouble. As you can see from my photo it will not hurt me a bit to lose a few pounds anyway.

The state supplies us with one roll of toilet paper per week, one bar of life soap every two weeks and one packet of chalky toothpowder once a week. Other than that if you don't have the money to buy the things you need you do without. I *must* trade food to be able to get some decent soap that doesn't make me itch all the time. I also need proper toothpaste. We get a shower every other day so I can manage without deodorant since we do not have cell partners here. I can also use the "real" soap for shampoo so that is another problem solved.

No, we don't go outside if it is raining, we just lose out for that day. There are so many men here on death row that there is no way to reschedule an outside exercise period if it rains.

My mam was sending me twenty-five dollars per month and I was getting by very well on that. Not only could I easily purchase all the necessities I needed but there was money left over so that I could buy some decent food. The selection isn't all that great but to me a fresh bread and bologna sandwich is like a Christmas feast would be to you. I do believe as I get older I think, even more than sex, I miss food more than anything else since I have been locked up. I think even now if it were a choice of a night with the woman of my dreams or a home-cooked meal of my favorite things, well I'm afraid the poor lass would go unfulfilled. She had just better not be within my reach after I finished my meal though.

Now, as I told you in my first letter, I will never ask you to do *anything* for me. I am perfectly happy just to have your warmth and caring concern and friendship. I want you to know that is not obligatory or necessary for you to send me money. All I ever expect is to get your letters and share whatever time I have left with you through correspondence. I am quite amazed that I have become so fond of you in such a short time. I feel as if we have been friends for many years and yet I hardly know you. Perhaps it may be partly due to how lonely I have been these past six months and am just desperate for any display of kindness and concern. That is only partially the reason as I think we have a natural affinity for one another. Friends such as you are a distinct rarity in this day and age and I consider myself very fortunate that you have become a part of my life. This is also causing me a certain amount of consternation. I am thinking that as we grow closer as friends my execution will be especially painful for you. I feel as if I am being selfish and only thinking of my own happiness and elation at having such a new and exciting friend to share things with. I had even thought of not writing to you any more to spare you the pain losing a good friend will bring when I am executed. But I guess I am just not strong enough to even think about not getting your letters any more. They mean all to me.

Yes, I had one half-sister. She committed suicide in 1981. She had come to visit me twice as she lived in Florida, in Tampa which is about 200 miles south of here. She foolishly got involved with dope and as it happens to so many of our youth these days her habit finally killed her.

My real name is not Clark, it is Partridge. My mam divorced Frank Partridge when I was four years old and shortly thereafter married Harry Clark who adopted me and I have been Raymond Robert Clark ever since. Harry Clark is still alive. We were never all that close even when we were living in the same house and he was acting as my father figure.

Peace,
Ray

Dear Mary,   October 30, 1990
. . . Well, my dear friend, I think I now feel very relaxed and comfortable with you so I may as well go ahead and tell you how I came to be

on death row here in Florida. Even though you have been very discreet and polite by not pressing or even asking for the details of my crime I am sure it has crossed your mind a time or two as to how such a "seemingly" intelligent man could manage to get himself sentenced to death. After I tell you of this you may question my sanity, certainly my supposed intelligence will be put in the "disputed" category.

In March of 1977 I was a 35 year old high-rise window washer working in San Francisco, California and living in Redwood City, California, which is located about 20 miles south of San Francisco. I had been working with a young fellow, N.F., for about two years and we had become close friends. He was from here in Florida, St. Petersburg, and when his father passed away in 1976 he went home to St. Pete and never returned to California. We did keep in touch through letters and telephone calls and when my two weeks vacation came up in June of 1977 we decided it would be nice if I spent it here in Florida with him. At that time he was living with a young lady and I was introduced to her older sister and we all got along famously. Since all three of the others were not on holiday and had jobs to maintain I was alone one day when N. came in about lunchtime and said he had a sure-fire way for us to each be fifty thousand dollars richer inside of two or three hours.

He said he had heard his boss in a telephone conversation saying he would be picking up one hundred thousand dollars, in *cash* from the bank that afternoon to purchase a beach house on Treasure Island, which is an upper-class district of St. Petersburg. My first thought was, "Why would a man pay cash money for a house and not just have his bank or a realtor take care of it for him?" When I put this question to N. he told me his boss (who owned his own aluminum recycling company) was one of the high muckety-mucks of the drug dealers there in St. Petersburg and that cash money was the way drug dealers did business. Since I had never been involved in drug dealing and my only knowledge of such was what I had seen on the telly and in movies, this sounded very plausible to me. His plan was to abduct his boss as he came out of the bank, drive him to a secluded spot, tie him up, to be found later (or not), divide the one hundred thousand cash and go our separate ways. This sounded feasible to me and this is also when my mind ceased to function normally. I should have realized at this point that there was no way possible N. could leave the man alive to identify him as the one who had abducted and robbed him. Anyway, all went well, the man came out of the bank and he was carrying a large briefcase. As soon as [he] got into his car N. leapt out of his car and into the man's car. (While we were waiting for the man to come out of the bank N. had ascertained the passenger side door was unlocked.)

At gunpoint, N. had the man drive to a densely wooded spot that was located, of all places, adjacent to a police pistol and rifle range. On reflection I must admit this was rather clever as the shots from N.'s pistol would hardly be noticed. I followed in N.'s car and when we reached our destination we all got out and N. told me to put on a pair of the plastic gloves from the side pouch in his car. N. was already wearing a pair he had put on before he got into the other man's car. When I had the gloves on N. instructed me to open the briefcase and put the money into a pillowcase we had brought along for that purpose. N. had told the man to sit on the ground and kept him covered with the pistol while I transferred the money. When I opened the briefcase it contained miscellaneous legal documents, one crossword puzzle book, two packs of cigarettes and three ballpoint pens and not one penny in cash. I looked at N. and he was trembling and shaking as if he were having a seizure of some sort. N. said to the man, "I heard you say on the phone you would pick up a hundred thousand dollars cash from the bank this afternoon." The man actually *smiled* at N. and said, "Sorry kid, I gotta go back tomorrow morning and pick it up." It was at this point I realized the man was in serious trouble. N. told me there was some wire in the boot of his car and for me to get it and tie the man up, hand and foot, with it. As I reached into the car to get the keys to unlock the boot I saw N. walk around behind the man. When I got the boot lid open and my view was blocked I heard a shot and froze in place. This was followed about five seconds later by a second shot. N. had shot him twice in the back of the head. He then got into the man's car and said, "Follow me."

We left his car in a market parking lot about 30 miles away from the scene. On the way back to N.'s house he told me if I ever said a word about what had transpired I would end up the same as his boss did. Looking into his eyes, I believed him!

If it had not been for N.'s incredible greed and stupidity I believe we would have gotten away with murder. It was a week later, the morning of the day I was to fly back home to California. The man's car had been found but not his body. Naturally, the police suspected foul play and the man's work phones as well as his home phone had been tapped in case anyone called to demand a ransom for his release. And would you believe that is exactly what N. did? Not only did he call the man's family, he did it from his own home phone! To this day I have not figured out why a man who was clever enough to shoot a man to death right next to a pistol range, use plastic gloves during the crime and relocate the dead man's car 30 miles away from the scene of the crime would be so incredibly moronic as to try and extract ten thousand dollars from the dead man's family for his safe return. That was callous enough but to do it from his own home telephone is beyond belief.

Of course it took the police about 60 seconds to trace the call. We were all four sitting in the living room watching the Saturday morning horror movie on the telly when, WHAM-BAM both the front and back doors are burst from their hinges and there are six policemen swarming around us with 357 magnum revolvers and shotguns pointed at us. They shouted "FREEZE" and I must say, as I looked into the business end of a loaded shotgun I did a world class impression of a mannequin.

Both girls were released later that day when it was established both had been accounted for at their jobs at the time the crimes (I say crimes as they charged us with murder, kidnap and extortion) were committed.

N. and I were kept separated while we were in jail but his girl came to see me and told me not to say a word or admit anything as all that could be proven against us was extortion. I agreed to this and when the police offered to let me plead guilty to a charge of 2nd degree murder (which carries a term of between 7 and 25 years here in Florida) I told them to go suck on a great fat turd. However, when N. was offered the same deal he jumped on it like white on rice! When I found out about this and started screaming to see my lawyer and that N. had lied and reversed our roles in the crime it was looked upon as "sour grapes" on my part. They said if I had not had any part in the actual killing of the man I had already given up my opportunity to set the record straight. And, as there were no living witnesses to the crime except N. and myself the jury believed him and not me. Of course it didn't help my case at all when I foolishly got on the stand and kept saying N. shot the man, not me. I just looked like I was trying to blame him to save myself from a probable death sentence. The prosecutor brought up the fact I had been given the opportunity to tell my side of the story and of my snide remark and "arrogant attitude" and that really soured the jury against me.

I've had four death warrants signed on me thus far. One in March of '85, one in January of '88, one in April of '88 and the last in January of '89. No one currently alive on Florida's death row except myself has survived four death warrants. Two others had five and they did not survive them. It is very unlikely I will be the one to survive a fifth warrant. So it goes . . .

You asked me if I could sell the stamps you sent me. Well, with a sheepish grin on my face I will admit to you I have already had four more oranges than I was officially allocated. I love oranges, and I just could not resist the chance to get some extra while I had the chance. I'm not all that crazy about the apples but I do have a weak spot for oranges.

No, I have never married. I have a son who is 30 years old now, if he is still living. He was born 3 days before my 19th birthday on July 9, 1960. The girl and I were not married but her parents were quite wealthy and used to taking command of any "emergencies" in their or their offspring's lives. The baby was put up for adoption as soon as he was born. I don't even know his name. If it weren't for the girl who had him I wouldn't even know if it was a boy or girl.

Since that time I have had many different relationships with women. The longest lasted almost six years but I have never felt in my heart a love for any of them that was strong enough for me to make a lifelong commitment and to propose marriage. You know, I never realized it until I came to death row and had so much time to do nothing but think about my life and ponder the mistakes I have made, that I was afraid to have another child for fear it would be taken from me once again. This took me quite a long time to accept as I didn't really even know my son and had not actually formed any sort of paternal bond with him.

Evidently there was something at work, perhaps on a subconscious level, throughout my entire adult life that has prevented me from ever truly falling in love and siring another child. How very sad that I must be on death row awaiting my execution before I could uncover one of the biggest stumbling blocks that has plagued me for 30 years.

Well, I have just this minute received some very distressing news. One of my friends about eight cells down from me just hollered to let me know that the United States Supreme Court has denied my appeal. He said mine and another guy here on the row were two of eight cases they had denied. The other six were men who are on death row in other states.

What this means is that now the madman Governor can, and most probably will, sign my death warrant at any time. As avidly as they have been attempting to get me executed I will expect them to come for me before the week is out. Perhaps even as soon as tomorrow.

Please excuse me if I seem to be trembling and a bit disoriented but this has come as quite a shock to me. Even though I have been through the deathwatch procedure four times previously it is something one can never really grow accustomed to.

I will answer your letter the minute I get it although I doubt my next one will be nearly as long as this one. Also, if it is necessary, I will send you a last letter to say "good-bye" on the night before I am scheduled to be executed.

This seems so unfair, not especially for me but for you. Here we have the beginning of a new and warm friendship and chances are it will be terminated before we really begin to enjoy ourselves.

Perhaps this will change your mind about becoming friends with a condemned man; in the long run it can only cause you grief. What you must ask yourself is, are a few months or years of correspondence and friendship worth the pain and anguish that lies at the end of the appeals process? I am not trying to tell you what to do or to convince you otherwise. I am only trying to point out that the stressfulness over the end of these friendships could ultimately become very psychologically harmful to you. I only ask that you give this some serious thought. Take care, my dear friend.

Love,
Ray

Dear Mary,   November 1, 1990

Once again my previously flagging spirits are soaring! Yes, it is because I have just received your letter of October 24 in answer to mine of October 17. I must sound like a foolish child but when I get a letter from you I feel a burst of warmth that begins in my stomach and slowly spreads outward to my extremities. I have such a strong feeling and fondness for you it is really hard for me to understand. We are barely more than strangers and I have so very quickly begun to think of you as an old friend I have known all my life. Not only do I think of you in this manner, but I'm sure it shows in my writing that this is the way I feel also.

Before we began corresponding it really didn't make a whole lot of difference to me if I was executed or not. But now, I sit here and gaze upon your dear, sweet face and I want to scream at the blatant futility of it all. If I were to be locked up for the next twenty-five years it would make not a bit of difference as long as I knew you were there for me and that I would be hearing from you on a regular basis. This situation is rapidly becoming one of insanity. To find such a dear and caring friend and not be able to spend years nurturing and building upon that friendship is so damn unfair!

I'd better get off this subject and calm myself down a bit before I become actually hysterical.

So far the Governor has not signed my death warrant. When that does happen I will be moved to another wing of the prison where the electric chair is. So, now, every time I hear the guard put the key in the gate at the end of the corridor to come on the floor I get a butterfly stampede in my stomach. This happens about 5 or 6 times a day so my nerves are pretty much in a frazzled condition by now as you might expect.

Susan Cary came to see me on Tuesday, the 30th. She had heard of the U.S. Supreme Court's denial of my appeal and she knows I have no family or friends so she came to offer her condolence and tried to reassure me. She has done this on each of my previous four death warrants also. If *anyone* here on Florida's death row gets a warrant signed and has no family or friends to come visit them while they are on death-watch she will come to see them. She is a genuinely good and caring person. She thinks of every one of us 318 death row prisoners as her children. She's a great lady.

Yes, my dear, you do have my promise that I will notify you immediately when my death warrant is signed. As much as I dread bringing you those dreadful tidings there is no way I could not tell you of it. It grieves me deeply to think of the pain this is going to cause you but we have come a very long way in such a very short time. I guess we are just going to have to see it to the end together. If only we had met years ago I'm sure we would have recognized we were kindred spirits . . .

Love,
Ray

My Dearest Friend,   November 5, 1990

I had hoped it would not be so soon but I'm afraid this is the letter we both have been dreading.

The Governor signed my 5th death warrant on Saturday, November 3. I am scheduled to be executed on November 14.

One of my friends here got some cards in and offered some of them for sale. When I saw this one my thoughts immediately went to you and I could not resist buying it.

This card is a perfect depiction of how I feel when I look at your picture or when I am thinking about you or writing to you. I feel all nice and warm and snuggly, inside and out.

You have awakened emotions in me that have lain dormant for many decades.

If the worst does happen I will send you a good-bye letter and a lock of my hair. I will leave this with Susan the day before and if I am executed she will post it the same day.

Until then, I will answer any mail I get from you between now and then.

Love,
Ray

My Dearest Friend,   November 7, 1990

Last night I received your letter posted on October 30 and along with it a receipt for the $25 international money order.

Since my execution is scheduled for one week from today I may be several pounds heavier at that time for I plan to eat every penny of this twenty-five dollars before that time. I will not eat any of the "garbage" they serve us at regular mealtimes but I will now be eating nothing but sandwiches and canned goods I can buy in the canteen. They let a man who is on deathwatch purchase canteen items every day whereas on the "regular" death row we can only make canteen and sandwich purchases once a week.

For the past three days I have been kicking my own behind for not thinking of it earlier. If I had your phone number I could have called you collect the night before my scheduled execution.

When it becomes apparent a stay will not be forthcoming, along with the last meal they grant the condemned a final phone call to a family member or loved one. Since you fall into the latter category I would have at least been able to hear your voice before we were separated by my abrupt departure.

I will *try* to see if they will let me call overseas information between now and then but I'm not too optimistic they will permit me to do that. It's possible you may get this letter on the 13th. If you do, please stay by your phone between 9 and 10 P.M. on the eve of the 13th as that is when I will call you if I am able. If I am not permitted to call you, then you can call the prison on the morning of the 14th to see if I received a stay or not. If you are told that I did receive a stay be sure to ask if it was a temporary or an indefinite stay. A temporary stay means a stay of from 24 to 48 hours, and I could still be executed. An indefinite stay means I will have found new issues to present to the courts and that takes months and sometimes years.

My last warrant was signed in January 1989 so it has taken almost two years to exhaust my appeals through all the available courts.

My thoughts are of and with you constantly in these final days as the 14th draws closer. Most of all I feel so terrible because I know how painful my death will be for you. Please think of me as beyond any further pain and depressions caused by being confined for so many years. As I told you before, if this does come to pass I will leave a last letter with Susan to post to you.

Love,
Ray

My Dearest Friend,   November 14, 1990

About an hour before your letter was delivered to me last night I received a call from one of my lawyers and was informed we had received a 24-hour stay of execution. This will all be old news by the time you receive this letter. I fear this stay is only prolonging the agony but every 24 hours more to live and think about you and so gaze at your picture is worth it.

I'm sure you must have called the prison today to see if I had been executed or not. I'm glad I had the foresight to tell you beforehand to be sure to ask if the stay was temporary or indefinite. It would have been terrible for them to tell you I had received a stay and you would have thought I was safe for a while only to find out later I had been executed a day or two later.

I have already written you a letter of good-bye and Susan will mail it to you if and when I am executed. There is a lock of my hair in the letter.

I must tell you, dearheart, your call to me yesterday morning was the same to me as a draught of the elixir of life! Even though my execution was imminently impending I was elated and in high spirits the rest of the entire day. I was so happily and wonderfully surprised to hear your sweet voice.

It is almost unheard of for an inmate on deathwatch to receive incoming calls from anyone other than an attorney or his minister. I had written a letter to the Warden the day before your call and had requested I be permitted to make a collect call to you as you were my dearest and closest friend and I wished to be able to tell you good-bye with my voice rather than after the fact through a letter. I guess my letter must have struck a compassionate spot in him somewhere as your call was allowed to be put through to me. Whatever the reasons, it was so good to hear your voice, I'll never forget.

If by some grand stroke of luck I do get an indefinite stay and we are able to continue writing I am certain the fact I am a nonbeliever will not be a factor as to whether we remain friends or not. I'm sure you care for me because of how well we relate to one another in our letters and not because of any personal beliefs or nonbeliefs. I love and respect you for the person you are and how you treat me, not because of what you believe. You are not a shallow-minded person and this is one of the many qualities about you that I admire so much.

I am still quite upset that if I am executed it will mean the end of being able to converse with you through our letters. In just a matter of a few months your letters have come to mean everything to me. This is not balm for your ego. I am only speaking from my heart. I was very fortunate indeed to have you as a part of my life even if it was for only a short time. You are a clever, witty and extremely intelligent woman who is not afraid to express her feelings and be willing to be honest and open with a new friend.

If my life must end I am very grateful that I was allowed to make your acquaintance. My life was made richer and fuller from it.

Hopefully, my dear, if it is, please know that I loved you and regret deeply it is over so soon.

All my love,
Ray

My Dearest Friend,   November 15, 1990

I can hardly believe I am still here to write that date at the top of the page. Once again I have been given a temporary stay. My execution is now set for Saturday, the 17th at 6:00 P.M.

As I can only speculate as to what you are doing or have done during this very trying time, I assume you are keeping up with all these short, temporary delays, by phoning the prison to see what is what.

If I get another letter from you tomorrow night, Friday, the 16th, I won't answer that one as I do not want to leave any letters here for the prison officials to mail for me. If I receive one tonight, of course I will answer that one immediately.

I must tell you I was deeply touched to learn that I have become an "honorary" member of your family and that there are others there besides yourself who genuinely care what happens to me. This has engendered in me feelings I have not experienced since before my Mom and aunt passed on.

Take care, Dearheart, if it makes you feel better, please do pray for me, I am convinced it can certainly do no harm.

All my love,
Ray

Raymond Clark's execution did not proceed as scheduled on Saturday, November 17. Instead, he received another forty-eight-hour stay until Monday, November 19. This meant that he faced four execution dates within the space of five days. The fourth date, and eighth in all he had faced, proved his last.

My Dearest Friend,

If you are reading this letter it will mean that the State of Florida have finally exacted their "revenge" upon me and I have been executed.

As I had promised you, if I was indeed executed I would send you a final letter to say good-bye.

I want you to know that the last living image in my mind was your dear, sweet face.

Enclosed, along with a lock of my hair is a photograph of myself and Susan Cary whom I have mentioned in previous letters. She puts on little Christmas parties each year for death row inmates who do not get visits from family or friends. The photo was taken at the same time the one of me by myself was taken at her party in December of 1988.

I am really at a loss for anything to say at this point so I will close by saying I deeply regret we did not have more time to correspond and share more of our love and feelings together.

I wish you many more years of life and I sincerely hope they are all happy and prosperous.

Love,
Ray

10

Facing the End

Raymond Clark was executed in Florida State Prison at 6 A.M. on Monday, November 19, 1990. Before this, his execution had been scheduled for 6 P.M. on Wednesday, November 14. Then it was deferred for twenty-four hours to 6 P.M. on Thursday, November 15. Then it was deferred again—for forty-eight hours—to 6 P.M. on Saturday, November 17. And then it was rescheduled for, and occurred on, Monday, November 19. Four execution dates in a five-day period.

In the last week of his life, Ray Clark twice spoke by telephone with Mary Grayson, his pen-friend in England. They had been corresponding for less than three months, but during that time she received eleven letters from him (see Chapter 9, "The Pee-Pee Dance"). Apart from Susan Cary, the full-time prison visitor who had accompanied many men to their executions in Florida, and of whom Ray spoke with great warmth, it was to Mary that Ray turned in his last desperate days. He had no one else. During his eleven years on Death Row, his parents died, and his relatives and former friends deserted him. So he used his last official phone call to contact a woman whom he had never met and had known on paper for little more than two months—but who had extended to him the hand of friendship.

Many prisoners come within hours of their scheduled execution before they are granted a stay. Occasionally two or three stays might be granted in quick succession in a final flurry of legal moves. But to have one's death scheduled once and then rescheduled three times within five days must rank as one of the most hideous experiences any man has been required to endure in his last week on Death Row.

Some prisoners deliberately cut themselves off from others, for they do not want to be too close to someone who is then executed—as they themselves may be. Many write of the pain of initially getting close to people and then making sure they never make that same "mistake" again. This attitude seems especially common in large Death Rows, such as in Texas, where executions can almost pass the men by.

Prisoners on smaller Death Rows can feel a great sense of solidarity with each other, so that each and every inmate is dragged down with the person facing execution. A man in Georgia writes: "Whenever there's a date set for someone to be executed, my insides are very empty, for the people that are on Death Row are very affected when anyone is put to death. You know exactly the hour and everything is very quiet."

Death Row prisoners also follow what is happening in other states. In March 1988, Willie Darden, a well-known black prisoner, was executed in Florida. He had been on Death Row for twelve years, having survived a number of execution dates before the final one that March. The following is an account of the reaction in Parchman Penitentiary, in Mississippi, to Darden's execution:

I'm going to respond to all you spoke of in your letter plus add my two cents to a few other things but, before I do I need to talk about something more immediate. Namely, Willie Darden. I guess that by now you've heard that he has been killed. He was killed this morning (it's Tuesday, 15 March now as I write this—the news of his impending death had me so depressed last night I couldn't continue writing this then) at around 7:00. I didn't know him personally but I couldn't help from crying. They also killed a man in Louisiana this morning shortly after midnight. His death drew very little publicity but Willie's has been on the news all morning. You spoke of feeling "impotent" and your "helplessness" over what this system is doing to all of us here and, for the first time since I've been here, I acutely feel all that you speak of. Before now I still had faith and hope in this system and that it wouldn't kill its innocents but now, after Willie, the faith and hope that I had is at its lowest point and, frankly speaking, I'm a little scared. Not of dying—death certainly will visit all of us—but of this system and its bloodlust spreading worldwide to destroy all in its wake.

After what was done to Willie, "innocence" has no meaning at all. A concept devoid of substance. I think that in killing Willie, America made its statement to the world that it doesn't care anything at all about what the world thinks of it. People from all over the world wrote in support of Willie asking that his life be spared and the authorities paid no heed to any of what was said. A late night news program did a feature on Willie giving his "last words" and Willie maintained his innocence all of the way to the end. He said that he could do nothing to stop them from taking his life but that he would die with dignity.

I think that all of the guys on the gallery cried when they saw it. I know that I did. It hurts very deeply to see someone helpless as he was and it hurts even more to know that you're equally as helpless and probably face the same fate. I won't ever give up hope but after seeing Willie and seeing what happened to him I can't help but wonder if there's any use in maintaining hope. I wonder about this but I won't give up. If possible, I intend to fight even harder now.

What happened to Willie has muddled my thoughts considerably and my conception of "justice" or "the American way" for the Blacks and the Poor of this country. I think of slavery and how it was. The only difference that I can see between slavery then and now is the time. Things are no different at all really. We're enslaved in a more subtle manner now than then but we're still enslaved.

I'm at a very low point right now and I'm not writing a very good letter. I don't want to depress you because I'm depressed and I ask that you understand and forgive me for not saying more in this.

In the course of 1988 it became plain that Leo Edwards in Mississippi was running out of time. In October, he came within twelve hours of being executed. At noon he learned from the radio that his execution that midnight would not be going ahead. Sam Johnson, who knew Leo well, wrote of this occasion:

This past week has been a very traumatic one and one of the brothers here came within a day of being executed. I stayed up with him day and night until the night that he received his stay and that took a lot out of me. He was in A-14 which is directly behind me and one cell away.

I had to talk to him through the "vent" that separates our cells and I had to stand on the toilet-sink in order to do this. He was in very bad shape.

In June 1989 another date was set. Sam wrote:

We've spoken about the probability of this day coming but speaking about it didn't and can't really prepare any of us for the actuality of its coming. We knew months ago that this day could come but, now that it's here, I'm not prepared for it. I've experienced the trauma of all the executions/murders that have been carried out within this State and witnessing three others doesn't inure me to the pain and heartbreak of what may turn out to be the fourth. There are many things one can do where repetition causes them to be routine. Witnessing death, served up in such a cruel, callous and inhumane fashion, certainly isn't one of the things that become routine as it increases. There are no words, Bro.

Previously Leo had survived no fewer than four death warrants, one of them served with chilling indifference over Christmas in 1982. By the time of his execution he had just completed three thousand days on Death Row, waking each day to the knowledge that the state was trying to take his life.
In his last letter to Suzanne O'Callaghan in Cambridge, England, in May 1989, Leo wrote as follows:

As I start this letter I have many, many thoughts and feelings I'm experiencing. By now you may know that an execution date, 21 June, has been set.

I can't say what I'm feeling during this time because I don't know myself, but for some reason or another it doesn't bother me as much as it did the first time. But to tell you the truth, Suzanne, if I am executed I'll be at peace to have it all over with, I say all because one of the greatest joys of life is to be loved. I'm speaking of total love which in the past I didn't recognize, and now that I do, I don't have.

All the time it takes for letters to reach you and me, this will probably be my last one to you, I am at a great loss of words on this occasion,

Suzanne, because your friendship and concern have really made my heart smile with the life you've brought it and it's extremely difficult to say good-bye to you but I must.

I leave this life with nothing as I came into it but I hurt for those whom my death will hurt, their pain is what I feel and fear most. I'm very disappointed that I must die for a crime I did not commit, but death will put an end to all my lovelessness, emptiness, heartache and pain so I am grateful for that.

It's very ironic that one must face death to *know* life; since I've been here I've come to know and feel every aspect of life and love, only to die before I can share it.

May God be between you and harm and all the empty places you walk.

Leo

One of the other prisoners who knew Leo well wrote as follows:

You asked me how Leo was coping. They still have things set up to execute him on the 21st of this month. I saw him today in the visiting area. I was seeing my mother and Leo was there with a visitor. We spoke only briefly, but at least we had made contact. He is quite withdrawn and introverted. I have wanted to break in on him, but what could I do to help him? It would only disturb him to break in on him. It would be like violating his privacy. To be seen at the mercy of others, those exercising absolute power over one's life, and them still being unmerciful. I know all too well how powerless and naked Leo feels. It is like watching terror, unable to stop its horror and unable to turn away.

Sam Johnson wrote of the execution and the loss of a man who had become a close friend:

I couldn't help but cry when they murdered Leo. Death can come in some most horrific of forms but none as horrific as to "systematically" and "methodically" kill someone as they killed Leo. They caused him to sit in abject agony for almost nine years and then murdered him.

The ??? (I don't know "what" to call them) who came and took him to the gas chamber acted as if they were attending a picnic or some other social event that gives great pleasure or joy. The looks on their faces were something similar to sexual fulfillment and it radiated from them like a beacon through an evening mist. It was sickening.

It's at times such as this that it's very hard to *not hate* "the doers of the deeds" when *hating their deeds*. I've searched my heart and the deepest recesses of my mind and I don't hate these people even though I hate *what* they are doing to us here and all across this country. God doesn't teach us to hate and I know that were I to hate them I would be just as evil as they are.

Mark Robertson in Texas, writing to a friend in Ireland, recounted his experience of an execution:

Clearly I remember the first day that I arrived at Death Row. That same 9′ × 5′ cell I entered back in February 1991, seemed hollow, like a small cavern. Each time I spoke there was to me, an echo. I did not know anyone, I had not a clue as to what this place had in store for me, and I never imagined that a person I had come to know would be executed during my second year here.

This experience was very poignant for me and it opened my heart and my mind toward a radical change in life, for life and about life.

Others had been executed since my arrival, yet they were people I had not known and their executions seemed from afar. I felt as though one was seeing the obituaries in the newspaper. Distant. Then John Sawyers was moved in the next cell to me. We did not get along at first. We bickered at one another and lived silently close, but as the weeks went by, we found that we had common likes and dislikes. We shared a sense of humor which bonded a friendship of being neighbors.

After a couple of months I found from John that he had an execution date. What do I say? I'm sorry? That's terrible news? The obvious seems abnormal in this situation and I chose denial. We both knew the night was coming and chose not to speak of the date.

The days passed as others do on death row, yet the silent tension built a wall of solicitude as the days closed in on his execution. Three days before the execution, he started passing things over to me; mainly books, a new pair of shoes and hygienic items. He wanted me to have them and I felt morose excepting them. How does one accept a gift from someone who is going to die? My thanks seemed hollow. I wanted to say more things but what do I say? Hang in there? And about the gifts, I wanted to say, if you do not get executed, I will give them back, but this sounded like the emptiest of the worst. I did not know what to say and I think he did not either, because we both crept back into our silence.

I can think of a good number of words to say to John Sawyers today. Experience has shown to me, that we have too little experiences to pass upon an opportunity to express our friendship. I think John understood my silent plight and would be happy to know what I have learned after his death, yet eternally will I live with the regret of not saying; "fare-well, my friend." It is not bad to say good-bye to someone who is going to die, however painful this may be. We feel sad knowing this and odd speaking it, yet we must humble ourselves enough to show our feelings to whom we care for.

In May 1989, Emily Shaw, at that time sitting for her finals at Cambridge University, received a letter from Henry Willis, a thirty-year-old black man in Georgia with whom she had been corresponding for a year, telling her that a date for his execution had been set. The notice was short. By the time she received the letter, the execution was just two days off. This was Henry's final letter to her:

Dear Emily,

I trust that all is well with you, they aren't with me and I'm saddened that I have bad news to tell you regarding my situation here on Death Row. I'm very distraught right now and feeling depressed but I felt that because of our friendship I should tell you what is going on.

The State of Georgia has set a date to execute me between the 18th and 25th, which by the time you get this means I will have been killed unless we can get a judge to give me a stay of execution and grant a new appeal. One never knows what happens in these situations and all you can do is hope for the best up to the final moment.

Emily right now is a difficult time for me and there really aren't many things I can say. I know you are going to be sad as it is and I would only compound it with my babbling so I won't make this too lengthy.

I want you to know that I have enjoyed our friendship and hoped some day to meet you and if I'm fortunate enough to overcome this I will some day.

If this thing is reversed then I will write again but if not you can't change what was meant to be and you can write Clive and find out what is what.

I hope this isn't my last letter to you so I'm not going to say good-bye, but I will say take care.

Fondly,
Henry

Richard Townes was executed in Virginia on January 23, 1996. Three weeks beforehand he wrote to his pen-friend Mary Grayson:

For reasons I am unable to understand, I do not feel scared or threatened by the 23rd January date. People are monitoring my behavior and I find it annoying—I am not concerned about this to the point of cracking up or breaking down under pressure. Yes, the knowledge that I am scheduled to be killed for a crime I did not commit does bother me, but it does not control my behavior or thoughts.

In his final letter, written on January 20, Richard wrote:

I love you for the goodness and genuineness I can feel within you as a person, which I found has had a very positive effect on me. Perhaps it was your tolerance and extreme understanding and compassion that allowed myself to grow the little inside that I needed to be able to feel real as a person—not just an image. Thank you for giving so much yet receiving so little in return.

Four months before then, Mary Grayson had visited Lichfield Cathedral. In October 1995, Richard wrote:

I am pleased to hear that you lit a candle in the Cathedral in my name and left it there for remembrance. I am hoping to visit it (cathedral) one day and say a prayer with you and Peter as a form of gratitude and acceptance—I would be free.

Prisoners also face the day-to-day difficulties of other inmates; for some, it becomes too much. From Mississippi:

One of the Brothers filed papers to the Court today ending his appeals. It's saddening that he has done this and what is even more saddening is that it is the conditions of this hell that made him end his appeals. He says that he is tired of suffering and that death can't be worse than this. He doesn't deny his crime and this state, by killing him, is equally guilty of murder as he is. All killing is wrong and state killings can never be justified as being correct. I hate it that they are going to murder him and it really hurts to be totally helpless to do anything about it. I can't stop it but I feel driven to tell others of this hell and what I say will touch others enough to bring abolishment to this evil that is this death penalty. The depths of depravity and cruelty that people who wield power can knowingly and willingly descend to are unbelievable.

The terror of living in an atmosphere of continual uncertainty comes through clearly in this letter from Andrew Lee Jones in Louisiana— presented here unedited, as his authentic voice. Andrew once again received a date in February 1991, when he was granted a forty-day stay.

I think that its a very good idea that you are writing a book about Death Row. The world need to know about it, like here on the Louisiana Death Row. Its like having two death sentences, first of all we are locked in from five to six days at a time. Sometimes even longer, like we get three days yard call. A hour a day. We never come in contact with anyone. Every time we leave the tier we have handcuff top and bottom, and its so hard to get a tier change, like a person here have to look into the same faces sometimes for years. Its so bad until you can have a person saying the same thing over and over, like at one time we used to take a ride to the hospital. Now we don't.

Death Row here is cut off from everything. The way this building is made it would be weeks or months before you see a different face, unless you were on B-T or C-T, those two tier face the yard. The one I'm on I can't see nothing. When I'm in the yard, I can here a person calling but can't see him. Anyway since I came here 11/16/84, 14 people have been executed. The first thing I did wrong here was made friends with a guy that have the death penalty. That's one of the worst things to do, because it is no telling when its going to be the end, like in '87 from June 7 to August 24. Eight people got executed—the last one was on my birthday. My rap partner he got executed on the 9th June. Since then I haven't made a friend with anyone. I don't like the look in the eyes of these people when they have a date, and I don't think they like the look either, because four guys have lost their mind completely. One guy, named W., he talked to the toilet, he named it Diane. B. he can't stop talking about his case, he keeps saying over and over, I haven't done nothing. P. he keeps talking to somebody named Susan. E. he is all the way. Its no telling what he might do next.

Anyway, I have had seven dates. My last one was 8/28/89. The one before that I came within 20 hours of being executed, the lawyer I had didn't even have it set for me to go before the Pardon board, that's how I got the stay, and I felt that it was my turn to go. I remember for some reason I couldn't get off the bed, it felt like I was paralyzed. People were trying to talk to me, but I couldn't understand what they were saying, doing that day. Nothing was real to me. The only thought I had was, I was next, like they were getting ready to take me to the death house. I still don't remember when they told me I had a stay of execution. Anyway the last date that I had I got a stay on my birthday on 8/24, like I was on the phone talking to my lawyer about the pardon board when the call came from my other lawyer. For some reason it didn't effect me like the last time. I guess because I know that I could go at any time. Anyway, at this time one guy has a date for 8/12. He went to the pardon board and they need more time to look into his case, and the governor gave him a 30 day reprieve, and believe me that was a surprise to all of us, because people from everywhere were writing and calling on behalf of Dalton Prejean, he wouldn't even look into his case.

Andrew Lee Jones was executed on July 22, 1991. Jane Officer, his pen-friend from Birmingham, England, had flown to Louisiana and met him for the first time a few days before. She testified on Andrew's behalf before the Louisiana Board of Pardons. When she returned home, the following letter was waiting for her:

Jane

Its 8:47 P.M. I was setting here thinking about you and I wanted to write these few lines to you. Like I want to thank you very much for all the support that you has giving me and I'am sorry that it had to end this way. Like I felt uncomfortable setting there saying that I did something that I don't know if I did or didn't do. Like I guess this is the way the world work and like the charge that he brought up from the pass it was dropped on me but they brought it up. Anyway like I hope that my pass wasn't to shocking for you. Like it was rough but it was a long one. Like if I see you tomorrow you want know about this letter until it arrive at your house. Like what I want you to do is tell everyone that their prayers was really did help in a lot of ways like I told you before that I didn't have anything against anyone and I will go to my grave that way. Like I want you to always remember that your support kept me going. Like I'am not feeling to bad at this time I just feel bad about all the people that is going to be hurt by me being executed this way. Anyway my friend like when the book come out I want you to send a copy to my friend Dee Fowler. Also let her know how things was at the hearing. Also make sure that my mother gets a copy. Jane my friend I want to write more but I want to lay down for a while to think about you today. Your friend always.

Love
Peace/Friendship
Andrew lee

Christopher Burger, born in 1959, was sentenced to death in Georgia in 1977 for an offense that he committed as a juvenile at the age of seventeen. In 1993, six months before his execution, he wrote to Micheala Conway in Darlington, England:

First, nothing has happened on my petition to the U.S. Supreme Court. But I have to assume that my stay was extended as I have not received a death warrant.

However my co-defendant, Tom *has* received a death warrant. This is the first real date he has ever had on him, and it looks very bad. Many people over the years—including attorneys—have told me my age at the time of my crime is the paramount reason for me not being killed yet. All the judges and courts are sensitive to the juvenile death penalty issues—but prosecuting attorneys are hard.

Even though we are in different cell blocks, because we are co-defendants we can get together in one of the offices, alone to discuss our case. So, he has been asking to see me. He knows I have been through this shit many times, and we have been friends for 17 years, he needs me, to tell him what will happen. Not the external things—the internal ones. He is very scared (he looks bad—like he's 50 years old) he's facing his mortality for the very first time and I empathize with him. But, it is really pulling me in, and draining me emotionally. Don't get me wrong, I wouldn't't/couldn't leave him in his need for me. I want to help him—I need to help him but it is emotionally draining. Right now he is going through the most intimate experience of his life, the most emotional experience, and he needs to share it with me. It's an honor, and I'm humbled. I need to help him.

Two letters later he wrote:

As for you saying "how could I not hold the judge, the guards, and everyone involved in your death, in contempt. How can I not hate those responsible, it's human nature to feel that anger and bitterness. I know now exactly how I would feel Chris." I know sweetie, and it is natural for you to feel that way—and it will be ok. But, please, for me, but more so for yourself, try not to always feel that way, ok? Initially, for a while it is okay—it's part of the natural grieving process. But please, don't allow it to *stay* in your life. It is destructive if it is held inside for too long . . . and it will mean that my coming into and being a part of your life ended up being something bad, negative and destructive for you. I would hope that my principles and values would be held by you and shared with others. I am not a vengeful, hateful, judging and condemning person. These people don't know or realize what they are doing—they are just more blind than a lot of us—so they need forgiveness as much (maybe more) than the rest of us. Besides, if you hold them in contempt for taking my life, it just perpetuates the cycle. After all, they hold me in contempt for taking anothers life—someone who was also loved by family and friends. They are responsible for their own actions and some day they will have to answer for them. You are responsible for *your* hatred and contempt. *Please* don't care around anger and contempt for anyone . . . it will only hurt and eat you up. I don't want this. As I said, I'm not asking you not to be angry if it happens—you will be, you won't be able to help it—it's natural, good and acceptable . . . but only up to a point. You must let it go, and try to find forgiveness for them, that's what they need most . . . they feed on and get stronger with contempt.

On June 29, 1993, he wrote:

Well . . . they did it Micheala. They killed my friend last night. He was pronounced dead at 11:15 P.M. I didn't even know until this morning when they turned the TV's back on at 6:00 A.M.—and they put it on the news . . . and they showed the hearse—carrying his body—leaving the prison.

At 6:00 P.M. last night the 11th Circuit Court of Appeals gave him a three hour stay to review his petition. So that put the execution off until 10:00 P.M. (remember I told you it was scheduled for 7:00 P.M.) We didn't have any news on the TV after 6:00 P.M. so I didn't know what was happening. At 10:00 P.M. when the guard shift changed I asked one of the nice ones if he knew anything. He said that the 11th Circuit had extended his stay until 10:30 P.M. The rest I found out this morning . . .

The 11th Circuit denied his petition. So his attorneys filed to the U.S. Supreme Court. That court gave him another 30 minute stay to review his petition. But they denied him about 5 minutes before 11:00 P.M.

At 11:00 P.M. they hit him with the first of three jolts of electricity. The execution only takes about 2–3 minutes, but they have to let the body cool down before they can touch it. So he was "officially" pronounced dead at 11:15 P.M. But I have to/need to believe he was dead at 11:00 P.M.

I've got to tell you, I'm not doing real well with this. The last sleep I had was Sunday night, I've cried, been angry, apathetic, depressed . . . and all I can think about is Tom.

Usually I seem able to find some "wisdom," some profound principles and virtues to hold on to, reflect upon, and share. But, right now all I can do is *feel* all of this. I can't rationalize it, I can't dismiss it or excuse it away. I can't find rightness or justice in it at all. Quite frankly, I don't feel very forgiving toward all of the people who played a part in this crime!

I know, I know . . . I just talked about all of this with you in a previous letter, and about how I would want you to feel afterward in the event of *my* execution. This is not a double standard, I meant *all of that*! In a few days I know I will find some peace, and emotional comfort, but like I said to you, it is hard right now, and I have to accept my grief and loss. Right now I only feel hurt, pain and anger. The state just killed a friend of mine, and I am hurting . . . I can't accept that he is gone; I want to talk to him again, but I can't. I miss him . . .

May I ask you a question? Have I made your life more difficult, harder, by coming into your life? Especially now that you know they have murdered my co-defendant . . . ?

A month later there was a further development:

Now I'd like to share with you some thoughts and feelings I have been left with since Tom's death. The anger has gone. The frustration is gone. What I have is a lot of guilt . . . for being alive. Micheala, it took *years* for me to find forgiveness for myself for the part I played in R.H.'s death. The day after Tom's execution there was an article in the paper, in which they spoke to R.H.'s sister (who was six years old in

1977). She said "They should both have been killed over 10 years ago. Not only did they kill R.H., they killed my mother too, because she grieved herself to death." First of all, this shocked me because I had never—in all these years—heard anger like this from R.H.'s family. During my trial in 1977, his mother, auntie and older sister even said they didn't want me to get the death penalty, because it wouldn't bring R.H. back. But his younger sister, the one in the paper who was only six at the time, so this is the first time I've heard anything from her. I could feel her anger and hatred toward me. Even though I understand it, and she has every right to it, it hurt me to feel it—especially at that time.

But, what it all did afterward is, not only did I have to accept and take responsibility for R.H.'s death, suddenly now I feel responsible for playing a part in the lives and deaths of *three* people: R.H.'s, his mother's and Tom's. How am I to deal with this?

Eddie Johnson in Texas describes how it feels to receive a death date:

On 16 April 91 I went to Rockport, Texas where my first conviction and death sentence was handed down, and was given an execution date for before 11 July 91. Just 20 days before my 39th birthday.

How does it feel to be able to count the days of your destiny? I don't know. Only that the family still doesn't write and after sending both my wife and sister copies of the execution order, they still haven't written.

It feels scared with the guys telling me that "They're taking you fast," after all I've been here 2 years and one month this month! and am lacking family for consolation or moral support.

It is my first date. Some say it's nothing to worry about but when you don't have counsel or had incompetent counsel from day one, it sort of bothers me. It does get weird after executions are proceeding as your date with death lingers.

Later Eddie wrote:

Yesterday I just didn't have the answer to several questions when the captain had me in his office to sign a form regarding if I needed a will to dispose of any property on the street and in my cell. I had no answer to who would pick up the body. I immediately stated I wanted to be cremated and "Who's going to pay for it?" was the other question.

No one in my family has corresponded with me. I told you previously that I was alone in Texas and my wife's in Minnesota. She doesn't write, my family doesn't write. I thought things would change once I received an execution date. That's weird huh? Hoping your family would talk to you, visit you, write once they knew your death was imminent? I notified them and received *no* response. I was hesitant then. And now I'm positive I'm never going to write again.

I lost my only friend yesterday. The girl you found for me to write. Just out of the blue things started messing up. Just falling apart. Who could pick up the body scared the hell out of me. I never wanted to be buried and I had told my wife that. I guess that don't mean much to many but that's a last request I can't even have. I have no intentions of mailing this letter today. I guess I just need someone to talk to.

Sometimes death takes a different form. Judy Haney wrote to her British pen-friend, Margaret Nicholl, in August 1995:

Last week my room mate Anne died of a massive heart attack. She was 47, and had never been sick since she lived by me, She woke up about 12 that night choking and couldn't breathe. I got her help but it was over in about 30 minutes. They moved that other Death Row inmate out of segregation up here last night. We have talked a lot today. I think she cried just about all night last night; I just left her alone and let her get it all out.

Bill Bonin, executed at San Quentin in California in February 1996, wrote to his pen-friend just before the end:

I talked to one of the counselors this morning. He had some questions to ask so that he could fill out a form that had to be filled out. One of the questions he asked was *"Do you want to be executed?"* I told him that I thought the question was one of the most stupidest questions I ever heard, and *No, I did not want to be executed.* He told me that it wasn't a stupid question, as some people find that they are tired and want to be executed. I told them that was their problem, not mine.

After an execution in Alabama, one inmate wrote to his pen-friend:

Yes, the execution did go on and another life was taken. It is such a waste and you are right, it does put a gloom over death row. You asked what effect it has on the executioner. Well, here the warden and assistant warden are the executioners, but the day after the execution, the assistant warden said he could not be a part of it any more and he quit his job. He made the statement that he felt it was easier to house a man for the rest of his life than it is to put a man through the last week of his life. My hat goes off to him for having the morals to know that death is not the answer to crime.

A prisoner in Illinois describes the impact of an execution in 1995:

I was up the morning they took him out of here—I shook his hand but he wouldn't look me in the eye. I really miss him because he was like the father I never had. Even at Mass—his chair sits empty for no one will sit in it. It just wasn't right—not right at all.

The preoccupation with execution has been well described by a man at Mecklenburg, Virginia:

The knowledge of probable execution hits like a brick right at first and your first thought is to get it over with right then. Depending on the person that part of it goes away and you want every bit of time you can get your hands on. But you never forget for a second where you are and the most likely outcome. It's only when you lose all hope of anything but the execution that it really gets to you, unless you can't help but dwell on it. Its kinda like a terminal patient, you have an illness and know you are going to die from it, what makes us different though is one day we'll be told exactly what day and time and we are told this not less than a month in advance, usually up to three months in advance. A terminally ill person never knows from one day to the next, a blessing I think.

The how is no question. The mechanics of my execution will be identical to all those before me. They are all done the same. For at least 15 days prior to the execution you sit in a cell some 30 feet from the chair. In the cell is a sink/toilet combination, and a bunk (bed). You can have a book or two but other than that it's just you and an officer sitting outside the cell. You can have coffee or juice when you want, just ask the officer. You are fed three times a day. You can make as many phone calls as you like. On the last day at 8 A.M. the death squad comes in and sits facing you watching every move you make the rest of the day. At noon you get your last meal. At 10:30 P.M. you are shaved, head and left leg, given a shower and the execution clothes, then moved to the end cell which is completely empty except for a toilet. At 10:55 P.M. the entire death crew comes in and one way or another you are escorted to the chair. Two officers are responsible for getting you strapped in. The stomach and chest straps go on first, then the arms and wrist, then the legs. The wire to the left leg is connected and then the head piece is fitted in place. The warden asks if you have any last words and then the leather mask is placed over your face. Then you sit there until the warden gives the signal. If it all works out right you get to the chair at 10:59 and are dead by 11:03. If there's a delay you could sit there till midnight. Except for legal visits and family visits this is how they all go. Of course, it's different in states with lethal injection, but in every state with the chair, this is the procedure.

The question of how I or anyone would behave during those last 15 minutes is a question only answered after the fact by the officers who kill you. I have no idea, and by the time I know, I'll not be able to tell anyone. Over the years you can think and talk about what you are gonna do, but when they come for you what happens happens. For obvious reasons the administration always tells the public that "he went like a man." Sitting here waiting I think, no way. Peacefully walk to my death? They best plan on taking all day just to get my hair off much less getting me into that chair. But you can't say just what happens to the mind at that point and time. Every single one may go out yelling and screaming to the end, or the mind might go blank. Ya just can't say unless you are one of the guards that kill you.

One prisoner describes how it feels as an execution draws near:

A friend and I discussed this about 4 A.M. one morning two years ago. Why? Because the state, along with its carefully thought out (premeditated) plan, had him scheduled to be murdered at 7 P.M. the following evening. I asked my friend point blank, "Because you supposedly took someone else's life . . . the state is going to kill you to show that killing is wrong. Am I correct?" He nodded and stared abstractedly through the cold gray bars. "Okay," I said, "and who is this perverted message supposed to be directed at?" This time he turned his head slowly toward me, peering through tired eyes. I thought of all those who had died previously, and then of the ones who had walked in to take their places. Were the earlier ones killed to show the new ones not to kill?

The following day at 7 P.M. my friend died. He was tortured in a wantonly vile and inhumane way. He suffered depravity of mind and cruel and unusual punishment . . . all the things that he, as a human being, had been condemned for were suddenly condoned. But what was equally as sad was seeing all the new faces that drifted in over the next few months.

I'd ask myself each time a new face appeared, "Did my friend really have to die so that you wouldn't kill?" or "Did the murder of my friend here really accomplish anything other than more hurt and pain for his innocent family at home?" and "Can you replace something to one family by taking away from another?"

The constant preoccupation with execution also comes through clearly in this passage by Enrique Garcia, in Florida. Enrique, convicted in 1983 at the age of twenty-two, was the driver in a four-man raid in which a storekeeper and his wife were killed. Two of the four plea-bargained and received twenty-five years; the fourth person was also given twenty-five years. Enrique believes himself to be innocent of murder and thoroughly wronged:

As I mentioned before I didn't even know we had capital punishment until I was facing it and by then it was too late for it to have ever made a difference in my judgment. Half the people on death row have told me that they didn't know about capital punishment because it wasn't being carried out any, until we are finally living with the fact we could be the next one to be executed.

We live with the fact each day of our lives. When we wake up each morning that's the first thing that comes to our mind, not what's for breakfast or if it's going to be a fine day but if this will be the day my warrant is signed. The rest of the day we spend trying to keep our mind occupied so we don't keep on thinking about the situation we are living under. That alone can be hard to live with each day, a handful have committed suicide, the rest of us I guess are a little stronger or else we would have done the same.

Most lose themselves in the soap opera they watch all day or other TV programs they happen to get into. Others like me do it reading a good book or playing some kind of board game or card game. I enjoy a good game of gin rummy once in a while myself but my neighbors don't win enough games to make it interesting enough to keep playing each day. Now that our library has reduced how many books we can request each week, that has taken that pastime away from me and I'm stuck with not much to do all day.

Every time someone is executed part of us and our hopes and dreams just die with that person. In that man's last couple of hours we're each placed in his shoes and when it's time for him to be taken to old sparky, "our electric chair," we take each step in our own mind, living the horror he is. When these people finally pull the switch everyone in this prison knows it, as all our power shuts off for a few seconds so they can switch over to their generator for power as "the Electric Company won't allow the state to use their power to execute inmates." I can't explain to you what one feels or thinks at that moment.

So far I've been lucky as I haven't had my warrant signed once yet but I don't fool myself as I know it will be some day before I know what is in store for me my friend.

People on the outside don't understand that being executed in the end isn't the worst part of being sentenced to death. It's the waiting year after year that is the real torture, as you relive that execution often in your dreams and as I mentioned in other inmates' executions. In the end you just want to put an end to all this insane suffering. Being executed is the only way to set yourself free; I know that sounds crazy but it's the truth.

Whether you know it or not your friendship means the world to me and I wouldn't do anything to lose it. We may have been born in two different countries but were still both human, so just keep on sending me those letters as those are all I do ask you for my friend.

Such solidarity of course also applies to the prisoners themselves. From Texas:

I try not to think about it in too sappy a way, but dammit, these guys are my comrades here, they're my brothers in arms so to speak. And every time one of them dies, some of me (some of all of us) dies with them. In seeing them stay alive or even suffering less I am helping myself stay alive and helping to lessen my suffering. And when they get neglected or fucked over, I do too. To feel anything less would mean that a very essential part of myself is dead. Again, it's back to the point that I fight not because I expect to change the world, but rather to keep it from changing me, even from in here, even in minor ways.

But to get back to the point. One of us is possibly going to see freedom again. I remember Tuesday night when L. and I were playing dominoes. Yeah, that's kind of a mindless activity but it gives us something to do while we're discussing Mideast politics or current law. Anyway, when he came out Tuesday he was laughing that he'd read in the astrology horoscope section of the newspaper that "some important legal matter would soon be resolved to (his) satisfaction." We both laughed about that a lot. I even vowed that if he got reversed "tomorrow" (this was Tuesday and the CCA rules on Wednesdays) I'd be reading my horoscope from then on. Well, I'll be damned if he didn't get his reversal the next day. When I came back from the media visit that morning with the news he didn't believe me at first. He thought I was joking because of the laugh we'd had over the horoscope the evening before. Hey, I may have a hyperactive humor gland but there are some things I'll never joke about. We've been laughing about that damn horoscope since then.

The following tribute to Lawrence Buxton, an executed prisoner, comes from a black inmate in Huntsville, Texas, who, on his own admission, was virtually illiterate when first imprisoned:

Lawrence Buxton: Criminal, Victim, Singer
by Name Withheld

For the men on death row, with every execution comes a quiet panic. It's like a northern cold front sweeping the death row population, sending chills up the spine. This seem to be especially true with the execution of Lawrence Buxton who was executed 2/26/91 for an alleged grocery store robbery and murder.

To everyone, free and confined, executions bring into sharp focus the finality of death and the mortality of man. But for the condemned man there are added elements—the ever present aura of death and the uncertainty of escaping it. For this reason, with every execution comes the unnerving situation in which one desires to forget, yet remember simultaneously. After a day or so the execution is no longer discussed, but intuitively each knows that the other remembers.

If this behavior pattern can be described as a rule, then it is safe to say that Buxton's death was an exception to it, as his name continues to pop up at frequent intervals.

Based on the many conversations that I have heard, Buxton is best remembered for his uncanny ability to laugh and make others laugh under such oppressive conditions. He would sometime amuse the fellows with his adlibbed blues singing; the lyrics testifying of a gloomy present and of a hope for a brighter tomorrow. But more important than the words itself, the tone in which he sang echoed loudly the mental, physical, and psychological stress and strain that are naturally associated with such burdensome circumstance.

Prison guards were bewildered by his ability to sing while death loomed over his head like a black, ominous cloud. His heart, thought the guard, had to be calloused. Hence, death is a justified sentence.

Being, myself, a condemned man I understood Buxton's reason for singing and joking, in spite of my inability to explain it. But in my modest effort to do so, I ask the reader to read with care, for there is a much deeper underlying meaning than I am capable of conveying.

I mean not to undermine the holocaust of the Jews nor the slave trade experience of the African people. But in truth, living on death row is in many ways like living in a concentration camp; in a human slaughterhouse waiting to be slaughtered. Meanwhile you're treated with the ultimate disrespect.

During the holocaust, Jews were often the subjects of human experiments. Here, on death row, there is a real fear of doctors administering experimental drugs. It is believed that once these drugs leave the rat-labs they are first brought to prisons, nursing homes, refugee facilities, and the likes. Be it real or imagined is irrelevant. The point is, the fear is real, as well as all of its ailing effects.

Death row prisoners are like the African slaves in that they are torn from their families, stripped of virtually all human rights, systematically dehumanized and, in a sense, forced to work. For refusing to do so results in consequences.

The one undeniable common denominator of all three systems is that they are all physically, mentally, and spiritually crushing. As did the Jew and the African in the past, the death row prisoner today looks for survival methods, means of coping, ways of relieving stress and frustration, and maintaining sanity.

Frederick Douglass, an ex-slave and abolitionist, wrote in his autobiography of privileged slaves being transferred to a lesser oppressive plantation known as the Great House Farm, "The slaves selected to go to the Great House Farm, for the monthly allowance for themselves and their fellow-slaves, were peculiarly enthusiastic. While on their way, they would make the dense old woods, for miles around, reverberate with their wild songs, revealing at once the highest joy and the deepest sadness. They would compose and sing as they went along, consulting neither time nor tune. The thought that came up, came out—if not in word, in the sound;—and as frequently in the one as in the other. They would sometimes sing the most pathetic sentiment in the most rapturous tone, and the most rapturous sentiment in the most pathetic tone. Into all of their songs they would manage to weave something of the Great House Farm. Especially would they do this, when leaving home. They would then sing most exultingly the following words:

> I am going away to the Great House Farm!
> O' yea! O' yea! O!

This they would sing, as a chorus, to words which to many would seem unmeaning jargon, but which, nevertheless, were full of meaning to themselves. I have sometimes thought that the mere hearing of those songs would do more to impress some minds with the horrible character of slavery, than the reading of whole volumes of philosophy on the subject could do.

Understanding why the Jews and the slaves sang enables us to understand why Buxton sang. Their voices served as fetching buckets with which to retrieve strength from the wells of their beings.

If it were I who delivered the eulogy at his funeral, I would have simply said:

"His crime made him a criminal. His government's decision to kill him to show that killing is wrong, made him a victim. And the deplorable conditions of death row made him a singer."

Note: This writer does not write without the many innocent crime victims and their loved ones in mind. This article was written for the express purpose of sharing what it is like to live on death row.

11

The Murderer Lives

*R*eprinted in this chapter are two tributes to Edward Earl Johnson, the subject of the BBC documentary Fourteen Days in May. *It was this film that first inspired the correspondence with Death Row prisoners, ultimately leading to this book. The first tribute is by Clive Stafford Smith, Edward Earl's attorney. The second is by a fellow-inmate, Samuel B. Johnson.*

Perhaps telling this final story will operate as a catharsis. But to understand his final story, first I must tell you who Edward Earl Johnson was. I could mention that he was an 18-year-old black kid, from a shockingly poor background, who nevertheless somehow pulled himself all the way through school and into the little world of Leake County, Mississippi, without ever getting so much as a parking ticket on his record. He was the first person I have ever represented who had absolutely no record. I could tell you that he was only 18 when they first decided that he should be sent to Parchman to be gassed, and that he spent all his adult life in the confines of death row. I could discuss for hours his family and friends—all the wonderful people who gathered around him in those final hours before he died. I could analyze the psychiatric reports, which showed him to have a serious organic brain dysfunction, perhaps the result of his alcoholic father kicking his

From *A Punishment in Search of a Crime.* Avon Books. © 1989 by Ian Gray and Moria Stanley. Reprinted by permission.

pregnant mother in the abdomen just before she was full term. Then, of course, as Edward's attorney, I could relate one sham court hearing after another which the American legal process offered in apology for this rank injustice.

But that would be a one-dimensional view of Edward. The more important Edward was the one who responded so incredibly to those last days of life.

Death row at Parchman, Mississippi, has all the appearances of the death camps with which the postwar world is all too familiar. Who can enter a high-security prison without the claustrophobia of someone drowning? Yet the presence of the unseen death chamber adds an additional morbidity.

After entering through the barbed-wire fencing, and then through the heavy main door, I found 15 of Edward's family members sitting around in a small room, usually used by guards. As I entered, I did not even notice Edward, since he fitted in so normally with all the others.

Immediately before I got to the prison, I had called Jackson, and learned the details of the Fifth Circuit's decision—they had of course denied Edward's appeal, but in their misbegotten effort to hammer in a few extra nails had made a couple of very serious legal errors. Paradoxically, the court's perverse zeal had lent one more chance that Edward's life could be saved in the United States Supreme Court.

The family members were all in good spirits, nobody showing it if they thought that Edward's death might be imminent. The rock upon which they all leaned, though, was Edward himself, sitting there as calm as could be. I sat with him and explained the situation as optimistically as I could, also partly for the benefit of the family, and for myself. He just gave me a hug and smiled.

I had talked to him about his games of chess with Paul Hamann, the producer of the BBC film crew who had been at the prison for two weeks previously. Edward had beaten Paul twelve times straight, so I asked him whether he would like a game.

The family gathered round, certain that someone with various university degrees would have little trouble beating Edward—certainly, filled with misguided beneficence, I had no intention of beating him at such a time, expecting the pressure of the moment to get through to any normal human being. Edward was never just a normal human being. As if we were just playing to pass time one quiet evening, he made me look like a beginner. I admired him all the more.

Two telephone calls to Washington, D.C., and the Supreme Court still had not ruled. Each time I walked to the telephone, I had to pass half a dozen guards in the antechamber of the death row unit. Everybody avoided my eyes, ashamed.

As nine-thirty approached, the "major" in charge of death row, needing to assert his authority more loudly than necessary, said that the family had to leave. Why, reason could not really explain—but to hide behind rigid procedures depersonalizes, and somehow obscures the absurdity of something so purposeless.

Edward's small nephew began to cry, but Edward took him in his arms and told him to stop such nonsense. The little boy calmed at once. The rest of the family and friends put on brave smiles, and said they would be praying over at the prison chapel, brightly lit a half mile away, but thankfully hidden from our windowless cell block. Perhaps it was best that they would have to go. As the final moves of the legal appeal played out, Edward might find the flow of their tears harder to stem.

A guard told me that there was a telephone call. Edward smiled at me, and I walked briskly back along the cell block, out to the telephone at the front door. When I picked up the receiver there was no response. Finally, I could hear Rob's voice in the background as he came back to the phone. Seven to two, he said. Only Brennan and Marshall dissenting, as they do in every death penalty case. Justice Brennan wrote a four-page dissent on one issue we had raised. Small comfort. Somehow it would have been easier if some more of them had understood what this was all about, even in the two hours that they had considered Edward's life.

It was much farther back to the cell than it was leaving it. And yet, I arrived there too soon. Edward looked at me and smiled when I said, "They turned us down, seven to two."

"So it's just the Governor." I told him all the reasons why the governor ought to grant clemency—no flattery, but simple truth.

—"The Governor denied." So expected, yet so harsh. How to move? How to go to tell Edward that the last heartless, shameless, barbarian had decreed that he should die? Probably after coffee in the Governor's

mansion, with due consideration of the favorable press the next morning. Truly, truly, a sick world.

—"He turned us down." Edward seemed totally unmoved. Only
Sandy [Edward's spiritual adviser] suggested that we should pray. She
said some things which perhaps some can believe, and from which
perhaps Edward drew strength; yet I find it small comfort to be told
that God has a purpose for this senseless, senseless barbarism.

In the end, after Sandy told Edward that God loved him—true, I am
sure—I told Edward that Sandy and I, and many others, loved him also.
He looked straight ahead, and said, "It's strange, but I feel absolutely
no fear." So we sat on the bed once more, and Edward agreed with
Sandy that there was still time for miracles.

What can I say? The time passed. A handwritten note came around
from the next cell and another was delivered by a guard. Willie Reddix
wrote that everyone in the unit was praying for him, and just thanked
Edward for being such a friend. It was actually only ten minutes before
Commissioner Cabana came to say that it was time to go to the isolation cell, just a few short yards closer to the gas chamber.

Why do they make up these names? "Isolation Cell." Hardly designed to make anyone feel more human about such a human tragedy,
but then that is doubtless the purpose. It was just a small whitewashed
room, two heavy solid steel doors, and a tiny window above a prayer
bench and a simple wood cross.

It is so hard to know what to say. Paul Hamann pretended to be
interested in who made the wooden cross. "Another inmate," said Cabana. Although Edward still talked about hope, Sandy read some verses
from the Bible concerning how God is with us in Heaven as well as on
earth.

Indeed, Cabana, who I must suspect abhorred the death process as
much as anyone, tried himself to be human. I admired him for his good
intentions, but again the words seemed so tactless at the time when
nothing could really be appropriate:

"Edward, I have to tell you that I have a tremendous amount of
respect for you," he said. "And you'll remember what you promised
me? You'll put in a good word for me with the Man Upstairs?"

As each person spoke, and each statement seemed so out of place, I
tried myself to think of a way to break the eternal silence which period-

ically seized us all. Edward looked at me, and I smiled and told him, "It ain't over till it's over."

What a strange ebb and flow between hope and the need to prepare for the seemingly inevitable. As Paul and the two others from the BBC crew prepared to leave, Paul turned away to hide his tears. Edward noticed, however, and told him, "Hey, Paul, keep your chin up." At this incredible display of courage and humanity, the tears welled in the eyes of the other BBC men.

Cabana came in and presented the strangest monologue of all. "Edward," he said, "I'm going to tell you this so you won't be surprised by anything. In a few minutes, two medical personnel will come in, and they will tape two stethoscopes to your chest. They'll also tape two EKG terminals to you. They may have to shave a little hair off to do that. They'll put them on so that they can tell when your heart stops beating. Okay? I just want you to know what they are doing."

Now, it is no reflection on Cabana, who had to try to think of something to say on an impossibly cruel stage. But I wondered then if maybe it wouldn't have been kinder to use the apology used by those whom history already has condemned, who told their Jewish victims that a shower awaited them in the gas chambers.

It was all so unreal. Edward sitting there so calmly, nodding as Cabana spoke, and everyone else just listening as if this was really something quite normal for a civilized world to do. Against reality, I just kept waiting for someone to call it to an end and tell Edward he could come home with me.

Edward turned to Cabana, and I am sure his words reminded some there of Jesus Christ: "Mr. Cabana, I just want to thank you for everything you've done for me." My mind was far from such analogies to the Bible, as I was simply astounded that a human being could really be so kind.

Edward then thanked Paul, and joked about beating him at chess. He hugged the other two BBC men, and said good-bye. As they left, he turned to Sandy, and said he had something he wanted to say to her.

"You've done a lot for me these days, but I want you to remember that you've got a lot more to do out there," he said, gesturing to where the other 45 men waited on death row. "Don't ever give up. You've got to remember that. Don't ever give up. And tell my family not to take it too hard. Okay?"

I sat there afraid of what Edward might say to me. We had tried, goodness knows we had tried. We ought, in a fair world, to have won it for him, and stopped all this hours before. But there is always something else you can do, and if I had just taken on his case earlier, if . . .

But he turned to me, and thanked me. He said we'd done everything we could have. Then he smiled, and said, "It ain't over till it's over." I managed to quell the tears before Edward could see them coming, that anyone could want to kill a man like this.

The room was hot. I used a legal pad to fan the air a little, as Edward seemed ashamed that he was sweating. It was oppressive, and much quieter, now that the BBC people were gone. I was thankful when Sandy suggested we sing something, pointing to a verse in the Bible. She led us, but neither Edward nor I knew it. But it was strengthening to hear voices, strong and calm, even if out of tune.

We sat together again for a while, and I held an arm tightly around Edward's shoulder, while Sandy gripped his hand. Edward looked straight ahead and said, "I suppose everyone wonders what a man thinks about when he is about to die." It was a question thrown out, without an answer. And then, "Well, it ain't over till it's over."

The silence descended again. I suggested another song, and Sandy asked Edward what he would like. Edward thought, for what seemed a long, long time. I remember that I had the sense that he was being put on the spot—it is so hard to choose a favorite something at the best of times, and yet to choose a song at a time like this—"Amazing Grace" suddenly came into my mind, and, at the same second, Edward suggested that. I was grateful that we had a song we all knew, so that we could sing loud and long. Sandy even had the words, on a little card she had been given by another prisoner.

Somehow the words she had did not have the part about saving "a poor wretch like me." I remember feeling glad since I just did not want the word "wretch" spoken in a context in which it could be associated with Edward. So inappropriate to describe him.

Then the "medical technicians" came in, and told Edward to lift up his shirt. I'm glad Edward did not look at me at that moment. I was so angry. How could those sworn to save lives assist in this gruesome ritual? What had happened to the Hippocratic Oath?

They took heavy gray binding tape which one might use to wrap a parcel, and wrapped it twice tightly around Edward's chest. He even helped them, politely holding it for them. One of those faceless men—though his face will remain with me always—then shaved a little hair next to each of Edward's shoulders, and attached the EKG contacts.

I was grateful that Sandy had the thoughtfulness to tell Edward to put his blue shirt back on, restoring his dignity after this horrible scene. Edward just smiled, saying they had done it rather tightly, and maybe they wanted to suffocate him already.

Almost immediately, Cabana came back in, and said, "It's time."

Edward reached over and hugged Sandy. Then, childlike, he kissed her on the cheek and said good-bye.

He turned to me. I said no, I would come with him. So we put an arm around each other's shoulders and walked in there.

I was glad to be there with him. There seemed to be a dozen gray-faced guards in the small room which surrounds the gas chamber. I—and I am sure, Edward—had never before seen the gas chamber. I would that I will never see it again. No description of the roughly welded oval, something like a diver's bell with four windows for the spectators, can capture the gray evil of that sight.

I put my arms around Edward, and we hugged each other. He whispered in my ear. At first, I did not hear, and asked him to repeat it. He said, "Do you know something that I don't know?" He looked at me hopefully. For a moment I did not understand. Then it hit me—somehow, he thought I still knew something that would put a stop to all this.

It is impossible for anyone to know what to say, me least of all. I mumble something, sincere but innocuous, about him knowing more about so many things than I would ever know. I hugged him once more and said good-bye. As they strapped him into that disgusting chair, he looked at me. I smiled and signed thumbs up. He smiled back at me.

Then the guard told me I had to leave.

The door led outside. I felt an overwhelming nausea. But the air was so fresh and cool, and the stars so full of life. A guard motioned for me to go into the witness room.

I just felt an urge not to follow the procedure that was making it so damned easy for them. So I walked over to where Sandy was standing—and she suddenly burst into tears, letting emotions from the hours of brave encouragement flood out. As we leaned against a van, its engine still hot from bringing some person who apparently wanted to be here, she sobbed that she could not go in. I told her of course she should not—what purpose would it serve?

Myself, I wavered. I similarly felt that there was nowhere on earth I would rather be less than in that witness room—"Observation Room," as they called it. I knew that I should be there. There was a phone. Once before an execution had been stopped because they botched it, and the lawyer was there. Who knows, in an insanely unreal world, what might happen? So I went.

Fortunately, I had a chair next to the red and black telephone, right at the back where I could not really see anything. The air conditioner was on, and a large black curtain (black, to be appropriate at least) over the windows into the chamber. I took off my glasses and held my head in my hands, unable to believe that I was really in the witness room to Edward's execution. How could this be?

Rather than miss any sound someone turned off the noisy air conditioner on the order of some official. He seemed to be the master of ceremonies for this perverse occasion, and took his job seriously, explaining the minutiae of the minutes to come. I could not listen, though others seemed rapt in attention.

There were five media people there. Three guards from the prison. The attorney for the prison, who I had met at a party in the house of a friend in Indianola, Mississippi, a year before. And others I did not know. Nobody cared to look in my direction. When they caught my eye, they turned away—ashamed, I liked to believe. Although the only ones who truly looked uncomfortable were the guards, who at least knew Edward in passing his cell.

One media person, whose name shall not be mentioned, did acknowledge my presence. He wanted an interview. Was there no human decency? Could a person be so ignorant of human emotion?

Then, boisterously to his fellow journalists, the man began to ask a series of phenomenally absurd questions as to the details of this media event. The curtain was drawn, and this semi-human was interested in the color of Edward's shoes, the cloth of his trousers . . . it was the depths of depravity.

I was drawn between a desperate need to look at Edward in case I could reassure him, and a terrible desire not to look, and not to rob him of his dignity at this most undignified moment. In the end, when he spoke I could not but look. He said, "I guess they won't call. I guess they won't call." Only now, only now, did the reality of this horrid nightmare come to him, and I could not help him. He was strapped so that he could not see those who had chosen to watch him die.

I never looked again. I did not look at my watch. After five hours of not wanting to see time go by I wanted every second to go faster. I could not understand, they just kept him sitting there for *eight* minutes, doing nothing. At one point, Edward said, "Please let's get it over with." But the timetable could not be changed simply to comply with the elements of human consideration.

The telephone rang. Before a fleeting hope could cross my mind, the guard said that was the signal for it to begin. I wondered later if the sound registered with Edward through the far-from soundproof walls, and if for a second the cruel thought came to him that this was the call that was never to come. Just another sadistic coincidence in the procedures which legitimized Edward's death.

Those next 17 minutes would be those upon which the media would dwell. The only questions they would ask would be what death was actually like. From the sound of gasping for breath, and the excited chatter of the ghouls in that ghastly room, it could not have been easy, even discounting the hours and weeks of psychological torture leading up to it. But I was far away. We can leave it to others to downplay the terror of the death of a man they will never know, and ignore the courage of a friend who goes silently to a better place.

"The prisoner is officially dead." Edward could not even die without the permission of the official procedures. I wanted to be sick.

I was in front of everyone as the door opened. The reporter tapped my shoulder for an interview, but I was too sad even to tell him of his depravity. There was an eager discussion among those who never knew Edward, but I walked as fast as I could from one locked gate to another, and waited until the lock clicked back on each. And at last I was out, heading to my car, those terrible people and that terrible place behind me.

A group of guards were laughing around their vehicle as I left to drive to the chapel. I recognized some family members as I drove up. As I got out and walked toward them, the reality set in, for them and for me. Edward's cousin screamed, his sisters started sobbing uncontrollably. And at last I could weep too. For a long, long time. No words were spoken, save for exclamations about good Edward.

A long time later everyone was beginning to decide what to do. The sadness and anger was once again building up in me, and I asked Edward's uncle if I should make a statement in behalf of the family to keep the press, already snapping at the fence, from further indecencies. He said he thought it would be a good idea. I knew it would be a catharsis for me, and I doubted I would regret next morning anything I might say.

So I drove to the finale of this strange, revolting history. The press was gathered in an auditorium near the prison exit, cameras trained upon the spot where Cabana would soon make the next official statement regarding "the prisoner," my friend. The five media witnesses were lined in their seats, smugly anticipating their opportunity to describe, in fine objectivity, their wonderful journalistic experience. It was not easy, it seemed, to separate this from a press conference after a football game.

Cabana took no pleasure from a brief official announcement. However, then the journalist from the witness room went into an eternal discourse on how easy it all seemed, and how he had noted in intimate detail the remains of Edward's last supper of shrimp, such a fine treat for such a poor black boy. Oh, how the blood boils.

There is neither the time nor the eloquence when one most needs it. I could tell the hundred and fifty reporters just a tiny part of what I wanted the world so much to hear. How much better a person Edward was than me, and, I suspect, most of them. How absurd taking his life was. How truly incredible and sickening it was that *anyone* would want to watch Edward die and then describe it by emphasis on a shrimp dinner.

And their question: "How does his family feel about it?" What is the point of talking?

I was grateful for the BBC crew who all cried outside. I was grateful for Tom Brennan, from the Jackson newspaper, who said he did not want to talk about it at all. I was grateful for the tears that periodically overwhelmed me, and forced me to stop the car. But, as I drove one hundred thirty miles back to Jackson in the early morning, how, oh how, could they have done this to Edward?

Edward, age twenty-eight, had been on Death Row for seven years. During that time he had grown particularly close to Sam Johnson (no relation), who was nearly twenty years older. The two became like brothers, and Sam later wrote this tribute to Edward.

I knew him as "Chui" (chewy), but to many people, Edward Earl Johnson was many things.

To the Trest family, Edward was the author of unquantifiable grief, the focus of intense feelings of revenge. He was these, and more—not because the Trest family knew that he had killed their family member but because they were told that he had.

The only certain "crime" that Edward committed on the night that town marshal Jake Trest was killed was to suffer an automobile breakdown in the neighborhood where an unnamed white woman was attacked and Trest subsequently murdered. A telephone call Edward made for repairs made known to authorities his presence in the vicinity.

To his family, Edward was "Squeaky." He was a grandson, a son, a brother, a nephew, a cousin, a friend. He was a good child, a big brother, a help to those in need; a loving and caring person, a non-violent person who would "talk it out" or even run rather than fight.

Edward was reared by his grandparents, and he and they were favorably known in the Walnut Grove, Mississippi, area. He was 18 years old at the time and had no criminal record, save a minor traffic violation.

His coerced confession and a white woman's dubious testimony were sufficient to convict Edward, who was inadequately represented at his trial and through his appeals process. When counsel finally was

Reprinted by permission from *The Other Side,* 300 West Apsley Street, Philadelphia.

appointed to represent him, it was so deficient that he couldn't have done worse attempting to represent himself. His attorneys admitted that they "ineffectively represented" him and that he didn't receive a fair trial.

But in the United States, inadequate and ineffective representation is not enough to prevent an execution.

On the morning of May 20, 1987, from 12:01 to 12:26 A.M., Edward was slowly and agonizingly murdered in the gas chamber here at Parchman by those to whom the people of Mississippi have granted a "legitimate" right to kill.

Earlier, we'd hoped and prayed that Edward's and others' death sentences might be found unconstitutional. The U.S. Supreme Court had accepted as evidence a study of more than two thousand murder cases in Georgia in the 1970s. The study showed a black person convicted of killing a white person was 4.3 times as likely to receive the death penalty as a white convicted of killing a black person. (In Mississippi a black person receives a death sentence for killing a white approximately eleven times more often than a white for killing a black.) By a five to four decision, the justices of the Supreme Court held that this Georgia study showed only "a discrepancy that appears to correlate with race" and that such "apparent disparities in sentencing are an inevitable part of our criminal-justice system."

So the death sentences of Warren McCleskey, the Georgia defendant, and of hundreds of other blacks (such as Edward) were upheld. Despite what Justice Blackmun, in dissent, called "a clear pattern of differential treatment according to race," Edward's legitimate murder was carried out.

Edward was indeed many things to many people. A black child, caught up in Mississippi's racist system, he was one of the many Americans who are afforded few, if any, of the many rights constitutionally guaranteed them.

Yet, to me, "Chui" was a man who rose above his tragedies and environment. He was a Christian who daily gave real meaning to love. As much as is humanly possible, he personified our Lord. He was the "kid brother" I never had.

When a good person dies, it is not their words but their deeds that are remembered. I loved and love "Chui" for the person he truly was.

If you had known him, you would have loved him too. I grieve for him. I grieve also, as he did during his life here on death row, for the Trest family and the pain they suffered and will always feel upon remembering their loved one. I grieve for "Chui's" family and their pain. I pray for both families. I pray, too, that all who haven't will learn how to forgive. "If we cannot forgive, we cannot expect to be forgiven."

Was the death of Edward Earl Johnson "the death of a murderer"? I think not. The murderer is the death penalty. It sits patiently, with its sardonic grin, waiting to touch you directly or indirectly through a family member or a loved one. No, the murderer did not die; the murderer lives.

12

A Simple Plastic Mirror

Michael Lambrix was born in 1960 and has been on Death Row in Florida since 1984. At the time of the writing of this book, he lost a critical appeal and was facing the very real possibility of imminent execution.

The crime for which he faces the death penalty was committed in 1983. There were no witnesses. He and the other party had both been drinking heavily. He states that "what really took place was an act of legal self-defense, as I was forced to hit the man while attempting to stop him from fatally assaulting a young woman on my property."

Although the facts are in dispute, what is clear is that the Mike Lambrix of 1996 is a very different man from the self-confessed drifter and no-hoper of 1983.

To See the Soul—A Search of Self

A simple plastic mirror hangs upon the door frame of my death row cell, faded with the age of years gone by. I could easily replace it with a new one, but I don't want to. That inanimate object has become my friend. I can look within its reflection and see a person I'm still coming to know. I doubt anybody else would ever understand, but I do. And that's good enough for me. You see, years ago when I first arrived and was placed within the confines of my solitary crypt, condemned to an existence of a seemingly endless state of judicial limbo, we had no mirrors. For reasons beyond my personal comprehension, any type of reflective object was deemed to be a threat to the security of this institution. For years I did not see myself, with the exception of a few opportunities stolen along the passage of time. But it was just as well, as even when confronted with the reflection of my own being, I couldn't recognize the person who looked back. It was a stranger I did not know, and could not understand. And it scared me.

My true friend, the mirror, is a patient being. Willingly, it has given me the time to look deep within myself, grasping in almost maniac desperation for the person that I knew existed beyond that shell of emotional void. So many battles in the past had tempered my ability to rationalize and overcome. I came to this crypt with a death wish, as I saw death as an escape. It would allow me to end the continuous cycle of adversity that plagued my life. As a crutch enabling me to survive, I had come to accept that I was not at fault for the way my life had painfully twisted its way through one nightmare after another. Responsibility for my personal actions was an alien concept. I had conceded that for reasons unknown to myself, my life was cursed. I came to accept that philosophy, no longer even attempting to defend against the plague of pain that continued to fall forth.

Yet, ever so slowly over the years I've gained a new and refreshing understanding of the man in the mirror. Oh, yes—I still fought what I did not want to see. I still created my own justifications for what I chose not to accept. But in its silent wisdom, that inanimate piece of plastic ever so patiently drew me back into its reflection of self. At times I would spend hours doing nothing but staring at this stranger I knew so well, but didn't know at all. In the stillness of night I lay awake searching the very depths of my soul for understanding. I expected a miracle. I anticipated the day I would awaken and hold all the answers. It never came. But ever so slowly I came to know that once-stranger. I came to understand the person who had blankly stared back at me as I looked within that plastic mirror.

I came to accept reality, no longer imprisoned within my imaginary world of excuses. I could at long last identify the paths I've traveled, ascertaining the many places along the path in which I've chosen to challenge the natural flow and do things my way. I've come to accept that the deceptive vehicle of illusive charm which I've followed and traveled upon so blindly is in reality the foundation of my life's disasters. In the ignorance of my youth, I had adopted the use of intoxicants as my crutch from reality. Rather than confront the problems of life, I turned in weakness for the closest available form of deception. Alcohol. Drugs. It didn't matter. I would use either without hesitation. And somewhere along that river of intoxicated stupor, I continued to flow even further apart from the person within. But I am not an old man. I have not spent a life of absolute intoxication. I am not the proverbial "wino" our society so quickly identifies as a model of alcoholism, or the "junkie" that haunts the depths of the inner city. I was only a young man—a working man, a husband, a father, an alcoholic and a coward who could not and would not face that truth; a teen alcoholic who had matured only physically into an adult alcoholic. I had become a person trapped and imprisoned by the compelling need to drown all time within a bottle, or whatever else might be readily available—any escape from the harsh truth of reality.

Now I look at the person within, and find someone I can identify with. No longer am I a stranger trapped within myself. Only, the search of self came too late. In at last escaping from the imprisonment of alcoholism, I have only awoken to find myself now condemned to death as a direct result. I cannot retrace that path of the past. I cannot recreate what has already been. Yet I feel as if a burden has been lifted. Still I can sense the inner freedom as I explore who I am, the one within. And over these years, I've kept journals about my solitary environment. Perhaps one day I will gather these thoughts and reflections together and allow others to look within as I have done myself. For now I'm satisfied with simply confiding my thoughts upon that paper, creating my own security blanket, another trustful friend who will hold my deepest secrets and always gladly spare a listening ear. And within those many pages I will form a trail to follow, a path in which I will be able to see the metamorphosis of self as it slowly evolves, as I come to know even more of "me." And as I see more of the true self emerge from the dark recesses of the past, I am inspired and motivated to push even harder toward a future. I am compelled to tell others of the experience, as I realize that I had been cheated out of my own life by a bottle, but even more so by the deceptive justifications I had so readily created to rationalize why I had fallen into the well of alcoholism.

In coming to know myself, I have realized what had first instilled within me the weakness that led to my addiction, and by identifying that weakness, I have found the strength to overcome the circumstances now present in my life. For the first time, even though imprisoned and condemned to death, I am in control of my life. I know what I want to achieve and can make plans to do so. I can look beyond the moment of today and into the eternity of tomorrow. For me, that in itself is a victory. Nothing I say or do can change the past. But I now know that I can use yesterday's battles as a source of strength in building a future, because I am willing to accept my addiction to alcohol, and how it can so easily become my master, enslaving me to an existence of irresponsibility and failures. For this realization, I owe a great debt to that mirror that still hangs silently as if in its wisdom, it knew all along that time itself would slowly bring about the unity of my body and soul. The piece of plastic could only reflect back what could be seen. It could only show me the physical being, but it was the stranger I saw that forced me to look deeper. Time, itself, brought about the gradual evolution of the stranger and the soul, each discovering the other along the path of a desperate search.

I can now only wonder what I would have become had I continued to live as I once did. Could any alternative path be worse than my present state of condemnation? Yes, I believe it could, as I can deal with what I face today. I may not still understand how it all came to be, but I continue to pray an opportunity will eventually present itself, allowing me to exhibit all the facts, all of what I now am willing to accept and confront. I have no doubt that if such an opportunity was to present itself, even this condemnation would be lifted. For now, though, I accept it. And I equally accept the truth that my prison of today is not at all as restricting or enslaving as the prison of alcoholism I had been previously confined to. In this small, solitary cage I am free not only to discover self, but to explore who I am, and to allow myself hopes and dreams of what tomorrow might bring. The prison of alcoholism had never allowed that. It not only mastered my body, but entrapped my soul. In my present condemnation I have found the true essence of life and in my solitary confinement I have found freedom. And all in the reflection of a plastic mirror.

The Yellow Brick Road

Outside the window a cricket sings out in its private celebration of life, as the humid aroma of recent showers steaming off the hot concrete barely overcomes the stench of a hundred living souls compressed into an abyss of lost humanity. Darkness, in its possessive manner, steals its way forth as I stand at the front of my cell. Beyond the bars that separate me from the rest of the world, I can bask in the simple pleasure of watching day give way to night in my own selfish celebration that I have endured—and even survived—yet another day. This is my evening ritual; my way of paying homage to the ability and inner strength of perseverance. And even in this shadow of condemnation, I do find strength. I accept that the definitive measure and molding of character is not simply the ability to survive adversity—but to overcome and even manipulate the essence of adversity into a productive entity of which I might find the strength to master.

I cannot see beyond this artificial hell in which I've been confined. The horizon I see is nothing more than a scattered number of lights flooding the compound grounds and dancing with glittering fire upon the honed edges of razor wire that lies between the statuesque "iron curtain" perimeters. The only sign of life in this world outside is a spotlight, as it lazily rakes its way across the grounds in an unpredictable, haphazard manner.

But even as they've confined and condemned my body, there remains a part of me that is rebelliously free; that no amount of steel and stone can confine and no man can condemn. Within the inner self of the man I am, just as within every condemned prisoner, there's a path that leads its way off into a different horizon. This path is landscaped and lined with the symbolic fruits of faith, hope, encouragement and perseverance; stolen moments of our humanity—and even sanity. For each of us, we strive to maintain some recognizable, progressive forward motion, refusing to succumb to the environment, finding inner strength to keep pushing ahead one slow step at a time. And all too often, it is a constant struggle, as this imaginative path takes its twists and turns through the highest of emotional peaks, to the lowest of emotional valleys.

For me, I call this imaginative escape from the reality of condemnation the "Yellow Brick Road," in personal reflection of the theologically symbolic nature and promise of the covenant of the rainbow; because even in the worst of storms, there's always the presence of a rainbow. And somewhere over the rainbow is the promise of hope. And this Yellow Brick Road is my odyssey through Oz—my exodus through hell. And somewhere at the end of the Yellow Brick Road is my redemption.

And it is a strange road. There's night and there's day. With the night comes the uncertainty and even fear of darkness; the long moments and hours of hopelessness and despair. The feeling that all has already been lost and to continue would be futile. The mocking echo of silence which serves to remind me that I am alone in this concrete crypt. Long nights of lying awake—unable to sleep as thoughts of what was and what might have been haunt me. The demons of darkness that stealthily creep in to rob me of my most prized possessions of hope, faith, and the strength of perseverance. But then comes the new day and with it mixed confusion. Darkness, and all it holds, has again been defeated—but there is no joyous victory as the new day does little to restore the gradual erosion of those values that compel me forth. The day brings with it the anticipation and anxiety of uncertainty; of hopelessness borne of living in an environment of forced conformity and dependence.

Life of the condemned is not life at all. Rather, it is an existence somewhere between hell and who knows where. A constant state of forced limbo, like a puppet on a string. Having been condemned by society, we now are not allowed to live—or die. Only exist . . . if being stored in a virtual warehouse devoid of emotion can be said to constitute an existence. If life is but the struggle for mere existence and its value judged by longevity—then perhaps by cheating those disciples of death that now demand the forfeiture of my life I too am worthy of that unknown cricket's celebration of life. I only wish I could find some justification and comfort in that argument. But I do not, as for me life is not merely a struggle for biological existence. Without the preservation of my humanity and individuality, such an existence would have no meaning, or worth. Here on death row, we do exist. Yet through the condemnation imposed upon us, society has deprived us of the recognition of our existence—denying our humanity.

It is not enough to condemn us. In society's demented state of moral consciousness, we must first be stripped of our humanity before being deprived of our life. To recognize our humanity is to create a reflection of their own inherent imperfection, as well as face the truth that they are taking a human life. But to make us less than human pacifies society's guilt. They don't kill any particular individual, but rather something less than an individual. And so for years on end a death of the inner self is methodically inflicted upon us so very gradually that it's practically imperceivable. An erosion of all emotion, until having been subjected to the endless rigor of administrative conformity, the person within is lost in a penologically conditioned sacrificial surrender. The strength to resist no longer remains and without realizing it—we have been subdued. Conformance, and compliance—even the acceptance of death—become a form of adoptive security, protecting us from confronting atrocities we've suffered in the name of justice and "We The People."

But for each of us, there is a Yellow Brick Road. An escape from the reality of our condemnation. A place of solace and security. The adversity we suffer remains and continues to plague us; continues to rob us of the humanity and individuality we so desperately cling to. But as long as we each keep sight of our own Yellow Brick Road, we will deprive our captors and executioners of the theft of our humanity and stand strong in our inner strength. Not only to survive—but to overcome.

13

Remorse

*P*eople often ask whether the prisoners on Death Row ever admit their guilt or display any remorse for their deeds. The following slightly abridged letter was written by a prisoner in 1995 in response to a letter he received from the victim's granddaughter. His name is being withheld not at his request but out of respect for the victim's family. The letter demonstrates the virtual impossibility of finding a way to address the victim's family that will not give offense.

By way of background, the prisoner wrote: "The girl who sent me a letter is about 25 years old. She was in the store where the crime occurred, and she left only minutes prior to the crime. She is the granddaughter of the man I killed. The enclosed letter is one which I sent to her and her family, after much prayer and deliberation. It was the most difficult letter I have ever written.

"I have never received a response to this letter, and I understand that I probably won't. I don't expect them to want to be my friend. I only hope that I have done my part to try and 'make things right' and I hope my letter allows them to find some peace and begin to move on with their own lives."

December 2, 1995

I'm sorry it has taken so long to answer your letter. This has without a doubt been the most difficult letter I have ever written in my life and I wanted it to be "right." I've done my absolute best to convey my thoughts and feelings to you accurately. If my thinking seems disordered or jumbled on occasion, please bear with me. There is a lot that needs to be said and deciding just what order to put it in is difficult at best. Thus, the delay in answering you.

Before I go any further I would like to assure you that no matter what I say to answer your questions or explain things, NOTHING is intended to JUSTIFY my past conduct. (In the words of King David in Psalms 51:3, "For I know my transgressions, and my sin is always before me.") There is no justification for what I have done and I accept full responsibility for my actions. What I did was wrong, HORRIBLY wrong, and it CANNOT be justified. This letter is NOT an "excuse."

For the killing of your Papa, I am as sorry as a human heart can be, and I apologize from the deepest depths of my soul to you, and to your entire family. There is not a day that goes by that I don't feel and agonize under the immensely heavy burden of what I have done. (And this is as it should be!) I know words are so inadequate in a situation like this, but the truth is: I did it, I am guilty, and I am sorry. I would gladly do anything in the world, make any sacrifice, to bring your Grandpa back to you. As God Almighty is my witness I swear to you, if my execution would bring your Grandpa back to life, I would willingly drop all my appeals this instant. But sadly, there is nothing that I can do. My death won't bring him back. It will only create another grave, another funeral, another set of mourners overburdened by their grief. (My family. I deserve whatever happens to me, but my family doesn't deserve any punishment, just as your family didn't deserve what happened.) I am sorry that I can't bring your loved one back to you. I sincerely wish that I could.

In March of 1989 I gave my heart and life to Jesus Christ as my personal Lord and Savior and was baptized in the prison chapel. This is not a case of "Jailhouse Religion" as there is no purpose to that "scam" on Death Row; I am not up for parole and religious conversion is not considered by the courts in appeals. It is something I had to do for myself and in response to God's promptings when the Holy Spirit convicted my heart. I write this letter hoping that my words will be of some help to YOU, and that you and your family will find peace for your own souls and be reconciled to Christ (not letting hatred or vengeance rule your hearts and lives), and I hope that you will then be able to move beyond your pain and go on with your lives.

Grief, anger, hatred, vengeance . . . all of these things eat at a person from the inside. They must be dealt with for the sake of your own health, both mental and spiritual. Also, I would encourage you to get in touch with members of an organization called Murder Victims' Families for Reconciliation. They are victims' families, just like you, and they can help you with your grief and pain. They put out a newspaper called *The Voice*.

Many things have happened in my life that have caused me to become so remorseful, caused me to be honest about my past, caused me to attempt to make my feelings known to you. And some of it has given me some insight into how you and members of your family might be feeling. While I have been living here on Death Row, locked in this little cage called a cell, both my Father and Grandfather have died. I was adopted as a child and these were members of my adoptive family who helped raise me. In addition, while here on Death Row, I have found my original biological family, the people who gave me away as a baby; but by the time I found them, both my biological Mother and biological Father were dead. My real father put a pistol in his mouth and killed himself when he discovered my mother was pregnant with me. He was not her husband . . . they were both adulterers . . . I am the product of an illicit affair that had been going on for years. I am a bastard. My Mother was killed, murdered, by a drunken second ex-husband in 1979. I never had the chance to know her. He broke in the home, chased her and beat her as she tried to defend herself first with a cast iron skillet and then with a butcher knife, both of which he took away and used against her, and then she fled into a bedroom where he caught her, beat her severely, tied her to the bed, breaking her arm as he bent it around the headboard so that bone was sticking out (it was from this hole in her arm that she bled to death), and he then proceeded to beat and rape her and finally raped her with a bathroom plunger handle and left her for dead. One of her other sons came home later that day to find her dead on the bed this way.

I never got to know my Mother, and a murderer like myself took her from me (Poetic Justice?), so I think I have some thoughts as to how you feel. (In addition this man served only 10 years in prison and has already been granted parole.) I understand your anger, your deep sense of loss, the dark hole you feel deep in the pit of your stomach when you think about it, and I understand your endless questions of "Why?" (Why was I never allowed to know my Mother? Why was I not loved or wanted by my real family? Why did they abuse me? Why were so many of them dead (Mother, Father, three Brothers, two Nephews) by the time I found them? I too have questions of "Why?")

I can also tell you that all the answers to your questions "Why?" won't make the pain go away. They will explain things better, but your grief will still exist. They can execute me (and most likely will), and in three months your pain will still be there. (Every follow-up interview with condemned men's victim's families bears this out.) There will only be another set of mourners, and still you will hurt. There are only two things that can ever make your pain go away. And in the memories of your loved one, a portion of that pain will always be with you, just as the pain of my Mother's loss will always be with me.

I'll explain all that I can, answer all your questions "Why?" and anything else that you may wish to ask. I'll do all that I can to help you—but until you deal with your grief and let it go, your pain will never end. I know that sounds harsh, but it is also the truth, and I would be doing you a disservice if I did not share this truth with you. As I've said, I want to do all that I can to *help* you, and to help ease your pain. I am *sorry* for what I've done, and this is the best thing I know to do to try and make things better.

And now I will try to answer the rest of the questions in your letter. I'll start with a specific question from your letter, and try to answer that specific question before going on to the next one.

WHY DID YOU CHOOSE TO DESTROY MY FAMILY?

The simplest reason for the crime is that your Grandpa was known to carry a large amount of cash in his pocket and this was a robbery that became a murder. And the main reason for the murder was that, at the time, I thought it would keep me from being identified later. If I couldn't be identified, it meant I might not get caught. At the time I was young, stupid, full of anger and emotional problems, not thinking about others, or caring about them or myself, and I was selfish, greedy, and sinful. You are right in saying I "chose" to do what I did. Although there are many contributing factors that made me who I am, etc., no-body was there to actually "make" me do anything. I "chose" and I chose wrongly.

WHAT WERE YOU THINKING WHEN I WALKED INTO THE GAS STATION THAT DAY? (IF I HAD BEEN ALONE WOULD YOU HAVE KILLED ME TOO?)

When you walked into the station that day I was "waiting" for everyone to leave. I was waiting for everyone who might identify me or attack me to leave the store. No, I would not have killed you too. I honestly don't think I could have killed a girl even at this extreme time in my life. Nor could I have killed a child. Even though I was "psyched up" to do a vicious and terrible thing, I was also filled with adrenaline and fear, and felt almost as if I was forcing myself to do something I knew was horribly wrong. Because of this fear, I didn't want anyone else around. I was waiting for everyone to leave.

TRY TO PUT INTO WORDS WHAT WAS GOING THROUGH YOUR MIND AND WHAT LED UP TO YOUR KILLING HIM.

I want to restate that none of what I say is intended as an "excuse" for what I did, but merely an explanation. Many things occurring in life contribute to who we all become as people. No one thing justifies anything we do later, but each "straw" on the "camel's back" adds to the total effect. Having said that, let me start with a brief history. (I don't expect you to feel sorry for me, but perhaps it will help answer your questions of "Why?")

I was born to a manic-depressive and alcoholic mother, the eighth child and the fifth one fathered by her illicit affair with her husband's boss. Her lover killed himself and this drove her into more despair and alcoholism. There was a lot of abuse in this house. I was left in a playpen alone, not fed or cared for properly, and beaten occasionally if I cried too much. I have an aunt who can remember coming to visit and seeing bruises on my arms when I was six months old. At the age of 11 months, the State of Georgia (where I was born) came in with the police and took me away from my family "due to severe neglect and abuse." I have seen the paperwork from the state welfare department on this. I was pulled from the arms of my (then) eight-year-old sister. The State took all children away from the family. Later, as they got their house in order, children were gradually given back to the family, beginning with the oldest first. When it was time to give me back, my mother told them "I've got too many kids already. I don't need another one, especially an infant."

I then belonged to the State, she signed away her parental rights, and I was put up for adoption. I was suffering from some mental, emotional, and physical deficiencies. I was put through two different foster homes until my health seemed better, and at the age of two was adopted by a man from Texas (a 20-year naval man), and his wife. At the age of four they divorced and I was sent to Texas to be raised by the people I call my grandparents. I was a victim of Fetal Alcohol Syndrome which causes emotional impairment. I was also born a manic-depressive, although nobody knew it at the time. In addition, one of the grandparents who raised me was filled with bitter resentment toward me because she didn't want me there, but wasn't asked about it first. Her overbearing resentment over the years, plus the fact that it was a completely dysfunctional family totally lacking in communication skills or the ability to show love, plus my childhood ailments that nobody knew about at the time, all created an emotionally bankrupt childhood that led to all kinds of emotional problems that essentially guaranteed I would be a "screw up" of one kind or another in my adult life. I never felt a part of a family knowing from childhood that I was "adopted" and that "these people" weren't my real family. I was always haunted by the fact that my real mother didn't want me and gave me away. I never *ever* felt truly loved or wanted anywhere in my life as a child. None of my emotional needs were ever met. In addition, although physical abuse was never more than an occasional slap or spanking with a board, switch, or rubber hose (once), as a 10-year-old boy I endured some sexual abuse by an older cousin that scarred me for life.

All of these things were contributing factors. As a young adult I quickly fell prey to the crowd of drinkers and drug users because of the "easy acceptance" available there. I became a drug abuser and alcoholic. I was suffering black-out drunks by the time I was 21. I dropped out of college because of drugs. I tried the army and later got kicked out because of my drugs and alcoholism. (I was physically and intellectually very capable, yet all the while the emotional problems were contributing to my slow downward spiral in life. I was steadily acquiring more inner rage, more alienation from society, and less feeling for the "world" that seemed to have done so much wrong to me.)

After the army I returned to Texas and bounced around from one job to another, partying and doing more drugs and alcohol. My life was going nowhere and so was I. I had talked to my Dad about going back to college, and he demanded that I earn my first semester's tuition myself. I began to save money. I began working out at a gym, quit drugs for two months, quit cigarettes for six weeks, and quit beer for two weeks (the hardest thing for me to quit). I thought I was fixing to get my life together.

Then, on the way to a job one morning, the pick-up motor blew apart. This meant that my money for college would have to go to auto repair. There went my plans to return to college and thus "fix" my life. Whether because of mental impairment, bad genetics, Satanic influence, Original Sin or whatever, when this happened something "snapped" inside me and on the exact day (June 13, 1986), I ceased to care about anybody or anything in life, including myself. I went out and bought a case of beer, five hits of LSD, some methamphetamine (speed) for intravenous use, some cigarettes, and began a *very* self-destructive "spree" of drugs and crime that ended 65 days later with me in jail suspected (and guilty) of two murders.

Why your Grandpa and not someone else? How did our paths cross? In late July of '86 I picked up an older woman at a bar and later we moved in together. In both my crimes it was a robbery for money and the murder was committed to avoid identification later. I had already told her about the first murder (the crime for which I've received the death sentence), and later when money was tight I asked her this question: "Who do you know that carries a lot of cash that we could rob?" I received the name complete with a plan to approach him. It was her idea to call him and pretend to be a buyer for the store that she knew was for sale. That day she called your home, but hung up in fear when she heard voices. (You had company, I think.) I later called and pretended to be a buyer to get your grandfather to come to the store and show it to me.

After everyone left the store I continued to pretend to be a buyer on a "tour." I obtained the sawed-off shotgun from behind the counter and pretended to admire it as we walked through the store. I asked about something in a back room because I thought the noise of the machines there (coolers) would cover the sound of gunfire. (May God forgive me . . .) I shot your Grandfather twice in quick succession, trying to end it as soon as possible. He did not live and thus suffer for a long period of time. It was over in less than 15 seconds. I do not say this to shock you although I'm sure it does (I'm sorry), but to let you know he did not suffer a long time in pain. I then took his wallet full of cash and left the store to get [the woman I'd met]. She was more than willing to help me spend the money (we went to buy groceries because the refrigerator was literally empty), but the next day when everything hit the newspapers she got scared and (via her daughters) contacted the police. They set up surveillance and I was arrested that night. I have been incarcerated ever since, and will most likely die here by execution, and I am heartily sorry for all the pain and grief that I have caused you. I will do all that I can to help you, and I wish that there was more that I could do.

God is the giver of life, and only God has the right to take it away (Psalms 24:1). I have "taken" life, twice. I was WRONG for what I did. I cannot restore those two lives, but if there is something I can do, I will do it. In my efforts to "give back" to life some of what I have taken, if the time comes for me to be executed I would wish to donate my organs if that were possible, so that others might live, even though I die. Unfortunately the law does not currently allow for this and to change it would require a bill to change the wording of the law. I would like to be able to find a legislator who would sponsor such a bill. My remorse is such that, if the law were changed to allow for organ donation, I would willingly drop all my appeals so that my death might "give life back" to others. I cannot bring back your Grandpa, but perhaps I can help others live as a way of making up for what I have done. But under current law, organ donation is not allowed, and the poison they'll shoot into my veins to kill me makes all my organs unusable.

I am telling you this in my continued efforts to convince you of my true and heartfelt remorse. I think it is important for you to know how badly I feel about this. There is not a day that goes by that I do not think about what I have done. When my own Grandpa died, and I was here, unable to attend the funeral or be with family, it caused me to think a great deal about *you* and what I had taken from you. Likewise the death of my adopted Father. And when I discovered my natural parents and their deaths, especially my mother's death being a "murder" that robbed me of the chance of ever getting to know my mother, I was truly moved to consider the things that I have done.

In my photo album here in my cell I have a photograph of the tomb-stone of the [other man I killed]. (And also photos of the tombstones of my dead grandfather and father.) They are there to remind me, whenever I look at the photos of friends and loved ones, of the true magnitude of what I have done and what I have taken from others. I am truly sorry and I think you need to know this. I think it is necessary if you are ever to find in your own heart the ability to let go of your grief (and forgive?) and move on with your life so that your own pain will be lessened.

If you think there will ever come a time that you would like to confront me face to face (preferably to speak rationally), please write me and tell me and I'm sure it can be arranged through the Warden here if you contact him as well. (In case you are wondering, visitors are totally separated by glass and steel. You would not be in the same room with me and touch would be impossible.)

I am sorry; I repent of my sins; I beg your forgiveness. May God's grace and mercy and peace be yours, now and always.

14

Religion

Sometimes you can be so still you can hear the grass grow. Sometimes you can be so still you can hear the voices of the children who must once have played even in the fields of places like this.

> —Willie Reddix, in conversation with Jan Arriens
> Death Row, Mississippi, December 3, 1988

In December 1988 I went out to Georgia and Mississippi, where I met twelve condemned men. As the meetings progressed, I began to have a strange sense that a series of monks were being produced from their cells. It is difficult to put this into words; perhaps the prisoners can best be left to speak for themselves.

Leo Edwards, who two months before had come within hours of execution, and who was to be executed six months later, told me, "I thank God for having come here. It has brought me a realization of God, and an appreciation of life and love, that I would never have had otherwise." I expressed astonishment at his words and asked—as best I could—whether what he was saying might not be a psychological prop. He quietly denied that it was, saying that he had developed a deeply precious awareness of life and love and that he genuinely no longer feared death.

Willie Reddix, then on Death Row in Mississippi for nearly thirteen years (but no longer under the death penalty), spoke of the peace of mind he had developed while in prison, calling it "the quiet light." Developing the theme "To know that I am is to be still," he said how we might at a certain stage in our lives retreat to a cave (either meta-phorically or, in some cases, literally). When we emerge, we learn that we can be in a crowd and be just as still.

Then there was Willie Gamble in Georgia, who described his impris-onment as a "road to life" in which he had achieved fulfillment in spirit. He said the sacrifice had been worthwhile because it had brought joy and peace and something to look forward to beyond death. God he regarded as "thought manifestation in its purest form," to be approached by self-denial in the sense of nonattachment. Through a sense of acceptance, he observed, we have to work past our usual selfish attitudes toward religion. (Willie is also no longer on Death Row.)

For all their extreme isolation, the inner awareness apparent in so many was far from self-absorbed or introverted. Alvin Culberson in Mississippi said, "The fulfillment of life is other lives," and Johnny Lee Gates in Georgia spoke of how his self-awareness had changed his attitudes toward other people. You could, he said, hate someone only if you hate yourself. You might hate aspects of a person, or things a person did, but that did not mean you hated the person as such. Con-versely, you had to love your true self to approach others in a spirit of love.

As Sam Johnson in Mississippi put it, "The situation forces you to ground yourself. You can't run from it. Guys seek to escape by watch-ing soap operas and turning to the fantasy world, but it dawns on them at a certain point that reality is this."

I was not alone in my impression that imprisonment often wrought profound changes. Stan Runnels, the Episcopalian priest in Mississippi with whom I stayed, gave unstinting support to the prisoners near his parish and went so far as to say that part of him envied the inmates for the time they had for reflection. Their lawyers too drew parallels with a monastic order.

Over a breakfast of Mississippi grits one morning, I taped Stan's remarks about the existence of the men on Death Row and what it brings out in them:

I think that it is very much like a monastic existence. You haven't been able to go down where they live, but it's very much like cells, in the

monastic sense. They are individual, isolated and not able to see anyone else while they are in their cell.

As they go through that experience, I think some of them discover
what the monastics have known over the centuries and that is that you
change your perspective, you change your way of living and you discover the inner self more. And out of that, for some, has come this very
deep insighted human condition because they are confronted by their
own mortality in a very profound way, knowing that the conclusion of
this journey that they are on is expected to be death, but a death that
they can anticipate, not like the rest of us; we know we're going to die
but we've no idea when. They live year in and year out with the state
attempting to set a date for that. And because of that they have to face
that issue of life and death in a very profound way. For some of them
it has moved them to a very deep understanding of the human condition. Far beyond what you would expect of a person that has a 7th or
9th grade of education. Far beyond perhaps what you would expect
from perhaps a degree in philosophy. Because they are dealing with it
at a real human level.

*How do the men respond in religious terms to the experience of
Death Row? Sam Johnson in Mississippi provides some clues in these
extraordinary observations:*

God is the only "constant" and humans can change inequality into
justice and equality. Into "real love." In spite of what has happened to
me in America I still believe in mankind. These people and this experience have taken me so low until I have had to "reach up" to touch the
bottom but still I believe in mankind. A lot of the guys in here have
stopped believing in anything at all.

We certainly have been touched by some force or something greater
than we are and what we have been touched by is GOOD! I'm unable
to say "exactly" what it is but I can sense it and I know it's GOOD!
I'm so very thankful and happy that we're its beneficiaries.

Somewhere I've read: "If you seek to understand the whole universe, you will understand nothing at all. If you seek only to understand
yourself, you will understand the whole universe." The understanding

of self comes first. Doing these things allows one to understand and love all of creation.

I *strongly* believe in God—or whatever name there is for Him—but I don't and can't accept the god these people try to conceptualize and give to me.

Let's both keep our great grins and chuckles going and continue knowing that as that mystic, Julian of Norwich, said: *"All will be well will be well will be well."* Let's also "Trust in God, have faith in tomorrow and most of all believe in ourselves."

Sometimes it takes losing something in order to find it and I think that our sufferings have enabled us to really find ourselves and appreciate ourselves in relation to life. From this experience I have been able to look at my life as that of sand in an hourglass with each day being a grain of sand that filters through to the bottom. When all of the sand at the top filters through to the bottom my life won't really end but the hourglass will be turned over and my life will begin again with each grain of sand filtering through to the bottom identically as it filtered through before the hourglass was turned over and it's impossible for me to change any grain from falling as it fell before.

I don't know if life is like this at all but I do know that looking at life as being an experience that I will reexperience unable to alter anything at all makes me do all that I can to make this day and however many other days I have left within my hourglass the best that I can because this day is going to come to me again and when it does I won't be able to change anything about it but only experience it again. As I've said, I don't really know if life is as I've tried to describe it or not but, if it is, and if I love all that I can this day, if I laugh all that I can this day, if I give all of the happiness that I can this day, if I do the least amount of bad that I can this day, then when this day comes back to me I won't want to change it even if I could.

In the silence of Death Row, Sam has discovered a close affinity with Quakerism, especially the absence of creeds, dogma, and a priesthood:

Bro, if I'm never "formally" accepted I'll still always be a Quaker in my heart, soul and mind. From the small amount of knowledge I've acquired about the Quakers I know that being a Quaker is the *right thing* for me. People come into Religion or a Way of Life in some of the most strangest of places. I've come into mine in this hell. Bro, I can't begin to tell you what it means to me to know that people, such as all of you, who I've only dreamed about and imagined in my fantasies really do exist. Bro, I've done a lot of bad things/wrong things in my life but I've never stopped loving people or believing that people loved me. I can't take back any of what I've done in my life and, right or wrong, I did the things I've done because I had to do them. I'm not the same person now as I once was and, Bro, I won't do the negative things I've done again nor will I live as I once lived. It takes each individual to find, for himself/herself, The Better Way. In a way I hate it that it has taken me *so long* to find the Better Way for myself but when I think about it I have to realize that it took *all of this* to bring me to the point where I am now and *none of this* could ever have happened without *all of this*. I, sometimes, look at myself and say: "Wow! why did you have to get *so old* and be in such a predicament before you got some sense in that thick skull?"

Christianity, as I know it, won't allow us to do this but mandates that one follows directly in Christ's footsteps. Following directly in Christ's footsteps allows one to only experience what Christ did. I don't and can't say that this is wrong. I think and believe that there is *more* and I can only experience the *more* by being free of restrictions to feel it.

My brother, you're a translator and in translating you interpret as you see and know things to be. Meanings vary as often as their interpretations, as you know well. The Bible has been translated many times and who is to say that its meaning hasn't been changed during its translation? I believe in the Bible but there are things that I question in it as not being the Word of God but the word of man. Each day I am more attracted to the Quaker way of worship because the more I think about it, the more that it seems *right*. Love says it all. Love does it all. Love *is* all. Loving *fully* is what it's all about.

I am deeply engrossed in *The Upanishads*. I am being given new meaning and understanding to a lot of things that I've never been able to think of in the light and sense that I now can think of and see them. It's not a book that can be read "easily" and its depth is most profound.

I really do enjoy reading it and I've got to read it several more times at least. Jan, have you ever seen any of those cartoons that show a character getting an idea by picturing a light bulb above its head? Reading *The Upanishads* makes me feel as if there's a giant beacon above my head! I haven't and won't try to read it all in one sitting but think that it's best to let the knowledge and wisdom come to me from reading parts of it at a time. I read and then reread it and then reflect upon all that I've read. I enjoy reading it and, thank you for sending it to me.

This administration stopped allowing us to attend conventional Religious Services more than two years ago. When they did allow us to go to church and listen to the chaplain I wasn't completely sold on what he tried to preach and now that we no longer have conventional services I worship in a manner that's similar to the way you worship. I worship in this cell and my mind isn't warped by Racists guised as clergy. They, when they were preaching, would have me believe that because of Him I am destined to subservience—their euphemism for "slave." They also think I suffer tremendously because they stopped religious services but their stopping religious services for me is analogous to punishing the rabbit by throwing it in the "briar patch."

In his correspondence with Liam O'Gorman, a doctor in Carrick-on-Shannon on the west coast of Ireland, Edward Fitzgerald in Mecklenburg, Virginia (executed 1992), wrote:

I was brought up Catholic and still believe mostly in the Catholic ways. I am ashamed of some of the Catholic history. So as far as the religious question goes I would say I am Catholic. But I practice the way of the Dao, an Eastern philosophy. It basically has all the same teachings of the Catholic Church, but without man being the center of all things. Man is a part of nature, he didn't create nature and has no right to destroy it. The first line in the dao de ching is, "dao ke dao, fei chang dao, ming ke ming, fei chang ming." Which means that the dao "is." To give it a name or to define it is to limit it, it "is," it has no limit because it is everything and everything is it. I am not God, but I do possess the dao, so do you, a rock, a glass of water, and a tree. We are one because we exist. If I hurt someone, I hurt myself because I am they in the dao. If we destroy the earth, we destroy ourselves. Even a single grain of sand has a reason and a life of its own.

There's an old proverb that goes something like this. A young boy went into the woods and saw a tree. He cut it down and tried to make a table for his mother. He used up the whole tree but failed to make the table good enough to give his mother. Again he went into the woods and did the same with the same results. He did this year after year until there were no more trees. And still he had no table to give his mother. On her death bed his mother asked to be able to rest looking at the trees. The greatest gift he could have given her, he had destroyed trying to please her with. We only have one earth with one human race, thankfully two sexes, if we destroy each other or the earth we have no place to go.

In many cases, religion takes the form of turning to Jesus. Often, this is a fundamentalist, born-again belief; in other cases Jesus is a more symbolic personification of an inner awareness. The following touching letter by Joseph Amrine in Missouri to his new pen-friend in Taunton, England, is of the latter kind:

You spoke of my upbringing. Understand that in the U.S.A. it's hard for the average black person. I was one of five boys and five girls, with both parents, which is rare. We lived in the projects, also known as the concrete jungles. I was raised around nothing but discrimination, trouble and poverty. I had no religious upbringing, in fact I have *never* been in a real church.

I think my parents' philosophy was we would survive by any means necessary, even if it meant stealing, cause they more or less sanctioned our stealing. From grade school to the 9th grade I excelled, I was really smart. I then began to take notice of women but being 14 with two pairs of pants and maybe two shirts was embarrassing, so I started skipping school and stealing. I eventually quit school. I fathered a son at 17 and was determined to make his life better than mine, yet I was too lazy to work, so I resorted to a life of crime and the rest you know.

I have a very good relationship with my son, he don't like writing but I do talk to him at lease once a month. His mother is the best, she is very religious, God bless her soul, and because of that she's doing all the right things. I told you how I found the Lord after being on death row. I would like to share with you how I fell wantonly into the hands of the Lord. I was place in solitary confinement and there was other inmates there who didn't have a death sentence and they use to constantly heckle me about my being on death row. For about two weeks non stop they harassed me and I was mad and would cuss at them and unknowing pray that I could get my hands on one of them.

So one day one of them threw a Bible in front of my cell with a note inside, that read, nigger you better start reading this cause you won't be around much longer. So I ended up reading it out of anger and because I didn't have anything else to read. For over two weeks I would read it to pass the time away, until one day I came across John 14:27, and when I read it, it was as if God hisself had spoke them words to me right there in that cell. A few days later I tried praying and I felt the change in my whole being, and from that day on my life has been in the hands of the Lord.

Two years later I wrote the white guy who threw the Bible to me, and even though he only threw it as a prank I thanked him. He wrote me back and cussed me out. I believe he did it only because from reading my letter he could tell I was at peace with myself, the Lord as well as my situation.

In other cases the belief in Jesus is of the more evangelical kind. Walter Correll in Virginia, for example, wrote of his experience:

While I was in jail, people from the church came to jail to visit, but I had so much anger inside that I didn't want to listen. One day, Bill Garrett came up but I did not want to hear it so I started for my cell. But before I got there he said something that stopped me in my tracks. He said that he didn't come there for himself but to let us know that Jesus loved us then he asked if anyone wanted to pray for forgiveness and I walked to the bars and we prayed. Anyone who has been in jail or prison knows how great it feels to be set free. Well, when you accept Jesus as your personal Savior, you receive and feel a freedom that can never be copied again.

Right now I may be on death row, but with Jesus in my life it's Life Row. I may not live to see tomorrow, but I do know where my home will be when I die. Tomorrow is promised to any of us so today is the day to give your life to God. I may be behind bars and walls, but I am freer than most people on the outside because they have a prison of their own. I don't know when or if I will have to face the chair, but until that day comes I will do everything I can to reach others and share the Word of God with them.

My prayer is that someone will read this and decide to give their life to God, because time is getting short for all of us.

Arthur Lee Giles, on Death Row in Alabama, wrote:

There is no better place to start than at the beginning. Although I only had a mother, like most kids I lived and grew up in a Christian environment at home and attended church nearby every Sunday. I found that there was something missing which was the Christian guidance and teaching which I find to be essential for becoming a Christian. Without this guidance I began to stray away and was soon running with the wrong crowd, in doing so I began to drink a little of this and that. I began to use different types of drugs which in turn led me to carrying knives and toting guns. I started selling drugs as well and stealing and robbing, and it wasn't long before I hit the bottom of the "pit." In 1978 at the age of 18 I was arrested and charged with capital murder. Like most teenagers at the age of 18 I thought I was bad and tough and could handle anyone or anything. This was until I walked into the court room. What I saw, what I felt, and what I heard from so many people filled with hatred changed what was once thought to be a tough guy into a weak and frightened punk.

For the first time in my life I felt and knew that I was alone. My friends had abandoned me and my lawyers had already spoken with my family, telling them to stay away because of the anger of the people until it was time for them to testify. So alone I was. There was a law student who befriended me during my trial which was helping my lawyer represent me. I felt that they were as much afraid as I was, but they were right there everyday during the trial trying to get me through that terrifying trial. For to have been there one would have thought they were at a lynching. For all I could hear was, "Shoot, hang and burn the dog." It was a real nightmare straight from hell. I made it through the trial only to be awakened to yet another nightmare, the one of "Death Row."

I was given the death sentence which only separated me further from my loved ones. And being illiterate as well only brought on more frustration and fear and being on Death Row scared me even more. With no friends, separated miles apart from my family made it even worse. I was unable to either read or write for a 3rd grader could have done better than me. There was no one to turn to for help and in despair I found myself sitting in my cell on the floor and began to weep like one. And that Glorious One I thought I had forgotten eight or nine years ago came into my mind. I find myself weeping, remembering an old forgotten but familiar name, the name that came from my mouth was "God," "God," "God" and having forgotten how to pray I just said, "Please God, help me, help me, help me." And after I cried until I couldn't cry any more. Later I got up and washed my face and for some reason I felt better.

The next day there were three guys on Death Row who befriended me, they took a special interest in teaching me to read and write and within a few weeks I was able to write a few lines home, a month later I received a surprise letter from the law student who had befriended me during my trial. She had returned home and to school in Vermont and we correspond quite often and this helps me greatly, emotionally as well.

I say the very next day after sitting on the floor and weeping, my life began to get better and although I didn't come to give my life up to my "Lord and Savior" until some five years later, he didn't stop watching over me and during those five years my life didn't stop getting better either. When I look back at that day, sitting on that floor, crying, and what my God has done for me, watching over me and preventing me from being executed, I praise His name for blessing me with such wonderful friends from the free world, who took the time to write to me and let me know that not only did God love me but they also loved me and cared about me too.

From various sources:

And now I pray you also dear tender one—chew upon this faith with me—in that the most holy one kiss your soul and make thee Holy well again—and ever now on! . . . no matter how rough the road, how sharp the curve, how steep, how high the mountain or how low the valleys—Believeth as I—in this Life unto Death—unto life ever unending—we will be ever well—in the fact that we strive always—either we live or die we do it unto the precious will of God our Father—the most Holy one the Host of heaven our Christ Jesus.

Some people take life for granted and don't know how to live. Me, myself, I am thankful for my life, day to day, because there is so much to live for. Do be thankful for the things that you have and be thankful for everything that you don't have.

If we can't forgive one another how are we going to be forgiven by God? God still loves us no matter what we do or have done and if you hate someone you hate Him also because God is love. He loves all for who they are, not for what they do.

One of the most moving contacts between prisoner and pen-friend has been that between an Irish woman and a younger prisoner in one of the southern states. The pen-friend writes:

P. is black, was born in the South of the U.S.A. where he was baptized into the Southern Baptist Church. He had a normal childhood, learned to play the French horn and drums and later played in his high school band and sang in the local choir. After graduating from college he joined the army and spent eight fairly happy years serving in many different countries. He married and they had one daughter.

Now P. is 34 and he is serving his second year on death row. He is separated from his wife and has not seen his four-year-old daughter for two years (children under 12 years are not allowed into death row). His friends have deserted him and because of his feelings of shame he has requested his mother and family not to visit him. In his first letter P.

said he was lonely, scared and felt rejected, embarrassed about destroying his life and guilty about his past.

What had I to offer him? My life was quite ordinary but happy, living in the country with my husband and four children (ages 10 to one year). Others, I thought might write of glamorous life-styles and exciting holidays, but despite this I felt urged to write and share with him a God who I know to be loving and forgiving no matter what the crime. Having prayed about it and with encouragement from my husband, I wrote my first letter in late June '90.

P. writes about every two weeks. Our older children love to see his letters as he usually includes a very colorful drawing. The girls in return send him little cards—some home-made, others bought. I write about anything and everything always reassuring him that we are thinking and praying for him and that God loves him.

In one of P.'s letters he expressed a wish that he would like to write and say sorry to the victim's family but was afraid of rejection. He knew the pain and suffering he had caused and would understand their unforgiveness. I asked him to pray for the family and said I would join in praying that they would get the grace from God to forgive as I knew that true forgiveness can only come from God.

Can you imagine the joy he felt on receiving a letter from the victim's family to say they forgave him. Surely this could only be the work of God.

P. has reflected on many things since getting into trouble. He knows now that God has forgiven him and his soul is saved for Heaven. He may never see his daughter in this life but he looks forward to meeting her in Heaven where he will tell her how much he loves her.

I feel privileged to know P. and to be included in his prayers. I leave the last words to P. "Be faithful, be hopeful, be patient and be strong because God is with you all the day long."

This is P.'s own account of this remarkable episode:

How are you today? I received your nice letter through my wonderful friend [in Ireland]. Thank you for saying that I was courageous in writing to the victim's family asking for forgiveness. I wanted to write to them two years ago when my crime was committed, but was afraid to because of possible rejection. As time passed, I always knew that in time, I needed to address the issue of seeking their forgiveness. I knew them well before the incident, but still did not know what to expect from them. I asked God to give me the right words to say, as well as to touch their hearts so they would forgive me. As you know this response made me very happy, and came back very quickly. I have written to them two more times since then, and think that I am on the road to building a relationship with them. It's not complete yet, because the victim's brothers and sisters still hate me. I wrote the letter to the father and mother, because I remembered their address. They say that they forgive me, and are praying for me. In time, I will ask them for their children's addresses, and seek their forgiveness.

A black prisoner in one of the Deep South states has written:

To be sure, I would indeed be a very "bitter" man if I had not lived with this thing long enough conscious of bitterness being truly a worthless and useless thing.

Sometimes I do however catch myself nursing a quiet anger which never quite dies out, and just between us, if I did not see and understand that there is both good and evil—the evil truly to be overcome by the good—I would most certainly be dedicated to being a real hardened revolutionary who would do anything to further the cause.

I would rather practice healing, that peaceful path to liberation. I have seen so much violence cripple and destroy lives. Violence perpetuates itself.

Organized religion is not always a source of comfort. One prisoner in Texas wrote of a visit by a priest:

For some unknown reason I did not feel the earth shake when he passed by me. Do you think, as so many seem to, that I am just another lost soul on the sea of iniquity? Can you feature a man being in here for capital murder, and telling me that I should be afraid of being so disrespectful to that priest that I refused to stand up when he passed by?

Believe me, it happened. I very calmly told him that the priest was not with me when I came in here, and he definitely will not be with me when I leave.

From Florida an inmate writes of how he copes:

I pray to God every day to maintain a compassionate heart. When your heart goes hard, you no longer are a free being. You become controlled by environment and circumstances; your will is not that of your own, but that of a condition and situation.

They have my body, and even though they try to destroy my mind through humiliation and other tactics, they can't because that's free and guided by a Higher source.

From Florida, Linroy Bottoson, who has been on Death Row since 1981 (when he was forty), has written to his pen-friend Irene Morgan:

Each day I live by Faith and not Feelings. You see, when everything is pleasant and bright and the things we do turn out just right we feel without question that God is real, for when we are happy how good we feel. But when the tides turn and gone is the song and misfortune comes and our plans go wrong doubt creeps in and we start to wonder and our thoughts about God are torn asunder, for we feel deserted in time of deep stress without God's presence to assure us and bless. And it is then when our senses are reeling we realize clearly it's Faith and not Feeling for it takes great Faith to patiently wait believing God comes not too soon or too late.

Many people who know me wonder how I have kept myself together all these years in prison . . . I feel there is no difficulty you cannot overcome. How do I get through my troubles? Well first I try to go around it, if I can't go around it I try to get under it, if I can't get under it I try to get over it, if I can't get over it I just plow right through it—God and I plow right through it. I don't believe in defeat.

In Mississippi, Lazaro Faraga, a Cuban, has written to Suzanne O'Callaghan in Cambridge, England (to whom he writes in Spanish), about Christmas Day on Death Row:

Yes, I received your nice card for Christmas and the pullover and the gloves. Christmas Day here is a day like any other. The only good thing they give us that day is the food. The chaplains bring us presents, but they don't take us to church because the prison governors don't let us go anywhere, not even into the yard that day. You can't imagine what this prison is like. I didn't get a visit on Christmas Day because I told my family not to come. Visiting here is awful, you can only see people through a grill. You can't sit next to each other. I spoke to my family on the phone and wished them Happy Christmas—I know that families meet together and open presents to celebrate that special day, and then I feel sad and ask myself why I have to suffer like this. I look at the photos of my family, my children, and tears come to my eyes because I want to be with them—I wonder how long God will keep me in this place, because God is the only one who can get us out.

Many black prisoners turn to Islam. A Native American on Death Row in Oklahoma, John Walker Castro, wrote to his pen-friend in England in early 1996 about what Islam had meant to him on Death Row.

As you know I am not a Muslim in the true sense of the word, nor by my actions, although I have always gone to all of the Muslim services since I first became aware of them. I have not as yet actually taken the shadda (the declaration of faith), nor do I follow all of the tenets of Islam. But of all religions I know something of, I do lean toward Islam more than any other. I respect it for what it is and the truths it teaches, i.e. that no one can take the responsibility for your actions except yourself.

One can practice almost any religion one believes in, as long as it doesn't conflict with the always and almighty prison (catchall) of security. You see this is a so-called Christian nation, and believe it or not even within these walls that seems to apply. The nondenominational stand seems to only extend to those who are of different sects of Christianity.

Up until a little over six months ago there used to be a few Muslims that came in this prison to try and teach us about Islam, but that was put to a stop. They have Christian services every week, but if you wish to follow Islam on your own, you're free to do that, just don't count on being able to get together with other Muslims.

The Holy Quran just teaches modesty in one's dress, and this applies to men as well as women. Any dress code I see seems to come more from culture than religion. But even if there is a dress code in Islam that would be hard to follow in here. It makes one stand out and in a sense gives you a sense of respect (self-respect) and that is the last thing they want us to have in here.

You ask "Are the men sincere about Islam, how do they see it helps?" Dang! This is a tough one. I can't really speak for someone else's sincerity or what they may or may not believe in, but I'll step out on the limb on this one, this time. And my own personal feeling is that there are really only a very few who actually take Islam seriously, meaning to heart, but remember I am confined to such a small piece of this prison that my knowledge is very limited. But I believe most that did go to the Muslim services didn't actually go to learn about Islam, it was more of a chance just to be among your own, and by this I mean among other black men. You see, here in the States Islam has mostly always been seen as a black man's religion. But there were a few who actually wanted to learn something about Islam as a religion. In my opinion, it's the strict discipline of Islam that I believe draws many, as well as pushes many others away. But for those few who stay with it, it seems to be the discipline and logic and self-respect that it gives them that causes them to stay with it. But I must admit that those five daily obligatory prayers can be hard to follow, especially as it wasn't programmed in from early childhood.

I know for a fact that the guards see Islam as a religion of fanatics and at least here in the States as only blacks, which they already have a deep distaste for.

More than anything Islam has taught me that I am the only one who can answer for my past actions. No one can take the blame for what I did, and it's just opened my mind to the reality that there are many out there who do believe in God but that with this belief you must act, just believing is not enough. I know now that knowledge is strength and that wisdom is given by God, if only one opens one's heart and mind to it.

Forgive my lack of being able to go any deeper into this, but my lack of education (mainly spelling) holds me back like these walls hold me within this room.

Finally, a letter that goes beyond any particular faith to a level of profundity, based on experience, which must surely be very rare. It was written by Mike Lambrix, in Florida, in February 1996, after he had lost a critical appeal.

It is true that my childhood was lousy. There's probably not many who have been through worse, and survived. For a long time, I felt somewhat responsible or guilty about that childhood—and I guess now it's evolved into shame. To be honest, I really don't have many memories of that childhood and that's my greatest blessing. But it wasn't just my childhood. The way I try to explain it is that we all travel paths through life and rather than focus on whether specific events are "good" or "bad" experiences, I elect to see all experiences as opportunities to grow. The truth of the matter is that had it not been for the hell I went through the years prior to prison, I probably wouldn't have had the strength to learn and grow in prison. I see too many here essentially stagnate and go to waste, passing the time one day at a time with no effort to grow and expand, and I feel fortunate that I have the strength to continuously stay productive. I feel that in spite of the circumstances, I have accomplished a lot. Looking back, I don't like the person I was, I had no sense of direction and didn't see beyond that instant moment.

More importantly, it's really all part of my collective spiritual orientation. I truly believe that there's more to life than life, and that there's a purpose and meaning to it all. Most would find it very difficult to find meaning in being condemned to death—but I really feel I have. The way I see it is life itself is the mortal condemnation of an eternal soul. The purpose of "life" is to grow through our experiences. In the book of Romans it tells explicitly how we are all condemned by sin, and sin is the product of being human, and it's looking deeper and seeing *beyond* that state of imperfection that allows us to find true purpose and meaning in even the worst of experiences. That's the proverbial promise of a "rainbow" to remind us of God's covenant with man, that

"He's" with us through even the worst of storms. And my storm of life has been worse than most, but the greater the storm, the brighter the rainbow as there's a balance in everything.

But I pretty much gave up on the generalized concept of God. There's been too many times through this life when I've felt the depth of loneliness so overwhelming that it belied the existence of a personal God. And although that may sound as if I deny God—I do *NOT*. Rather, it's my belief that God is the collective consciousness, that eternal inner-self. In our mortal state, we are temporarily separated from the collective consciousness for the purpose of accumulating experiences that allow our consciousness to grow.

Just as much as I've felt the absence of God in a way so overwhelming that this absence could not be denied, so too have I felt the warmth of the spiritual presence with an intensity so deep that it was felt to my very soul. Even in my early childhood years, I made a habit of seeking "refuge" in religious retreat. I don't know if I told you before, but as a child, I was an "altar boy" at various Catholic churches. In my teens I left the Catholic Church and joined a Baptist church. I mean, I even actually carried a Bible to school and "witnessed" to others. But then I slowly substituted that spiritual refuge for "partying"—doing alcohol and drugs. This was especially true when I left home at 15 and went to work with traveling carnivals.

Actually I didn't really "leave home," as it wasn't a home at all. Since I was 12, I wasn't allowed to live in the house, but slept and lived in a small travel-trailer, and more often than not I would have to work at various local farms so that my step-mother could get the pay. For more years than I can remember, the least resistance to this domestic slavery was met with physical beatings from my father. But just after my 15th birthday the day came when I stopped taking it and stood my ground. I grew up with the abuse and didn't see it as abuse, as it was the only expression from my father. In a way I can't even explain, I suppose I interpreted this as an expression of love, as I had nothing to compare it to. I guess I can best illustrate this misconception by trying to picture a dog that's been beat all its life. If you've ever seen such a dog, you already know the dog not only accepts this, but even seeks it out, as that's the only relationship the dog knows. But the time came when I stood my ground and refused to just accept it, and I felt an anger that scared me more than I've ever been scared before. And what had scared me the most was I really wanted to swing back, but couldn't. And to this day, I don't know what it was that scared me the most—the desire to swing back, or my inability to.

When I left home, I also left my spirituality behind. Something died in me, although it's not something words can define. Years later I married, and our first child was born and there were a lot of complications resulting in her (Niki) being still born, but revived, but in a coma. For a month I could only see her through a heavy plastic incubator, with tubes all over keeping her alive. I never was much at showing emotions, but I'd go into the hospital chapel alone, and I'd pray. And it seemed like every time I'd try to pray and ask God to just let her live, I'd go back up stairs and Niki would slip into cardiac arrest and die again. Only after I stopped praying did she finally begin to recover. When they removed her from the incubator and put her in a regular crib, I was afraid to touch her. But eventually she came around and she became the most important thing in my life, although I had no idea how to show/express emotions.

The time came when I lost all of that—my wife, daughter and all that really counted. But I didn't turn to God. I just partied more no matter how bad it all got, my response was to drink or do drugs that much more. Looking back, I see now that it was what created the problem, not solved it. But when you're inside that bottle looking out, it's all just the opposite. Back then, reality was the problem and partying was the solution.

After I came to death row, I got the idea that maybe what really went wrong in life was I turned away from God. Maybe all the hardships was the way of getting me to realize that he was calling me and it took all this to get my attention, and I got really serious about getting my heart right with God. From '86–'87 I studied extensively and completed four years of college theological courses. I even fantasized about getting into evangelism. But it still kept getting worse and there were no breaks. In four years, I had a total of two visits and it was tough. But I survived and kept on. Then in 1987, after losing my first two appeals, I had to start getting into law as the "lawyers" were not.

Eventually, in late 1988 I had a death warrant signed. I hadn't even had my first collateral appeal filed yet, but still I came within hours of being executed—*three* times in one week. So, there I was on "death watch" during that last week. I had to order my last meal, my "death suit" and make out my will or in other words, I had to confront the reality of death—and I had to do it alone. It was by far the hardest week of my life, bar none. And nobody was there, not family, not lawyers, or friends—not even God. And that's when I finally accepted that this concept of God we talk of doesn't exist, and simply can't exist. For me that's the day God died for me. I can even tell you exactly when, as it was Friday, December 2nd about 7:00 A.M.—ironically, the time set for my own execution until I got a temporary stay until Monday. It was the first time I ever woke up literally in a cold sweat—from a graphic nightmare of my own execution. It was more than just a nightmare—it was an "out of body" experience. I didn't just dream it, I physically felt it, even the execution. And awoke just as the bright light consumed everything. The immense light I sensed as I was awaking was not a physical, environmental light—as that obviously would have been noticed by the guards who stood watch over me. This light I can only describe as that *sense* of light people experiencing "near death" experiences describe.

I had reached the point of accepting death, at a depth of the inner self that simply cannot be described. It's like something inside just lets go. And it was through that period of time that I experienced that "virtual reality" death.

I didn't die, though. But God did, as prior to that throughout my entire life I always felt a personal interconnection with God, even when I turned my back on Him. But not after that experience. That's why it's so hard to explain in words. It's that sense of His existence that made me believe He really was there. But that sense of the presence died in that nightmare/OBE, and I've never felt it since.

You know, you're the first person I've ever actually told all that to, and I didn't really plan to, it just rolled on out. I can tell you this. There is no experience more intense than death and it's that experience more than anything else that tells me there really is a God. So many times throughout my life I prayed in times of need. But not on death watch, so I really don't know why that nightmare came about. But I do know what I felt—and what I haven't felt since. I can't explain why everything in my life has brought only pain and loss. But neither can I understand why the consciousness of God "died" within me when I needed Him the most, when I was totally alone facing my third scheduled execution in one week. But that experience was more "real" than anything I ever felt in my life. It was so real, I *can't* deny it.

I must also admit that there are times since the "death" of that former perception of God when I really miss that "personal" feeling. The way this transformation of my spirituality came about, it allows me to relate to the anguish Jesus felt at the moment of his death—how he cried out "why hast thou forsaken me," as I think that he too felt that absence and emptiness of the spiritual inner-self. Yet equally so, I truly believe that I did not actually lose anything—but I gained a new and "more enlightened" perspective of what this thing we call "God" is, and more importantly, whereas before I could only wonder if there was life after "death," I am now unequivocally convinced that not only is there "life" after mortal death—but that we "lived" before this mortal existence. Our "personal" God is a reflection of our spiritual selfishness and as long as we want to possess it then we are limited in our growth and perception of collectiveness.

15

Life's Losers

Two hours after receiving a fax message saying that this book had been accepted for publication in the United States, I learned that one of its major contributors, Walter Correll, had been executed that day—January 4, 1996—in Virginia.

Walter was typical of many Death Row prisoners. He was convicted of a shocking offense, reviled by the community, and regarded by the legal system as having no redeeming qualities. But, as these pages have shown, this same man was capable of writing with great sensitivity and insight about his fellow prisoners. His long years in prison had seen the emergence of all sorts of qualities previously dormant or suppressed in his tearaway existence, centered as it was around toughness and terror. This is the man who was bounced on his head on his sixth birthday until he bled, and who would often wander the streets at night with his mother out of fear of his drunken father. By his own admission Walter grew up wild and disoriented. As related in Chapter 2, "Killing Our Mistakes," and Chapter 3, "Society's Debt—and Society's Response," he gradually became involved in at first petty and later more serious crime. Then, like so many, he started drinking and taking drugs and became caught up in the drug underworld. Again like so many others, he arrived on Death Row young, traumatized, and with little sense of his own identity.

Not all prisoners rise above their circumstances and manage to make something of their lives in the most improbable of circumstances. The extraordinary thing—as their letters show—is that so many of them do.

Through the letters we obtain a vivid glimpse of what could be done if they were treated as individuals of potential worth—something that many of them have never experienced in their lives.

The strains, however, are enormous. In early 1990 I received a letter from Sam Johnson on Death Row in Mississippi. It was the first letter I had received from him in two months. Before then he had been writing once a week for the past two years. In his letter Sam wrote:

"I'm still not completely out of that pit of blackness I was in to but I'm at a level now where light shines upon me and I am able to see. A conglomeration of things helped to take me to the brink of insanity. At that time I withdrew into what I thought was myself but, later, found out that I had withdrawn (or was taken by all I was experiencing) far beyond myself into depths I pray I never enter into again in my life. Hell, I felt and thought at that time, was a penthouse apartment a thousand stories above me in comparison to where I was."

At that point Sam had been on Death Row for eight years. For the first time I began to wonder whether the inhuman system of leaving people to rot for ten, twelve, or even fifteen years before killing (or releasing) them might be destroying even this remarkable man. Here is a person who reads medieval mystical tracts and the Upanishads, corresponds with at least twenty people in England and Holland, and has displayed extraordinary resilience and inner resources—especially if, as he steadfastly maintains, he is innocent.

Sam came off Death Row in late 1992 when his sentence (but not his conviction) was overturned. He had spent eleven long, dark years under constant threat of death. But Sam was still something of a new boy. John Irving—one of the other two prisoners to whom I originally wrote—had his sentence overturned in November 1995 at the age of thirty-nine, having spent nineteen years on Death Row—his entire adult life. There are others on Death Row now who have been there for twenty years.

What this means is that these men are punished not once but three times. Often, they serve the equivalent of a life sentence with parole. This they do in appalling circumstances, under the constant threat of death, which leaves some of them talking to their toilet bowls, braying like donkeys, or sedated into doing the Thorazine Shuffle. And finally they are executed.

When Britain still had capital punishment, there was a convention that executions had to be carried out within ninety days of passing sentence, or the death penalty would automatically lapse. It was felt that to leave people waiting for execution any longer than that was inhuman and inhumane. In the United States many prisoners have been on Death Row eighty times longer than that.

The reason so many prisoners spend such inordinate periods on Death Row in the United States is the elaborate (though still deficient) system of appeals. Cut the number and length of appeals, and the number of wrongful executions is bound to rise. The need for exhaustive appeal, however, does introduce an inherent and insuperable flaw in the death penalty. Capital punishment cannot be both swift and just. If an execution is swift, justice cannot be ensured. And if an execution is not swift, it cannot be humane. The Eighth Amendment to the United States Constitution rules out "cruel and unusual punishment." But how can years and years on Death Row be classed as anything other than cruel and unusual punishment? No matter what a person may have done, we can no longer regard ourselves as a civilized society if we imprison people like penned animals for periods, typically, of three thousand days, serve formal notice on them during that period some five or six times that they are going to die on a set date, and sometimes reprieve them within hours of the appointed time before finally proceeding to the macabre, ritualistic execution.

One of the less-well-known facts about Death Row is that many of those condemned to die come off Death Row. Since the death penalty was brought back in the United States in 1976, 4,700 men and women come onto Death Row. Of those, about 7 percent have been executed. And of those 4,700, 1,600 have had their convictions or sentences overturned. In other words, the state is saying in 30 percent of all cases (a figure that is bound to rise further), "We got it wrong."

Whatever our instinctive reactions may be to the crimes these men and women have committed, the fact is—as I hope this book illustrates—that many of them have a great deal to offer and that they can plumb extraordinary depths of human emotion. As the letter from Mike Lambrix reprinted in Chapter 14, "Religion," shows, some of the prisoners embark on a spiritual journey in which they touch depths far beyond ordinary experience.

The most unexpected thing for many of the pen-friends has been to discover how reciprocal the relationship can be and how much they themselves get out of it. People initially prompted to write out of compassion or indignation at the death penalty rapidly find that they get just as much out of the correspondence as the prisoners. This of course varies—the prisoner's anger can get in the way, the correspondence can become sexually charged, unreasonable demands for money can be made, or differences can arise as in any relationship—but when the correspondence goes well, as it so often does, the pen-friends can find the relationship one of the most important things in their lives.

Nearly all the prisoners are male, and most of the British correspondents—85 percent—are female. The combination of needy, intensely deprived men and compassionate women is obviously a potentially explosive one. LifeLines goes to special lengths to warn prospective female letter writers that the organization is not a dating agency and that the prisoners may "come on strong" in their letters. For many of the prisoners, the experience of "straight" friendship with a woman is a new one. Difficulties in forming relationships with the opposite sex are often an integral part of their stories, and they may feel they have to be macho and overtly sexual in order to prove themselves. One woman wrote back that there was no need for the prisoner to do this, but that she accepted him as he was. He wrote back saying that no woman had ever said this to him before.

Romantic problems are, unquestionably, one of the biggest difficulties that female correspondents suffer. Some enter the correspondence looking for love—consciously or unconsciously, only discovering their real agenda as they go along—but to most women, the men's attentions are unwelcome. Time and again, women have found that if they can hold firm at this point, the two can then work through distorted and unrealistic romantic feelings and fantasies to reach the clearer waters of genuine friendship: something that many of the men say they have never experienced before, and something that they come to regard as one of the most valuable things in their lives.

At the same time, there are also women who succumb to the strength of feelings expressed in the letters. In some, I would say fairly rare, cases, the feelings may be mutual and genuine. In other cases, the relationship comes unstuck—sometimes with devastating consequences for the prisoner. One thirty-four-year-old man in Florida became engaged to an American woman who had begun writing to him. When he lost a critical appeal, the woman backed out. Although it is impossible to establish a direct connection, three months later the prisoner had a heart attack.

To survive with one's sanity intact after ten or fifteen years on Death Row calls for very special qualities. To those fortunate to be in contact with such men, it is an unforgettable demonstration of the triumph of the human spirit in adversity. Quite apart from surviving the experience of waking daily for a decade or more with the knowledge that the state is trying to take their lives, these men must also come to terms with the appalling reality of their crimes. In many cases, that means a highly painful acknowledgment of shortcomings, facing the consequences of their deeds, remorse, and, for most, looking back over a childhood of intense pain and deprivation.

The pervasive attitude among the authorities, however, appears to be that Death Row is an end-station in which there is little if any room for humanitarian treatment. At one (primitive and retributive) level, this may be understandable, but one third to one half of those on Death Row eventually have their sentences overturned, while the punishment they are in for is execution, not imprisonment.

Given the fact that so many do eventually get off Death Row, there is, surely, an overwhelming humanitarian and practical case for permitting them to make something of their lives. In Texas, at least, there is a work program. Participants are able to work in better surroundings, mix as groups, and pursue courses of education and Bible study. The work, however, is unpaid, and many of the inmates take the view that participation in the work program and stitching guards' uniforms means selling out to the authorities.

In a number of states, including Texas and Mississippi, prisoners are limited to six books and magazines. This makes it impossible for an inmate to undertake a serious course of study. In addition, many of them conduct their own legal appeals but are denied permanent access to the law books they need in order to fight for their lives. The United Nations Standard Minimum Rules for the Treatment of Prisoners, to which the United States is a signatory, are ignored or violated at every turn. Never mind the leg irons, lack of ventilation, and denial of religious services, the men are regarded as trash, failures in a throw-away society. In some prisons—such as in Mississippi—obtaining medical or dental treatment can be inordinately protracted; if a tooth hurts, it is pulled, not filled. In summer, the cells are so hot that the men have to lie on the cement floor to obtain any relief. Little if any cool water is provided in the heat of summer. In winter, they are extremely cold. The men are shackled the moment they leave their cells.

No effort is made to help prisoners cope with the appalling stresses of coming to terms with their crimes and of spending years under the threat of execution. Apart from those who are innocent and eventually have their convictions overturned, many of those on Death Row are there because of a single act of uncontrolled behavior. Many go through agonies of remorse or denial, have no means of making amends, and far from being given any hope are humiliated and brutalized.

Numerous inmates in their thirties have spent their entire adult lives on Death Row. They are subjected to an existence that is, as they put it, "hell." The treatment they receive does nothing but breed anger, hate, depression, and violence. If released or transferred to different custody, they face their new lives without any preparation whatever.

The taking of life by the state is a brutalizing act that creates a climate of intimidation and callous indifference toward life. There are even recorded instances of disturbed individuals who developed a bizarre fascination with execution in childhood, later committing atrocities that enabled them to live out their fantasy of being strapped into the electric chair.

The death penalty is part of a climate of violence in which gun control is regarded as a fundamental violation of human rights and the violence and alienation that individuals suffered in childhood are met with the ultimate violence of execution. From this treatment by society of those utterly at its mercy it is but a short step to the human rights violations in the form of state torture that are so widely condemned by the civilized world, including the United States.

The main argument generally advanced in favor of the death penalty is deterrence. The United States provides a particularly effective test case for the deterrent argument, because there are neighboring states with and without the death penalty. If anything, the evidence suggests higher homicide rates in states that have the death penalty.

It is no accident that most of the executing states are in the South. If you shade in the executing states on a map of the United States, you will have the old Confederacy—the states where slavery was practiced, where blacks were generally held to be inherently inferior, and where black life was held cheap. True, whites may be executed in Louisiana and Georgia too, and Missouri and Illinois are now among the main executing states. But the motivation for the death penalty, and the willingness to use it, surely has some of its origins in the expendability of life in the former slave states and in white solidarity.

The death penalty is not just cruel and unusual punishment. It drags down all concerned. Not only the prisoners but also the guards, the legal authorities, and even members of the clergy are forced to adopt a hard, unfeeling veneer. On the day that Edward Earl Johnson was scheduled to be executed, BBC director Paul Hamann—who had been profoundly affected by the gentleness and dignity of the man whose last days he was filming—was asked jovially by one of the prison chaplains if he would like to join him for some target practice on the prison's pistol range.

Nor does the death penalty take any account of the devastating effect on the prisoner's family. This became painfully apparent to the British public in April 1995, when Nick Ingram was executed in Georgia. His British mother appealed to Prime Minister John Major and became a familiar face on Britain's television screens, her bewilderment and anguish evident to all.

At the LifeLines conference held in Edinburgh in May 1995 one of the main speakers was Betty Foster, the mother of Chris Burger, a juvenile offender executed in Georgia in December 1993. Betty had gone through a nightmare of seventeen years before her son was eventually executed. She recalled: "The last day at the prison with Chris was agony. We had about thirty visitors with him that day and we were told that we had until 3:30 P.M. to be with Chris. Chris spent time with us all individually, and when it came to my turn, Chris called me over and said, 'Mama, I'm sorry I wasn't the kind of son you could be proud of.' My heart went out to him," said Betty. "I said, 'Oh Chrissy (a name I called him when he was little), Chrissy, how could I not be proud of you. You've grown up in this place and you've grown into a kind, loving and compassionate young man. I'm so very proud of you."

In some instances, members of the victim's family become so dragged down by the degrading process that they, too, turn against the death penalty.

But what, it may justifiably be asked, about the victims and their families? Are we in LifeLines concentrating our energies on the wrong people?

The victim's family was a major topic when Sister Helen Prejean spoke to a LifeLines conference in 1992 about the two prisoners she had befriended on Louisiana's Death Row (since written up in *Dead Man Walking* and portrayed in the film of that name). In the United States there is now an organization called Murder Victims Families for Reconciliation. Its members are people who have lost loved ones to a heinous crime but who nevertheless have turned against the death penalty and seek to recognize the murderers as people with a story to tell.

I remember a woman in Ireland who was writing to a prisoner, also in Georgia, who was deeply troubled by what he had done and asked her whether he should write to the victim's parents for forgiveness. He wished to do so, but was held back by the fear of rejection—which had been such a big theme in his life. Slowly and prayerfully, she—an Irish Catholic—persuaded her Southern Baptist friend to take the risk. He wrote. By return mail he received a letter saying that the parents understood and forgave him.

Within LifeLines, one of our members, Lesley Moreland, asked if she could write to a prisoner on Death Row after her own twenty-three-year-old daughter, Ruth, had been murdered. Lesley came to a crossroads in her life. As she saw it, she had three options: to commit suicide to avoid the pain, to go under and be a perpetual victim, or to go on and strive to live positively. She decided to write to someone on Death Row because she felt the need to hold on to the difference between the act of murder and the whole person. In writing to someone on Death Row, she hoped she would stay in touch with the whole person. The man in Texas to whom she wrote happened to have lost his own mother in a murder; Lesley has been to Texas to meet him and his family. After years of discreet and patient negotiation, Lesley eventually managed in 1995 to visit in prison the young man who had murdered her daughter.

Equally as remarkable is the story of Leanne, another LifeLines member. While a teenager, Leanne was raped and stabbed by an attacker in a park, who then tried to hang her from the rafters in a park shelter but wasn't strong enough to hold her up. During the long, anguished night that followed, she managed to talk to her attacker and perhaps got to know him better in that short time than many other people who had encountered him in his short, confused life. "I'm not sure exactly when I was stabbed," Leanne recalled, "but he declared his intention to kill me somehow. I do believe, however, that he *let* me escape a last struggle." To this day she feels forgiveness and hopes that he has overcome his anger, although she knows that he has gone on to rape again. She too is writing to a prisoner under sentence of death.

What has the correspondence revealed about the men and women we write to? As expected, many of those on Death Row are deeply disturbed or retarded. Many are unable to enter into, let alone sustain, a correspondence; illiteracy, sexual distortions, and intense hate and anger get in the way. Some of these people can hardly be said to bear real responsibility for their actions, and society must certainly be protected from such people. But surely they require skilled psychiatric care and should not be on Death Row at all. Most countries stopped executing the mad in the nineteenth century. Death Row lawyers estimate that as many as a third of the inmates are mentally retarded. Lawyers also note that a high proportion of Death Row prisoners have some form of brain damage resulting from hereditary or congenital causes or from a blow to the head.

Brain scans have revealed significant differences (especially with respect to the limbic system) between criminals suffering from Attention Deficit Disorder and the general population. Experiments with animals have shown that stress in the early stages of life affects chemicals in the brain that inhibit or regulate aggression. Especially in children, a good deal of evidence suggests a link among diet and hyperactivity and antisocial behavior. Our understanding of the physiology of criminal behavior is still in its infancy; it may be that in a generation or so we will look back in horror at the way criminals were dealt with in the twentieth century.

We also know very little about the role of gender. However, the overwhelming majority of prisoners we write to are male. Of all the factors associated with the death penalty, none correlates more closely than "maleness": 98.5 percent of those on Death Row are men. But this is not something we look at seriously. Many of the women letter writers have felt the full weight of disordered "maleness" in their correspondence with the prisoners.

Then there are those whom we might term "conditioned": men whose values have been warped by their upbringing or what they have been through. Several prisoners have described in these pages how they became desensitized as children to violence between their parents. Similarly, a Vietnam War veteran wrote to his pen-friend, "But the same rules apply to me now as they did in 1966 in a place over 10,000 miles from the Mississippi State Penitentiary. Don't get too close. Don't let them hurt you by taking someone with whom you have more than a casual relationship. They are trying hard enough to kill me. I'll not let them do it slowly, a piece at a time, by being overly affected each time they kill somebody in the name of the Law."

To some, unfeeling violence and brutality can become an accepted way of life. Their carapace is not merely hard but very thick, so that the real self lying below is almost impossible to find. Such men (and women) tend to be cold, calculating, and apparently lacking in remorse. But they are not found only on Death Row. To varying degrees, they are to be found throughout society: on the white South African right, among soccer hooligans and neighborhood gangs, among the prison guards and police who smile while torturing "dissidents" in Indonesia or Somalia, and indeed among the forces of law and order in any country. In Rwanda and Bosnia we have seen that people formerly leading peaceable lives can commit unspeakable atrocities in huge numbers.

The staggering cruelty that "ordinary" people can display shows, surely, that those on Death Row are not a separate subspecies but that the monster lurks in us all. There are many recorded cases of notorious criminals who turn their lives around against all expectations, and the correspondence in these pages shows the trapped potential of many of those whom the state has condemned as worthless and beyond redemption.

Most of all, perhaps, the correspondence shows the men to be life's losers: those who have been thrown out of stride by life. This surely is the ultimate infamy, when those dealt a losing hand in life strike out desperately and are coldly executed in retaliation. A great many of the prisoners in this book fall into this category. Nothing brings this out more graphically than the observation made by a California Death Row attorney, Jay Pultz, at the LifeLines conference held in Darlington, England, in 1994. One of Pultz's clients told him that he was one of six boys from the same urban kindergarten class who had all ended up on Death Row. We are, surely, dealing here not with individual criminal pathology but with a social phenomenon. And although it is true that not all children from grim backgrounds end up as murderers and that not all murderers had grim childhoods, the intense pain and deprivation in childhood that comes through in the letters as the prisoners come to trust their pen-friends is a recurrent and striking aspect of the correspondence. Not only are they life's losers; they also end up losing their lives.

The correspondence also indicates that many of the men are where they are as a result of a temporary loss of control. Some have committed crimes of passion; others have committed crimes while under the influence of alcohol or narcotic drugs. In short, these people acted out of character; something went hideously wrong. It is my impression that this is true of many of the men on Death Row and is the reason why they so frequently protest their "innocence," in the sense that the crime was unintended and unpremeditated. One man wrote plaintively, "My brother-in-law has just been given a 9-months suspended sentence for a drunk-driving accident in which a person was killed. I also committed a drugs-related offense, but am here for my life. What's the difference?"

In the end, it comes down to a simple question: either the men and women on Death Row bear moral responsibility for their deeds or they do not. If they do not—because of brain damage or mental disorder, for example—the state has no business executing them. If they do bear moral responsibility, we are saying that they are one of us, have choices, and are capable of change. To execute such people is to my mind a doctrine of despair.

As we review history, we can see the progressive abolition of the death penalty with the advance of civilization. Apart from Japan, where the death penalty is barely used, the United States is now the last advanced country in the world to use the death penalty. The United States is certainly in no position to take the high moral ground about executions in, say, China. The way in which a society treats those most at its mercy is surely the ultimate touchstone of civilization.

The death penalty in the United States is not administered with compassion. It is administered vindictively, with pleasure and hate. People are encouraged to turn off their electric appliances before an execution to boost the voltage for the electric chair, and we have had the desperately sick spectacle of "Fry Ted Bundy" barbecues to celebrate an execution.

Which brings me back to where the correspondence and LifeLines started. Some of the truest compassion I have encountered in my contact with Death Row has come from the least expected source: the prisoners themselves. It is the Sam Johnsons of this world, deprived often of a decade or more of their lives and cast aside as the scum of the scum, who can see the worthwhile qualities of their fellow human beings on Death Row. It is they who can see that those administering the executions are the victims of a set of values equally as warped as those that led to murder in the first place. It is they who can feel compassion for those strapping them into the electric chair, while hating their deeds.

Writing to a Death Row Prisoner

LifeLines may be reached at this address:
96 Fallowfield
Cambridge CB4 1PF
England

The comparable organization in the United States is the Death Row Support Project. Founded in 1978, it facilitates correspondence between interested persons and prisoners sentenced to death. To request the name and address of someone on Death Row, write to:

Death Row Support Project
P.O. Box 600
Liberty Mills, IN 46946

16

In the Belly of the Beast

By Oconga Osuwo Omutu

In 1991 I entered the Oklahoma prison system. It was my first ordeal of imprisonment. I was nineteen years old and I had a sentence of death.

From the assessment and reception center at Lexington, I was sent to the Oklahoma State Penitentiary. I was transported on the prison bus, locked in handcuffs, waist chains, and shackles.

The Oklahoma State Penitentiary was the oldest prison in the state. Made of white stone and surrounded by huge walls that were buttressed with gun towers, it was an old, fortress-style prison. Throughout its history, it had gained notoriety for its crude indignities, rapes, beatings, knifings, and killings.

Death Row was in the F-Cell House. It was in that section of the old cell house where the condemned prisoners spent their last years, counting down their lives as they awaited the executioner's needle.

My Death Row cell was small. It had a barred and wire-meshed window, two metal bunks, two metal lockers, a desk, a stool, a sink, and a toilet unit that reeked with noisome fumes of bile, urine, and defecation. Etched into the walls were the names, numbers, and epigrams of prisoners who had been confined in the cell at one time or another. The front of the cell was made entirely of bars.

Death Row was a type of hell. On my first night, I listened to the noise, discordant voices, and screams of prisoners with disintegrating sanity. They were the harsh, jarring sounds of the damned. And I had joined them.

I had been sent to Death Row for a capital crime in 1990 when I was eighteen—a case of first-degree murder that had transpired during a botched robbery.

On Death Row, I hated the zoo-like existence of confinement, the regulation of time, and the inability to move at will. I hated being locked inside a cell for twenty-three hours a day and being fed through a "bean-hole." I hated the bunk that owned too much of my nights and days. I hated the inability to escape the cacophony of blaring radios and televisions, hollering prisoners, rattling keys, and clanging doors. I hated the lack of privacy and the tensions that erupted between prisoners who had not chosen to be confined together. I hated being strip-searched, manacled, and shackled. I hated the lack of control over my environment. I hated the pettiness and arbitrariness of prison discipline. And I hated the uncertainty of whether I was going to live or die. It made me feel dehumanized, mortified, and powerless. These feelings left me angry and easily agitated.

As I endured life on Death Row, I was often defiant with guards and fought with other prisoners on the yard. As a result, I received disciplinary infractions. I was sent to solitary confinement, lost my canteen privileges, my phone privileges, and my visitation rights.

Although I could not listen to a radio, watch television, purchase from the canteen, use the phone, or receive visits in solitary confinement, I did not find being there too terrible. I actually enjoyed the solitude that it afforded me. I liked being in a cell by myself. In solitary, I did not have to be locked in a cell day and night with another prisoner, be bothered or disturbed by another prisoner, put up with the mood swings of another prisoner, or deal with the interpersonal strife and hostility that arose when two prisoners who were incompatible were forced to coexist in a small, cramped cell. Instead, I was by myself, alone with my thoughts, memories, dreams, nightmares, anger, frustration, and pain. I spent most of my time in solitary exercising, writing letters, and reading the books that other prisoners had left in the cell. The books that I found were all novels, but I read them to pass the time. I even read some of the horror novels of Stephen King.

While I was in solitary confinement, some of the Christian missionaries who came to the prison to preach the gospel of Christ to the lost souls who were confined there would stop by my cell. They would talk to me about Christ and tell me how he was the son of God, who was the savior of mankind. They also offered me a Bible and encouraged me to accept Christ as my Lord and personal savior. Aware of my status as a condemned prisoner, they would tell me that Christ was the only one who could save me, but I did not believe this. I was skeptical about the existence of God and could not put any faith in religion, or give credence to religious notions. I wondered how he could save me when he could not even save himself.

One day after I had finished one of my stints in solitary confinement, a fellow prisoner lent me a book. It was not a novel, as were all the other books that I had read since I had come to prison. The title was *Soul on Ice,* by Eldridge Cleaver. I had never heard of him.

From his cell at Folsom, Cleaver had penned a collection of letters, vignettes, essays, and monologues. *Soul on Ice* was his memoir. In those pages, he bared his soul and revealed the tyrannies, inequalities, brutalities, and hypocrisies of the American system, and the psychological and cultural malaise and oppression that African people endured in America.

The period of time *Soul on Ice* covered was the turbulent sixties. Social upheaval gripped America and its ulcers were exposed like open sores on pale skin. The year in particular was 1965. In that year the Civil Rights Movement was at its apex, Malcolm X was assassinated, Watts erupted into the largest, most violent ghetto uprising since the Civil War, and America was escalating its war in Vietnam.

I identified strongly with Cleaver. I came from the world of the inner city as he did, and my experiences as a youth were similar to his own. Like him, I had been an outcast in American society, and I too had been alienated from the American system. The same circumstances that had led him to prison had led me there as well.

In *Soul on Ice* Cleaver spoke about the meaning that Malcolm X had to Africans who languished within the bowels of America's prison system, and how African prisoners viewed themselves and their imprisonment. I was deeply impressed by this particular passage:

Malcolm X had a special meaning for black convicts. A former prisoner himself, he had risen from the lowest depths to great heights. For this reason he was a symbol of hope, a model for thousands of black convicts who found themselves trapped in the vicious PPP cycle: Prison-Parole-Prison. One thing that the judges, police-men and administrators of prisons seem never to have understood, and for which they certainly do not make any allowances, is that Negro convicts, rather than see themselves as criminals and perpe-trators of misdeeds, look upon themselves as prisoners of war, the victims of a vicious dog-eat-dog social system that is so heinous as to cancel out their own malefactions: in the jungle there is no right or wrong.

Rather than owing and paying a debt to society, Negro prisoners feel that they are being abused, that their imprisonment is simply another form of the oppression which they have known all their lives. Negro inmates feel that they are being robbed, that it is "soci-ety" that owes them, that should be paying them, a debt. [p. 64]

For me *Soul on Ice* marked a turning point in my life. It was the first serious book that I had ever read. After reading it, I began to look at myself with a critical and analytical eye. For the first time, I saw myself for the delinquent that I was. I knew then that I had to turn over a new leaf. I was in prison with nothing but time. I knew that I had to use it constructively, as Cleaver had—use it to educate myself, discipline myself, and change myself as he had done.

In the days, weeks, and months that passed, I spent a good deal of time reading. *Soul on Ice* awakened in me a deep need to know more about the history of African people in America. I read everything I could get my hands on about it. In Lerone Bennett Jr.'s *Before the Mayflower: A History of Black America* and John Hope Franklin's *From Slavery to Freedom: A History of African Americans,* I found complete accounts of Africans in America. I also gained important insights into the African experience in America through Manning Mar-able's *How Capitalism Underdeveloped Black America: Problems in Race, Political Economy, and Society; Race, Reform and Rebellion: The Second Reconstruction in Black America, 1945–1982; From the Grassroots: Essays Toward Afro-American Liberation,* and *Blackwa-ter: Historical Studies in Race, Class Consciousness, and Revolution.*

I became acquainted with the term *colonialism,* a system under which one people dominates another people. The first book I read that described the colonial experience of African people in America was Omali Yeshitela's *Colonialism: The Main Problem Confronting Africans in the U.S.* From reading the history of African people in America, I knew that this description was accurate.

One of the periodicals that I read was *The Burning Spear.* Avidly I read its analysis of the contemporary colonial situation of African people in America, articles exposing American colonialism, accounts of the Civil Rights Movement and the Black Liberation Movement, and the counterinsurgency that the FBI launched against them under the acronym of COINTELPRO [FBI counterintelligence programs against political dissidents]. I also read the speeches of Omali Yeshitela that appeared in its pages, fiery speeches in which he passionately denounced colonialism and capitalism.

While I was beginning to understand my station in American society and my relation to the American system for the first time, a rebellion occurred in South Central Los Angeles. It caused me to think more and more about the inner-city hell of poverty, squalid housing, shattered hopes, and deferred dreams from which I came, the wretchedness of inner-city life, and the cold destruction of the human spirit. After the Los Angeles policemen who had nearly beaten Rodney King to death were acquitted in 1992, South Central erupted into the largest, most violent ghetto uprising since Watts. It was a spontaneous rebellion that revealed the extent of the anger and rage that had been simmering in the inner city.

During this period I read the works of Karl Marx, Frederick Engels, V. I. Lenin, Antonio Gramsci, Mao Zedong, Fidel Castro, and Che Guevara. I also read Albert Memmi, Frantz Fanon, Kwame Nkrumah, Amilcar Cabral, George Padmore, and C. L. R. James. I deepened my knowledge of capitalism, socialism, communism, imperialism, neo-colonialism, and racism, and heightened my awareness of social and economic injustices and national oppression.

As I further pursued my studies, I read the works of Howard Zinn, Noam Chomsky, Edward Herman, Ward Churchill, Angela Davis, and bell hooks, which acquainted me with alternative viewpoints and dissident politics. They also provided keen insights into the dynamics of class, race, and gender and the role that they played in capitalism, imperialism, colonialism, racism, and sexism.

Sometime later I reread *Soul on Ice*. This time I read it with an under-standing of American society and the American system, and an aware-ness of American colonialism and capitalism that I did not have the first time. This time I read it with consciousness of my subjugated status and the colonial status quo. And this time I read it with hindsight and knowledge of what had befallen and become of not only Eldridge Cleaver, but also Fred Hampton, Mark Clark, Jonathan Jackson, George Jackson, Geronimo Pratt, Assata Shakur, Sundiata Acoli, Huey P. Newton, and other leaders and members of the Back Panther Party and the Black Liberation Army.

After rereading *Soul on Ice* I reflected upon the milieu from which my generation had emerged. It was the post–Civil Rights era. Many of the most prominent leaders and the most eloquent spokesmen and spokeswomen of the Civil Rights Movement and the Black Liberation Movement were dead, in prison, or in exile. The causes to which they had dedicated their lives and for which they had put their lives on the line were disrupted and destroyed by colonialism's counterinsurgency. All that remained was a burgeoning middle class that clung tenaciously to their belief in the American dream, a coterie of petty bourgeois civil rights leaders who believed that America was on the road to being color-blind, and a superfluous underclass that was struggling at the periphery of American society. They were living and dying in poverty in America's inner cities, where underclass youth were consumed by drugs, alcohol, and crime, plagued by ignorance, parochialism, nihil-ism, and fatalism, and destined for cells in the penitentiary or graves in the cemetery.

Around this time I began to write. Sitting at the desk in my cell, I would put my thoughts and feelings down on paper and articulate my experiences as best I could. If I could not do anything else in prison, I could write and I could speak my mind, without reservation, circumlo-cution, or equivocation, regardless of whether anyone agreed with what I had to say.

As I looked out at America from my cell, I saw a land that was riven by a centuries-old dichotomy and structures of domination, power, control, privilege, wealth, and ownership that had been created by set-tler colonialism. I watched certain gains of the Civil Rights Movement being rescinded in a right-wing backlash. I listened to the inane cries of "reverse racism" that the settlers were uttering even as they showed a supercilious disregard for the baleful effects of the racism that was the sine qua non of the system on which their entire way of life was based. I watched the right-wing wave of conservatism that was sweeping over the empire as the "GOP Revolution" triumphed, and I heard the GOP's bold talk of a "Contract with America." I watched the crime-baiting and anti-crime fear mongering of right-wing politicians who used the canard of crime and punishment to win elections, and I listened to all of the rhetoric of law and order. And I watched the machinations of the foreign policy of the Clinton administration and the interventions of American imperialism in the Third World. I decided to focus some of my writings on America's most intransigent problem—colonialism and the relationship between the colonizer and the colonized.

In the midst of a cruel era of social vengeance, I listened to the clamor for capital punishment and I watched the severe limits that were imposed on the appeals of prisoners on Death Row. I also heard all the calls to speed up executions, and I watched as the rate of executions increased throughout America. Under the Clinton-Gingrich scheme, I watched as the stakes for the condemned got higher and higher, and the prospect of execution became greater.

The horror of Death Row was the specter of execution. It was the ghost that haunted every condemned prisoner. It was an act that would bring the life of a condemned prisoner to an end, and end whatever dreams, aspirations, and ambitions he or she may have had in life. Few condemned prisoners wanted to be executed. Most of them wanted desperately to live. Even though they awaited execution, there was always hope, hope that was based on the possibility that they would receive a favorable ruling on their appeals that would result in the reversal of their death sentence. It was this hope that sustained them from one year to the next as they lived under the threat of execution on Death Row.

Awaiting execution on Death Row as I did, I lived for the day when I would receive the news that my death sentence had been reversed. I did not know if that day would ever come, but I knew that there was a possibility that it could come with a favorable ruling on my appeal. That day came in 1999. Eight years after I had come to Death Row, I received news that my death sentence had been overturned by the appeals court. It was the best news I had received since I first came to Death Row.

In 2000, I was resentenced to life in prison without parole. As a lifer, I reflected upon the harsh mandatory sentences, "lock 'em up and throw away the key" media campaigns, "three strikes and you're out" laws, and new death penalty statutes that were part of America's frenzied and brutal lock-up binge. I also reflected upon the proliferation of "super-max" prisons, designed to house the "worst of the worst." I recalled the abandonment of any pretense of rehabilitation in a prison system that was the dumping ground for racial subjugation and capitalism's social wreckage and social dynamite.

Although I was to live out the remainder of my life in prison, I did not resign myself to that fate any more than I resigned myself to the ill fate of the condemned. As long as I was alive, I knew that there was a possibility that I would one day regain my freedom, just as I knew that as long as African people struggled, we would one day wrench ourselves free of the yoke of colonialism, and achieve self-determination.

In the bowels of Oklahoma's prison system I resolved to live my life to the fullest of my capability, making the most of each day, progressing in my personal development, moving forward with my eyes on the prize, and looking to the future with all of its uncertainties, potentialities, and possibilities.

17

Scraping Away Hope, Faith, and Dreams

This chapter deals with the effects of long-term imprisonment at a time when prison conditions have unquestionably become more severe. This has involved not just the construction of maximum-security units where prisoners live in extreme isolation and sometimes underground, without any natural lighting, but also the progressive whittling away of "privileges."
James Tucker in South Carolina summarized this in August 2003.

Prison is a milieu of mental torture, mind-numbing boredom, substandard health care, deficient diet, frustration, degradation, neuroses, psychoses, and attempts to create a homogeneous population to avoid individuality. Where policies and rules are created based on the lowest denominator of a paranoid view of "worst-case scenarios," and where the innocent and guilty are damned alike. In an era of failing state economies, prison systems are bankrupt: fiscally bankrupt, morally bankrupt, and humanely bankrupt.

Prison conditions have fallen into impoverished squalor. The first victim of the budget guillotining was "support services." This encompasses food service, medical service, education and religious programs, work programs, mail service, visitation, libraries, hobby crafts, canteens, commissaries, and janitorial and indigent supplies, etc. All these were maximally reduced or eliminated entirely. These losses created an environment of mental stagnation. The loss of jobs exacerbates this mental deterioration. Add to all this the stress of dealing with indolent, bungling, lying bureaucratic prison personnel deluded into a mass-punishment mentality, and the prison environment is a mental masochist's utopia.

I could fill a tome with the inanity and insanity that is prison. Suffice it to say that prison life is not "life" at all; it is mere "existence."

Daryl Wheatfall (Texas) wrote of the humiliation and degradation in 2002:

It is here I explore these bewitching and terrifying conditions and experiences, where prisoners are treated and fed like wild animals living in a zoo. Confined to your cage twenty-three and twenty-four hours a day, self-respect quickly dissipates when you are forced to strip naked in front of a female officer any time you have to leave your cage. Many female guards are out to prove to their male co-workers that they are tough enough and can be resilient working with prisoners. At times female guards insult prisoners during their strip-searches.

Prisoners are always handcuffed before leaving their cages. What truly makes you feel low is when a dog leash is applied to the cuffs before they are placed on you, to restrict your movement as the cuffs are being applied and removed. Yes! One does feel as if one is a dog on a leash, not a human being, just another wild animal. Try to visualize the brutal beatings so many prisoners are forced to endure at the hands of corrupt officials. You see, in these guards' eyes, this is the only way to treat wild animals.

The U.S. Supreme Court brought back the death penalty in 1976. Considerable numbers of prisoners have now been on Death Row for more than a quarter of a century. Others come off Death Row to face life without parole.

In 2003, when he had been on Death Row in San Quentin, California, for twenty-one years, Anthony Ross wrote of how he had come to terms with long-term imprisonment.

"The DA's offering you a deal—life without the possibility of parole. Trust me, it beats a death sentence."

My trial lawyer spoke those words to me right before my trial began.

The jerk had a stupid smirk on his face like he was doing me a personal favor. I could have broken his jaw for that. I remember the feeling of being trapped followed by a surge of anger that swelled up in my chest. It was at that moment I knew I was going to be found guilty. I glared at him saying, "What's the fuckin' difference?"

I cannot speak for everyone, but the Hobson's choice of execution or life without parole is a dilemma that plagued me for several years. I was twenty-two when I was sentenced to death and as far as I was concerned, life without freedom was not worth living. I would adamantly tell people that I would rather be executed than spend the rest of my life in a windowless cell. It was part bravado and part ignorance that fueled my stance. Later I found out it was also the sentiment of many death row prisoners. The specter of a lifetime behind 22-foot walls topped with razor wire and gun towers is something I didn't want my mind to adjust to. I mean, how the hell does someone do life without parole? How do I resist becoming one of the mechanical corpses I see walking around me every day? How do I combat the daily psychological abrasions of prison life? Abrasions that slowly scrape away your hope, faith, and dreams. These thoughts were an inseparable and ubiquitous part of the internal struggle I went through, and the only way I could legitimize what I felt was to detach myself from the emotions that made me vulnerable. I would become hollow and cold inside, erecting an impermeable barrier between myself and the outside world. I reasoned it was the only way for me to survive.

The first time I met my appeal attorney I told him that under no circumstances would I accept life without parole. I then demanded that he get me off Death Row within five years. I was dead serious. He looked at me the way a doctor looks at a patient who asks, "Am I gonna make it, Doc?" Okay, I admit I was a bit naive about the lengthy appeal process, but my heart was in the right place. Ultimately, time would temper my youthful fire and give me a more prudent perspective. My attorney just said, "I'll see what I can do."

The view that death is better than life in prison depends on how one thinks and feels about oneself. By its very function prison excludes us from the social community and attempts to impress upon us the notion that, in some qualitative way, we are subhuman. I, like many prisoners, internalized this psychology and began to resent not only society but myself as well. When I first came to Death Row, I was uneducated and unskilled and had absolutely no goals or vision. I didn't think I had anything of value to offer anyone. I did not think for a single moment that I could accomplish something positive. The pessimism, the diminishment of body and spirit, and the profound sense of repetition that is the miasmic environment of prison were all I could see and feel . . . and for a time, all I had to hold on to. Prison is violent and I'm not simply talking about the stabbings, the rapes, or the race wars. I'm talking about the violence of spending year after year in an area slightly bigger than an outhouse and the disturbing way in which the mind silently adapts to it. I spent ten years in the hole because I did not want to adapt, and it was in there that I decided to do something that would allow me to transcend my situation.

I would have never imagined becoming a writer but that's what happened. It was not something I consciously set out to do. Writing chose me. I was drawn to the acoustics of words and sentences in the same way a musician is drawn to sound. Reading opened my eyes and mind. It allowed me to travel and brought me in contact with information and knowledge I had never been exposed to. Writing became my medium of expression. Yet, in the beginning it was purely medicinal, like herbs taken to cure ailments. The effect was spiritual. I say spiritual because I immediately understood that it did not matter where I spent the remaining sum of my life; what mattered was what I did with it and how it would impact others. This inspired me to engage in life, not retreat from it. My present opinion about life without parole is that it does not have to mean life without choices, aspirations, love, hope, or commitment. It doesn't mean I have to oscillate between damning myself and hating others. I can construct a life that is worth living. A life that allows me to draw upon my creative and curative energy and be productive. There is no way I want to be locked in a cell for the rest of my life, but I do know that it happens that my life is not over. I have become a published writer, husband, a student of philosophy, an activist, and, most important, a better human being. This is the course I will maintain regardless of my fate.

To date I have spent twenty-one years on Death Row and during that time I have seen two men executed at their own request. I have seen nearly a dozen use suicide as a means to escape the suffocating reality of life behind bars. I've watched men—friends of mine—slip into insanity or multiple illusions that offer temporary respite from the vegetative and miserable existence of prison. And during this time I have grown up. I have made the alchemic transformation from street thug to a conscious, intelligent human being with a newfound intimacy for life and humanity. I realize that though I am separated from those I love, my life is not an island. It is deeply interconnected to others in a way I can neither ignore nor deny, and it belongs to them as much as it belongs to me. There are those who will choose death over life in prison. I cannot judge them. I know the difficulty of finding something meaningful and something that has the restorative power to sustain and nourish one's will inside hell. No one wants to be rendered invisible or insignificant while still breathing. I am one of those. I love life passionately even if all I have is but a sliver of it.

Another prisoner in San Quentin who sees a profound transformation in himself is Anthony Jones.

I look at my life and during these fifteen years that I have been incarcerated, I have changed dramatically. Some of you may think that a convict cannot change, but you would be wrong. I am speaking from my own experience, as someone who has made that transformation from a so-called "thug" who did not care about anyone or anything but himself to someone who has compassion in his heart for others— someone who does not want to see anyone else in a situation like mine. In the beginning of my incarceration, I did not want to do anything constructive, nor did I want to hear anything that anyone had to say that might help me. It's not that I knew everything (in fact, there is so much that I did not know, as I would soon find out), I was just comfortable being me.

I was not trying to change because my thoughts were "I am on Death Row, why should I better myself . . . they're gonna kill me anyway." So for the first few years, I ran around like a simpleton, being cantankerous toward everyone. A lot of people think that we (inmates) have no redeeming qualities, but believe me, that could not be further from the truth. The truth of the matter is, if a person feels as though no one cares about him, then he will not care about himself, let alone anyone else.

You know the saying "Each one, teach one." Well, a friend took the time to show me that regardless of my situation, I can still become a better person. Just because I am on Death Row does not mean that my life does not have meaning or does not matter.

Steve Champion, in San Quentin for more than twenty years, describes Death Row as "the decapitation of hope."

I absolutely do not want to be executed but, more important, I do not want to cling to life with paralyzing fear, or with mental scars that are so intense that I see the world only from a postmortem viewpoint. No, for me, life must register on a conscious level where I continue to exist as subject. I refuse to exist where denial or pretense is the only viable stimulus, and where avoiding the truth leads to an even darker prison.

Death Row can push its occupants to contemplate their own mortality. For most men here, including myself, it is the first time in our lives that we philosophically reflect on the profound question about death. This creates for many a continual influx of emotions that cannot be intellectually sorted out, and leaves some of us pulled and wrenched by inner conflict. I've seen guys become constantly engaged in psychological battles with their thoughts and avoid mental quietude for fear of what they will find, and an even greater fear of who they will meet. I've watched men impregnated with fear and despair isolate themselves in their cells and start living like recluses. They reject all contact with the outside and shun any association with other prisoners and guards. They begin sleeping most of the day, staying up all night, neglecting their hygiene, and talking to themselves. This mental deterioration leads a few of them to spend inordinate amounts of time trying to achieve the maximum level of escapism, which begins with self-mutilation, and ends with suicide.

Jason Walton, who has spent more than twenty years on Death Row in Florida, wrote of his struggle to survive in January 2003:

In a few days it will be my twentieth anniversary. Nothing to celebrate there other than being able to say that after twenty years I am still alive and well. It's not easy keeping the dogs of death at bay, as I have seen people come to this place after me, and they are no longer here, having been killed by the machine of revenge.

Strange how that happens, and over the years I have learned to keep to myself, not to get too close to anyone as it is always hard to have to watch them take a friend over there and kill him. I do have friends, it's just that we're not that close. Rather sad I have decided to choose that path, but I think it's best at this point.

A prisoner in Arizona wrote to his pen-friend in 2002:

This is far worse than death. I am here all alone in this box with nothing but my thoughts. Being without my TV has pushed my mind into over-drive. I am sorry, I shouldn't be laying all this on you. I am just in so much pain right now.

But do you know what it is like to be truly alone? I grew up lonely, but now I am alone. I'm alone in this cement box with the worst cell-mate. And that cellmate's name is silence. Silence is not what you want when you are alone in a box. And all the stress and pain is tearing me apart. Does this make any sense to you? I just want to say thank you for listening to my problems.

Walter Dye (Indiana), sentenced to death in January 1998, had his appeal upheld in June 2001 but faces the prospect of never being released.

Life without Parole (LWOP) is substituting one death sentence for another. It is wrong and immoral. LWOP is in fact death by imprisonment.

LWOP results in life without hope. It means living each day without the hope that the person can ever rejoin society. LWOP removes hope not only from the lives of prisoners, but also from their families, and assumes that people's acts and lives are irredeemable.

We have an imperfect system of justice. Life without parole or release makes no allowances for changed behavior, or for reconsideration of the gravity of the offense. It is as final as death itself. LWOP is used not only as an "alternative" to execution, but as an alternative to life sentences *with* the possibility of parole. LWOP is used as an excuse for harsher behavior by officials against those imprisoned by legitimizing their status as irredeemable persons. The U.S. keeps building prisons that are, in fact, special colonies of isolation and inhumanity. Yet those convicted of capital murder who are released at some point, for any of a variety of reasons, seldom become part of the penal system again. Everyone should be viewed as persons of worth and value and should be treated with dignity and respect, regardless of their circumstances in life, or how offensive their behavior to others has been.

Larry Hayes, who chose not to appeal further, wrote to his pen-friend, Carol Mullis, in September 2003 shortly before he was executed.

The absolutely craziest thing has come to light. The warden came to me to say a pastor from Florida had called him to say that he was adopted as an infant, had searched and found his birth mother, and that she had told him I am his father. Wow! The warden asked if I wanted to meet him, and of course I said yes. So, he is to visit me on Monday the 8th.

After the visit he wrote:

He is a very nice young man, and a devout Christian pastor. I am pleased to call him my son; our visit today was as if we had known each other all his life. A real treasure. He will visit again tomorrow (Tuesday) and half the day Wednesday. Till they take me to the death house.

The following are excerpts from the final letters written by Eddie Castro (Florida) to his pen-friend, Catherine Till, shortly before he was executed on December 7, 2000.

November 18, 2000

Death Watch! We reside on a short floor, just three cells—a guard sits twenty-four hours a day. November 30 will be phase II—no privacy. Oh well, they treat us exceptionally well. I like the fact that there is just Robert and I on this floor, it's peacefully quiet. I love being away from the madness of the floors. I love this peace!

Hopefully this will not upset you—I am ready for this. You know this is what I have been wanting. I believe sometimes it takes the death of a man to get his life right. No fears, no tears. It is either this or live in a box for the rest of my life.

November 26, 2000

So friend, I hope I have been a friend to you through the years. I have always kept my word to you, never attempted to use or abuse our relationship. I have respected you as I respect my family. I hope you've learned the good side of a man gone bad. If you discover there were lies in my initial letters of my past it was not intentional. I did not know you, so I wrote letters with embellished truths. I am the thief, killer thug the state convicted. Through your affection I have learned compassion again.

December 5, 2000

Phase II inmates are treated extra well—they don't want us upset. On our floor are three video cameras. Hidden microphones tape our every word. And when we go to visit or wherever, the entire prison is locked down. Very eerie! Thus far, I have received nothing but good treatment. I think the guards respect me because of my facing up to this with dignity and integrity.

Dearest Kate,   December 6, 2000

This is my sign-off letter. Tomorrow will be busy. I am writing because I want you to know that I was thinking of you to the very end. It has been an honor having you in my life. Take care of yourself and your daughters. I carry you and them in my heart to eternity. I really do love you. You're family to me as far as I am concerned.

Enclosed is the death warrant. I felt after all these years of writing you'd care to have it for adding to my letters. I stayed with you because I grew to love you and cherish your letters.

There will come a day when the U.S. will recognize that capital punishment isn't a deterrent for guys like me. They'll never realize how very sick I was, but then they never cared.

This Death Row belongs to convicts who cling to the skin of life, the ones who willingly surrender their pride so they may live in a box . . . this was never me. I leave this beast of a building a better man, a freed soul. I leave this abyss of darkness to those of darkened hearts.

The extent to which long-term incarceration under threat of death can defeat the will to live is shown in the following powerful account, written by Kevin Zimmerman when his scheduled execution on December 10, 2003, was postponed. He had then been on Death Row for thirteen years. He was eventually executed on January 21, 2004.

The Ride

At the end of my visits with loved ones on December 10, 2003, which was at noon (the day of my execution), the major said, "It's time, Zimmerman." For me, it was a welcomed blessing in my personal spiritual faith—a strength of peace, assurance, preparedness, and excitement for a journey into the promised land that humans are ever searching for here on earth described as utopia. Nevertheless, as this was to be genuine relief for me, it was chills to the bone for my family. Comforted in my assured peace, yes, but cringing at the thought of losing me. Feelings they could not hide.

Being handcuffed and taken back to Building 12, where Death Row is housed, I was strip-searched, electronically checked, and then given State-issued boxers, a jumper, and cloth slippers. A waist belt was put on me that had chains running down to the leg irons already in place while my hands were cuffed to the waist belt. With the wardens, captains, and several officers present, I was walked outside and put into a caged area in the back of a van. After official papers were exchanged and signed, the back gate of Building 12 was opened and we proceeded to the main prison's back gate. What seemed to be an hour was only minutes as we waited for front and back escorts to arrive with enough firepower for W.W. III and the quick ride to the Walls Unit in Huntsville, Texas.

Though I was chained like a dog and had to hear the remarks of self-righteous officers and their feelings/beliefs of me (and murderers in general), and what we all deserved, none of it bothered me at all. For I was in a zone no one could rob me of. So I thought!

As we traveled down the highway, my excitement of peace and joy increased and left me smiling as I saw people walking, sitting out on their porches, kids playing in their yards, adults getting into their cars to come and go as they pleased, etc. A sign of what was sure to be my physical release from a chain around my neck for more than sixteen years. An oppressed confinement where the label "Death Row" keeps you from earning privileges regardless of your behavior. Spiritually free, indeed. Yet a physical restraint that was rapidly coming to an end was every reason to smile for. So I thought!

Just like that the van was cruising through a narrow maze that came to an end deep within the prison where the death house was located. The back van door opened and then the cage door. I was helped out of the van with only three feet to the building door I'd enter to the hall of death. I remember looking up into the clear blue sky saying to myself, "Beautiful day." I then took a deep breath and walked into the death house—a hall of five or six cells, with one covered with a screen used for attorney/spiritual visits.

I was unshackled, strip-searched again (to make sure I didn't stop at a local U.S. Army Surplus store, I guess), to make sure nothing could be fashioned into a weapon since a key was no longer necessary. Ay, yes, once you're there you're treated like a human being with no chains, cuffs, or leg irons before they kill you. How courteous of them.

I was then fingerprinted to make sure I was the right Kevin Zimmerman because what a mess that would be for them if they killed the wrong Kevin Zimmerman. I washed up, put on better clothes, and went into a cell where I was to wait at full attention for the warden to come in. It was no doubt that a "good ole boy" pep talk was at hand, about how death was done out at the Walls Unit in Huntsville, Texas. I took it all with humor, of course, and a couple of officers were amazed by my cooperation and joy. All praise of this observation is to God, who prepared me as a light.

The warden walks in, introduces himself, and sincerely asks if I'm all right, which I confirm with a yes. "From here on out you'll come and go without restraints, and if there is anything you need, ask, and we'll get it for you, within reason, of course." He then explained that at 6:00 P.M. he'd come in and walk me to the death chamber, where I would be strapped down, which I could go to on my own, or by force. I assured him of my Christian walk and there'd be no problems out of me. I was then told my spiritual advisor, Kathryn H. Cox, could come in for thirty minutes, but the prison chaplain would be there throughout the day. Trying to hold back a tear, he told me there was still no change and asked if I did drugs, and if so, if I had any problems with my veins. Surprised at his genuineness, I found added comfort knowing he took NO pleasure in what would transpire. He then left, and the officers all relaxed.

Chaplain Lopez and I conversed for quite some time and drank tea. At 3:00 P.M., the warden comes in and informs me the Fifth Circuit had denied me. "Yes," I said with a smile. I gathered he and the others thought I was a good faker or serious at being ready to go. He then left once again.

My last meal was brought in. An egg and breakfast patty sandwich, fried pork chop, fried chicken, french fries, lots of ketchup, four milks, and a chocolate cake was what I ordered. All ordered and based on small portions on our daily trays left me embarrassed, as there was so much there was no way I could eat it all. Chaplain Lopez bailed me out, and ate with me while we talked in depth on scriptures and the power of God. That time did allow him to assure the others I was truly at peace and on a spiritual level for a peaceful end.

With time winding down, I was able to make calls to the hospitality house, so I could speak one last time with my ex-wife, Connie, my Aunt Jonell, and my friend from Switzerland, Bee. I then called home to talk to my eighteen-year-old son, Kyle, then with my fifteen-year-old daughter, Kara, then with Kyle again, and I told him this was it, and then we said, " 'Til next time," and hung up.

Several minutes later, 5:45 P.M., I was told, "We're taking you back." I felt like a baseball bat hit me in the face, and then felt as though all of my spiritual and emotional life was sucked right out of me. One officer said, "Drama," to insinuate I was faking. "No, that's real," the major who knew me said.

A woman came in and asked, "How do you feel? Were you surprised about the stay?"

"I'm disappointed. I was ready to go. The stay only means eighteen more months of this crap," I responded in a low voice. Which for clarity here, I meant eighteen more months of the oppressive conditions on Death Row with its modernized dungeon (Building 12) at the Polunsky Unit in Livingston, Texas.

Instantly, I was chained like a dog once again, thrown into the van's dog cage, and on my way back to a place I prayed I'd never see, touch, or feel ever again. I cried in confusion, asking God, "Why?" I cried even more so as we came within distance of the prison lights that made me realize what it all meant. The strangest of it all was the combination of feeling let down and/or rebuked by God. The yellowish, grayish tint of this large moon hung so low, as though I could get up on top of the building, reach up, and touch it.

In my fast-paced life, learning I was adopted at age seven or eight, my severe head injury at age ten that messed me up so bad my grades dramatically declined, and I became freak, retarded, Frankenstein's other half before my school peers who rejected me, and losing my grandfather at age fourteen who was the one family member I truly bonded to, left me cursing God. None of the above events, single-handedly, was as cruel as what I went through with four months of preparation, physically, spiritually, mentally, emotionally, only for it to be taken away. Not two weeks or even two days before, but fifteen minutes. Definitely the cruelest thing that I'd ever experienced.

For two days I was disappointed and depressed as I prayed for understanding. And I then came to realize it isn't about me, but rather God's purpose, which could have been for me, or maybe for the benefit of another person, or many. As I was then ready and willing to accept this blow in humbleness, I get hit in the face yet again on the fifth day as the Supreme Court vacated my stay. Yes, I lie not, my disappointment and depression were quickly turned to anger. I'm a strong Christian and my faith in God will be broken by NO man. Nevertheless, I am a human being with feelings, which includes anger. If people cannot envision what I have gone through to understand that anger, then let them remain ignorant in their self-righteousness. I WILL NOT act on that anger in any way, shape, or form, but I am angry and rightfully so.

As this Christmas day has come and gone I am slowly beginning to heal from the harsh reality of what I have experienced in the past fifteen days. Yet I'm still wounded indeed from "THE RIDE."

Appendix: The Appeals Process

by Clive Stafford Smith

To many onlookers, the eternal appeals process in the United States' application of the death penalty is both profoundly troubling and difficult to comprehend. Briefly, the process operates as follows:

Direct Review	State Habeas Corpus	Federal Habeas Corpus
(3) United States Supreme Court	(6) United States Supreme Court	(9) United States Supreme Court
(2) State supreme court	(5) State supreme court	(8) Federal circuit court of appeal
(1) State trial court	(4) State trial court	(7) Federal district court

In theory, only a murder can be punished with the death penalty. Furthermore, there are approximately 25,000 murders a year in the United States, and "only" about 250 to 300 death sentences handed down. Therefore—again, in theory—only a narrow class of murders should receive the death penalty. In practice, the decisions made are totally arbitrary and depend rather more on the race of the defendant and the victim than on any other single factor.

The death penalty is almost exclusively a southern phenomenon. Although thirty-eight of the fifty states have laws that authorize the death penalty, and there are sizable Death Rows in California and Illinois, the vast majority of the 3,000 people on Death Row today are found in the states of the former Confederacy—from Virginia down to Florida and across to Texas. For example, there are 400 people on Death Row in Texas, 340 in Florida.

A case begins with an indictment, sought by the local prosecutor— the district attorney. These men (as they nearly always are) are elected, and generally cover a district of four or five counties (there are 152 counties in Georgia, for example, and 45 district attorneys). They have absolute discretion in deciding whether to seek the death penalty, mostly for murder. In the overwhelming number of cases the prosecutor offers life imprisonment in exchange for the defendant's agreement to plead guilty. If this is accepted, that is the end of the case. Half of the people on Death Row were offered life imprisonment in exchange for a plea but rejected it, either because they insisted on their innocence or because their lawyers did not impress on them the likelihood that a death sentence would be imposed and carried out.

An indigent defendant is entitled to an attorney at first trial. (I will call the accused "he" because only just over 50 of the 3,500 people on Death Row are women.) Almost everyone on Death Row is indigent. The total payment received by a court-appointed attorney in a capital trial varies from state to state, but in several southern states the maximum payment is $1,000 for the entire case, so that a conscientious lawyer will then receive under $1 per hour for working on the case. My office sued the state of Mississippi because the federal minimum wage was $3.35 per hour, which meant that lawyers defending a person for his life were receiving a fraction of the amount one would get for serving burgers at McDonald's. Not that that disparity is necessarily wrong under an objective system, given the tedium of the burger-server's job, but it does not fit in with American values where a Wall Street corporate lawyer is paid over $350 per hour.

After pretrial hearings (which can last several months) the case is set for trial. A jury *venire* (panel) is summoned, normally composed of from 100 to 200 registered voters from the county where the crime occurred. The attorneys for both sides get to conduct *voir dire*, where the jurors are questioned, often over several days, concerning their attitudes and prejudices. (As a matter of interest to the French perhaps, an instruction to jurors that is required under Mississippi law reads as follows: "Voir dire [pronounced voy-er dy-er] is an ancient Latin term which means to speak the truth.")

An unlimited number of would-be jurors may be struck for cause—because the attorneys believe their prejudices make them unfit to be jurors. This includes anyone who expresses any reservations about the implementation of the death penalty. Then, depending on the state, both sides are permitted to exercise between ten and twenty peremptory challenges, which reject prospective jurors for any reason. This is generally how the prosecutors exclude black people from the process.

When the jury is chosen, the trial takes place in two separate parts. First, there is the phase where evidence is presented and the jury decides whether the accused is guilty. Then there is what is effectively a totally distinct trial where the decision is made about whether the accused should be executed or sentenced to life imprisonment. In most states, the jury has the final word.

Once the sentence has been passed, the defendant has an automatic appeal to the state appellate court. Here too he has the dubious benefit of legal aid, this time by lawyers who are paid even less than the state's trial lawyers. Once the defendant loses his direct appeal, he petitions the United States Supreme Court to issue a *writ of certiorari* to review the decision. The United States Supreme Court accepts only about one in twenty-five capital cases for direct review. From this time on, the defendant has no right to assistance by an attorney. A defendant with no money to hire a lawyer either must rely on a volunteer lawyer or must represent himself.

After denial by the United States Supreme Court, collateral procedures begin with a writ of habeas corpus in the state trial court. The writ is reviewed by the state appellate court. Every state court judge (in the South, at least) is elected, which does not bode well for the defendant's appeal in a much-publicized murder case. If the appeal is rejected, the defendant again petitions the United States Supreme Court for review.

For the first time in his appeals of right, when he reaches the federal district court, the defendant meets an appointed judge. This used to be the time for salvation for the defense in capital cases, for defense attorneys won 70 percent of cases in the federal district court and in the federal circuit court of appeals. In the 1980s, however, Ronald Reagan appointed right-wing ideologues to more than half of the federal judiciary. As a result, for example, in one federal appellate court we afterwards lost 67 of the next 70 cases.

Losing in the federal district court and in the federal court of appeals, and being denied again by the United States Supreme Court, the defendant comes to the end of his first round of post-conviction procedures. Until a few years ago, he would then embark on another round, starting with state *habeas corpus* (step 4 in the table), alleging new issues based on decisions handed down by the court while he was litigating his first set of appeals (normally a period of up to eight years, though no more than three in some states). Defendants have been known to repeat steps 4 to 9 (see the table) four or five times.

Congress has, however, severely restricted the availability of "successor" petitions. In 1995 Congress eliminated $20 million in federal funding for Post Conviction Defender Organizations, known as "Capital Resource Centers." Previously, attorneys from the Resource Centers had represented almost half of those on Death Row. Congress also attempted to impose time limits on the filing of habeas corpus appeals.

Why is the United States government trying to speed up the process of the appellate system? The average American thinks that all this legal finagling is just an effort to get the clearly guilty off on some absurd technicality. The reality is rather different.

In large part because of the lack of resources available to the defense, the quality of representation received by those who end up on Death Row is horrifyingly bad. Lawyers in the United States—not noted for their altruistic motivation—generally do not take cases for which they will be paid less than a dollar per hour. Therefore, most of those who try capital cases either are very young and seeking experience or are incapable of securing any other form of gainful employment.

Take two examples:

- Alfred Leatherwood was sentenced to death when he was represented by a law *student*, whose first words to the trial judge were, "Your Honor, may I have a moment to compose myself? I have never been in a courtroom before."

- In another Mississippi case the lawyer admitted to drinking alcohol during the trial, and—as part of his argument—locked handcuffs on his own wrists without determining that anybody had the key to take them off. He spent the rest of the proceeding with his hands locked securely together.

The courts have grown cynical and do not believe even the most blatant evidence of an individual's innocence. Death sentences are still reversed, but only for the most fundamental violations of the United States Constitution. Another important fact to note concerning the United States system is that although a court may grant relief, that does not necessarily end the case. The court may vacate either the conviction or just the sentence, but except in very limited circumstances the principles of double jeopardy do not preclude retrial from the start or just reconsideration of the appropriate sentence. One man has been sentenced to death a total of six times so far, although he has secured appellate relief five times. If his case continues to be reversed, and the prosecutor continues to prosecute for death, in theory the case could go on *ad infinitum*.

Finally, there is clemency. Usually, the decision is made by the governor of the state in question, and it is rarely made in favor of the defendant.

International remedies are currently almost nonexistent in the United States.

Once the last-minute flurry of efforts to stop an execution fails, each state kills people in its own individual way. The method varies from electrocution (still used in eight states), to gassing, hanging, shooting, and (the most common) lethal injection.